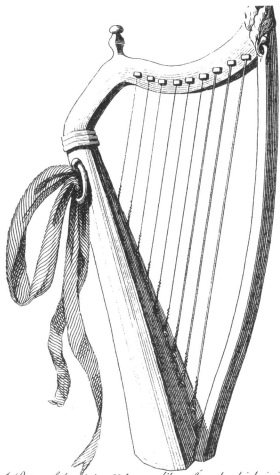

A Print of the Ariandlŵs, *or Silver Jewel, which is in the possession of Sir Roger Mostyn, in Flintshire; and has been from time immemorial in the gift of his Ancestors, to bestow on the chief of the Faculty. This emblem of Fame, which is crowned with Oak; is about six inches and a half long, and furnished with strings equal to the number of the Muses. It was gained at a public contest of the Bards, in the Reign of Queen Elizabeth, by* Siôn ab Rhys, Pencerdd, *principal Musician of the Harp, or Doctor of Music.——— See more in pages 32, 33, 46, 47, 49, 58, and 85, of this work!*

Herons.

Agnes Miller Parker, 1937

A BOYHOOD'S RECALL

Michael Ellis-Jones

1st Edition 2006
2nd Edition 2011

*With minor corrections in the text, also the addition of three photographs which have
since come to light, and twelve Agnes Miller Parker wood-engravings*

AUTHOR'S NOTE FOR 2011 EDITION

I am delighted, yet amazed, at the acclaim and interest my book has received. I humbly aspired that it would prove so and now deserves a 2nd edition to fulfil enthusiasm of further readers.

I believe having heeded 'Time's relentless Hour' by writing it, thus satisfying my wish to capture and recall some of its fleeting scenes of yesteryear that, hopefully, will pleasurably inform and occasionally amuse. My prime intent is for doing justice to the very dear memory of so many within the following pages, who, in my boyhood's heart, made Maesmawr an innermost and indestructible part of me.

I feel greatly favoured that this book was privileged to stand beside the National Museum of Wales' own publication in 2007 for its Exhibition entitled 'Things of Beauty – WHAT TWO SISTERS DID FOR WALES', concerning my late aunts Gwendoline and Margaret Davies of Gregynog Hall, Montgomeryshire. I trust you will enjoy reading A BOYHOOD'S RECALL and contemplating the many exquisite wood-engravings by Agnes Miller Parker, whose beauties grace its pages.

Michael Ellis-Jones 2011

A BOYHOOD'S RECALL

1937–1945

Maesmawr Hall.

W. M. Harris
July 1938

MAESMAWR HALL

Caersws
Montgomeryshire

Michael Ellis-Jones

Long, long ago I thought on all these things:
Long, long ago I loved them.

Mary Webb (1881–1927)

A BOYHOOD'S RECALL
1937–1945

MAESMAWR HALL
Caersws, Montgomeryshire

Michael Ellis-Jones

2006 edition ISBN 0-9553073-0-9
2006 edition ISBN 978-09553073-0-0

2011 edition ISBN 978-0-9553073-1-7

Published by:
Michael Ellis-Jones
Westfield, Lyonshall, Herefordshire, HR5 3JN

Typeset in Baskerville by: *Anastasi Ltd.*
Page design: *Anastasi Ltd.*

Printed and Bound in Great Britain by:
Berforts

Printed on: 120gsm Munken Pure acid free paper

IN REMEMBRANCE

of

All those so dear at

'A MAESMAWR GONE'

Whose received great

LOVE

Sustained me.

Courtesy: Tim Lewis

MAESMAWR HALL

Belov'd Maesmawr
of
Boyhood's brimful years;
Age now,
through
Time's relentless Hour,
Keeps cherish'd recall
of
Memory's All;
Becomes my fount
For sweet
REMEMBRANCE TEARS
that fall.

M. E-J

Ducks.

Agnes Miller Parker, 1936

CONTENTS

ACKNOWLEDGEMENTS

Special thanks to:

John Trevitt –
Valued initial guidance and introductions

Rick Woodcock –
Devoted Editing

Karen Stout –
Typing onto disc and editorial work

Tim Clement –
of ANASTASI LTD
Typesetting and Page Design

Hilly Clement –
for her assistance.

I am grateful to the following owners of copyright for extracts, quotations and many illustrations. Several others, who are closely associated with my family at Maesmawr Hall, have kindly lent me their precious and original photographs of beloved relatives who were devotedly employed at 'MM' over sixty years ago. Those several reminders greatly enhance the word 'portraits' that I have attempted herein. My dear friend Ieuan Owen of Caersws, whose boyhood coincided with mine at Maesmawr and was often happily shared there, recently found some attractive 1903 Ordnance Survey maps of the Caersws and Llandinam localities destined for destruction in a Bwlch-y-ffridd refuse container. He thoughtfully rescued them especially for me; they are included as a delightful graphic guide to many places mentioned in my text.

Written information about several interesting aspects of Maesmawr, notably its ownership by one family of Davies from about 1650 until 1920, was kindly given me by Tim Lewis at Maesmawr Hall Hotel. I am especially indebted to Margaret Stacey of the Newtown Area Library for invaluably drawing my attention to the anonymously written article entitled 'MAES-MAWR' in the Powysland

Club's *Montgomeryshire Collections*. It is ideal in providing me with a brief but nevertheless detailed insight into aspects of Maesmawr's distant past – far more distant than my relatively recent Recollections, which the article introduces in such an historically suitable context.

Granters of copyright material, together with those owners of loaned photographs, are individually acknowledged beneath each valued contribution. Finally, I warmly thank all who have wisely assisted my research, provided information, and suggested avenues of pursuit, which have all proved fruitful, and so advantageous for my quest.

AMGUEDDFA CYMRU (National Museum Wales); SAIN FFAGAN: AMGUEDDFA WERIN CYMRU (St. Fagans National History Museum, and the Librarian, Niclas Walker); John Attle; BEAFORD ARTS Archive; the late Ceridwen Bennett of Caersws; Gwyn Briwnant-Jones and Executors of the late Ifor Higgon and Stanhope Baker, respectively; Katrina Burnett (for the Estate of Eiluned Lewis); COMISIWN BRENHINOL HENEBION CYMRU (Royal Commission on the Ancient and Historical Monuments of Wales: RCAHMW); the COUNTRYMAN Magazine; Alan Crumpler; Lord and Lady Davies of Llandinam; Brian Demaus; Durham County Records Office; Norman Edwards; Alex Galloway (Clerk of The Privy Council); Reverend Jenny Garrard of Llanidloes; Gareth Griffiths (Montgomeryshire Group Librarian); Rhiannon Jones (for Nansi Richards; Telynores Maldwyn); Sharlene Jones; Henry Jones-Davies; Michael Key (BLACKSTONE COLLECTION); Andrew Lambert; Ruth Lambert; LLYFRGELL GENEDLAETHOL CYMRU (National Library of Wales, and senior staff member, Vernon Jones); NATIONAL TRUST Enterprises and Photographic Library; Elwynne Owen-Jones; David Owen Owen; Les Powell; THE POWYSLAND CLUB (Proprietor of *Montgomeryshire Collections*); POWYS COUNTY TIMES Newspaper (for *Montgomeryshire Express & Radnor Times* extracts of 1911, 1927, 1939, 1947); Jeremy Pryce of Llandinam; Bill Putnam; Ann Quickenden (for wood-engravings by Agnes Miller Parker); Dafydd Roberts, SAIN (for Nansi Richards; Telynores Maldwyn); the late Alwyn Rosser; Lib Rowlands-Hughes; SCOTTISH PROVINCIAL PRESS; SHEIL LAND ASSOCIATES Literary Agents (for the Estate of Dorothy Hartley); THE SOCIETY OF AUTHORS (representing Literary Trustees of the poet Walter de la Mare); SOCIETY of the SACRED HEART (for wood-engraving by Sister Tournour); Karen Stout, of her 'Weobley Bookshop'; Anthony R. Thomas (SENTINEL); THE TIMES OF LONDON Obituary Department (for extracts of the Obituary of Captain Richard Annand, V.C., 29 December 2004); VICTORIA CROSS, negative no. MH4720, with the permission of the Trustees of the Imperial War Museum, London; A.P.

WATT LTD. (on behalf of Michael Yeats and the line from the poem 'Easter 1916' by W.B. Yeats). Permission has been earnestly sought by the author, without present success, for the reproduction of the six miniature wood-engravings by Joan Hassall, together with the poems by Mary Webb which they preface: 'The Beautiful House', 'On the Hills', 'Very Early', 'Harvest Song', 'The Mountain Tree', 'Hazel Buds', and finally her poem 'Joy'.

For clarity, and my readers' sakes, in the context of the divers alterations and changes of room use that have occurred within Maesmawr since 1947, those room names that pertained during my boyhood are in this font. These include several utilitarian rooms that partly comprised the stableblock of those and previous years, together with some areas of ground adjacent to the house itself.

Magpie.

Agnes Miller Parker, 1937

INTRODUCTION

Maesmawr Hall, in the Welsh county of Montgomeryshire, was the home of my mother's family from 1910 to 1947, and my own happy home for several years during my boyhood. Before I begin my own account of the 'Maesmawr' I remember, by way of introduction to the house as it was when my family went to live there, I feel fortunate to be able to reproduce the following article, entitled 'MAES-MAWR', from 'Half-Timber Houses of Montgomeryshire'. Its authorship is uncertain, but it was originally published in *Montgomeryshire Collections*, Volume 17 of 1884, accompanied by a drawing of Maesmawr, signed and dated 'Thos. Edward Pryce 1883'.

The article confirms that Maesmawr's 'proprietor' then was John Pryce Davies, Esquire (1822–1896) and that the 'occupier' was his sister Jane Anne (1816–1898), who survived her brother by only two years. The article was thus written prior to both their deaths, but certainly after 1876, as I will now explain.

In that year was commenced or completed a major extension to the seventeenth-century Maesmawr by the eminent London architect W.E. Nesfield. The article devotes much space to a detailed description of the characteristics of the earlier house which were happily retained when the extensive Victorian accommodation was added to them, and mentions the (new) drawing room as part of it. My own descriptions, which will follow, cover virtually every room of the earlier house and the Nesfield extension, clearly recalled from my boyhood. Thus, my descriptions are partly pre-empted by those of the 'MAES-MAWR' article. Nevertheless, I am content to accept this minor duality in respect of a few rooms, rather than abridge the delightfully written article in favour of my own descriptions, where the two overlap.

Perusal of the Davies family's 'ownership tree' shows that it ended with the Reverend Herbert Davies (1871–1945), whose line continues to this day. Born in India, he returned to England with his father in 1887, inheriting the Maesmawr Estate from the aforesaid Jane Anne Pryce upon her death in 1898. That same year, Herbert was ordained into the Church of England and appointed to a curacy somewhere in the Midlands. However, having no training in estate-management, and feeling it unacceptable to remain absentee landlord of Maesmawr, he let the Estate to a series of tenants, the last of these being my grandfather, Edward Jones, who remained tenant from 1910 to 1920, in which year he purchased the Estate from the Reverend Herbert Davies, thus ending the Davies family's long ownership of Maesmawr.

I feel it to be of passing interest to mention that four owners of Maesmawr, from two respective families, were Appointed as High Sheriff of Montgomeryshire.

Davies of Maesmawr Hall
Owners of the Hall are in red

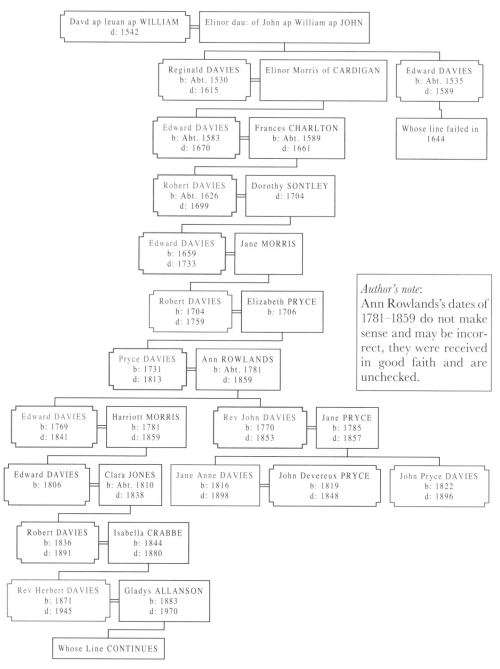

My taid rented the Maesmawr Hall Estate from the Reverend Herbert Davies from 1910 to 1920, and thereupon purchased it.

Courtesy: Tim Lewis

14

The first was Pryce Davies (1731–1813), followed by his grandson John Pryce Davies (1822–1896). Subsequently, in 1911, my grandfather Edward Jones (1854–1937) was Appointed to the office, followed by my uncle Evan Emrys Jones (1897–1947) in 1939. Facsimiles of the Appointment of Edward Jones and Emrys Jones respectively, together with the *Montgomeryshire Express & Radnor Times's* report of 11 March 1939 upon the latters' Appointment, I am proud to include. (see pages 206-209)

Kingfisher.

Agnes Miller Parker, 1937

HALF-TIMBER HOUSES OF MONTGOMERYSHIRE, 'MAES-MAWR'

I*t is agreeable to find a silver lining in a house that has been kindly treated and well looked after, and consequently does its duty as well as ever, and, set firmly four square to the wind, still shelters the descendants of its original founders.*

Standing some little distance from the modern turnpike road, and just on the edge of the old Roman road to Caersws, is Maes-Mawr Hall. Approached by a long avenue the width of its main front, the old house, with its broad central gable of cleft-oak framing and slighter quarterings cut to the fantastic shapes so dear to the eye of the Elizabethan carpenter, its curious stack of clustered stone chimney shafts towering high above the roof, affording plenty of shelter for the starlings, as the trees above do for the rooks, when seen through the framework of the branching elms of the avenue, forms a picture to which the accompanying illustration does but very scant justice.

Mont. Coll., Vol. xvii.

The half-timber house in 1883, seven years after Nesfield's extension (behind), whose triple-stack chimneys are seen (r.-h) on the dated drawing. Note the graphic evidence of bricks at the corner of the west gable, compared with the 'jettied' half-timber of the east one, and the (then) bare white iron railings on the west gable corner, as in photograph 1 (page 127).

On the right of the avenue, and a little in advance of the house itself, stands a range of buildings called 'the Dairy'. This is now used as a coachman's residence, with coach-houses and stabling for occasional horses; but formerly it contained the whole of the cooking appliances for the family and their dependants, the higher branches of the culinary art alone being undertaken by Madam herself at the hall fire. Here, too, were all the appliances for baking, brewing, cidermaking, home-malting, weaving and yarn spinning, blacksmith's forge and carpenter's shop, with tools of all kinds, from a lathe to a glazier's diamond, showing that the house was entirely self-contained, and quite independent of external aid.

The river then supplied an abundance of salmon, and the hooks to hang the nets up, with a large duck-gun of ancient date, still remain. The pastures, the poultry yard, the dovecot, the wide old garden with apple and pear orchards, and a profusion of damson trees, so abundantly supplied every want, that friends from less fertile Merionethshire were wont to term Maes-Mawr 'a land of Goshen'.

Many of the old fruit trees still remain, but are past their work. They do but stand and wait and bide their time, and every winter's storm thins their ranks.

The native oak and beech, together with hornbeams, Spanish chestnuts, limes, and walnut trees, flourished round the old place. A memorandum, written 109 years ago, is kept with many others, 'Sowed a pint of crab-seed under the big fir tree.' The 'big fir tree' is still here, and doubtless some of the crab stems grafted are now bearing rich fruit.

As for the gardens, so carefully cultivated and kept up in former days, little remains now to show their site even, except the ditches whereon the box-hedges stood. The thick box-hedges, through which, to use the expression of an old servant, 'never a bird could fly', have long disappeared; a few gaunt skeletons, becoming fewer and fewer every year, still linger on to tell of better days.

Four old yew trees tell where 'the Bower' was, and a quaint old table, cut out of a thick log of wood, with a hollow in the middle to hold the punch-bowl, used to stand here in the summer time.

The plan of this house is an unusual one. As a rule, the houses of this period were but developments of the simpler arrangements of feudal times, and consisted, in the first place, of the hall, which was usually entered direct from the porch, and formed the common sitting and dining room of the family. Next, at one end of the hall, were arranged the kitchen and domestic offices generally, whilst at the other end was a wing containing the parlour, and usually another small room as well, these two answering to the withdrawing rooms in the large mansions of the sovereign and the nobility. The chief stairs often led directly out of this hall, and there was usually another stairs from the kitchen to the bedrooms above. The plan thus took somewhat the form of the letter H, the hall forming the centre and chief feature, connecting the wing containing the kitchen etc., at one end, with that containing the parlour at the other.

At Maes-Mawr this arrangement is departed from, and instead of the different apartments being grouped round the hall, the hall itself, the parlour, and the staircases are all collected around a great central chimney shaft, while the kitchen forms a wing of its own projecting out at the back.

Entering the house itself, the visitor finds himself in a large porch or outer hall 16'0" long by 8'6" wide, which, with the rooms above, forms the great projecting centre gable of the front. Immediately facing him is a curious little narrow stairs, very steep, with delicately turned balusters and handrail, constructed against one end of the big chimney shaft, and leading to the rooms above. On the opposite side of the chimney shaft are the main stairs, about which more hereafter.

On the right, a low door leads to the 'Wainscot Parlour', a room about 19'4" long by 14'9" wide. The panelling of this room is still perfect, and covers the walls the full height to the ceiling with delicately moulded wainscot work. When the flooring was repaired in this room some years ago, a pavement of large river stones was exposed about a foot below the floorboards, ['an earlier technique widespread in the Trefeglwys area' – Pevsner].

On the left of the outer hall a doorway leads to the 'Hall', a room about 19'0" square, corresponding to, but larger than, the wainscot parlour, the great chimney dividing the two rooms. The wide, open fireplace, 7'0" long by 3'6" deep, remains, and burns wood logs as of old; but the panelling and mantelpiece, if they ever existed, have now disappeared. An oak mantelpiece, made up of old carved wood belonging to the house, having the centre panel of modern Swiss work, occupies the greater part of the space between the chimney-arch and the ceiling. The ceiling itself is plastered beneath the joists, but the main timbers, dark and time-stained, show prominently beneath, crossing each other and dividing the ceiling into compartments, with a rude plaster cornice, probably of Queen Anne's time, running round the room and between each compartment of the ceiling.

Crossing the 'Hall', and keeping to the left, a doorway leads through a small anteroom to the drawing-room, a modern addition formed out of a kitchen, which, with other offices, took the place of a range of buildings known as 'the Aisle', which fell into decay some fifty years ago. This 'Aisle' was doubtless built at a later period than the house itself; although that a building of some kind always stood there was evident when modern alterations exposed to view timbers without a sign of weather-stain upon them.

To the right of the 'Hall', and shut off therefrom by a small doorway, is the principal stair of dark oak, with massively moulded handrail and newels, and sharply turned balusters of excellent design and workmanship. Although on the upper floor the arrangement of the boudoir and bedrooms over the modern drawing room and offices has necessitated alterations, this staircase has been changed but slightly from its original form, and is curiously fitted in against the chimney stack on the opposite side to the little stairs in the outer hall.

Upstairs, it is evident the bedrooms consisted originally of two large family bedrooms, communicating with one another by a room over the outer hall, in which the little stairs terminated. These rooms at a later period, and with an eye to greater privacy, were divided into smaller rooms, and cut off from their fireplaces in the great chimney stack by the passage that now runs round it. This separation from the fireplaces was met by a variety of shifts, not the least curious and risky of which is the balancing of a fireplace and heavy chimney above it on the end of one of the beams over the 'Hall'.

There is little to be discovered of historical interest attaching to this house, and perhaps it is the more blessed in its old age on that account. It is mentioned by Sir R.C. Hoare, in his

18

edition of Giraldus Cambrensis, published in 1806, as then only a farmhouse, standing on the old Roman road. During this period of its existence it seems to have had its share of rough usage, but has stood it well; and now, in the careful hands of its present occupant, the sister of the proprietor, J. Pryce Davies, Esquire, to whom the author is indebted for the substance of this short description, it still remains, and seems likely to survive long, one of the most complete and picturesque of the old timber houses of Montgomeryshire.

Author and date unknown
Courtesy of The Powysland Club,
Montgomeryshire Collections, Volume 17 of 1884

The article laments the then vanished gardens of 'former days' with the aged and barren survivors of previous fruit trees sadly awaiting their gradual demise. Since it was written, the glorious gardens and extensive hedges of boxwood of the Maesmawr of my time, together with the generations of fruit trees which followed upon those the article refers to, have almost entirely vanished – for the second time in about one hundred and twenty five years. Moreover, Maesmawr's divers appurtenances of farmstock, electrical independence, fruit and vegetable orchard and garden, which existed until the Estate sale in 1947, now seem almost trifling when compared, in my memory of them, with the article's long-ago depiction of Maesmawr as the 'land of Goshen'.

Reed Warblers

Agnes Miller Parker, 1937

My mother, Elizabeth Beryl Jones, shortly before marriage in 1927.

Photograph: Bassano of London

PROLOGUE

...through grief and love we found it,
The spring of joy!

Mary Webb (see page 233)

After my parents' marriage on 14th June 1927 by the Reverend Dr. Richard Jones, D.D. at Llandinam's Presbyterian Church, the reception was held at nearby Plas Dinam, home of David (later 1st Baron) Davies. In proposing the health of the bride and bridegroom, Dr. Jones expressed this Benedictory sentiment upon them: ***Lovers may you ever be, and true comrades in pursuit of all noble ends. May the Spirit that seeks all which is true and beautiful, guide you and strengthen you. May the world be gladder and better for your wedded life***. *Montgomeryshire Express & Radnor Times* June 1927.

Flowers

Agnes Miller Parker, 1937

My mother had brought me to her beloved old home of Maesmawr many times from infancy until I was nine years of age. The following year, 1942, she died of spinal osteomylitis - a traumatic event for me as an only child. The ensuing three years brought me even closer to Maesmawr, as it became my home for that brief boyhood period. My acute assimilation of everything experienced there over that time, surely stemmed from an awareness, both conscious and otherwise, that Maesmawr fulfilled my deep need for a secure, happy and calm haven from the uncertainties plaguing my young life.

My Welsh father was a chronically alcoholic physician, trained in the 1920s at the old London Hospital's Medical School in Whitechapel. In the harsh winter of 1945, he was found lifeless in a Cotswold village lodging after self-admin-

21

Wedding group at Maesmawr Hall, 7th March 1928.

The marriage of Megan (née Jones) my mother's younger sister; to Lloyd Owen Owen of Garthgwynion, Machynlleth, Montgomeryshire.

Facing: standing far left, my mother and father,

standing far right, my nain Mary Ellen, and son Emrys, seated far right, my taid Edward Jones, seated close to the bride, her sister Mari.

Courtesy: Sharlene Jones

22

Myself, aged 5 (right) and Bride's God-son Richard Cotterrel (left), with my twin cousins David and Edward Owen Owen, aged 4 (centre), The Hon. Jean Davies of Plas Dinam, Llandinam (behind centre). Group photograph outside Llandinam Presbyterian Church in 1937. The Bride was Mari Elena (née Jones) of Maesmawr Hall, my mother's youngest sister. The Page-boys wore cream taffeta shirts and pale green velvet trousers. (Additional photograph since the 1st edition).

Courtesy; my cousin Ruth Lambert,
Elder sister of David and Edward.

My adored mother and I, circa 1933.

Photograph: Baine
of Aylesbury

My mother and I at Maesmawr, circa 1935, by the Hall window in the west gable. Note the window's louvered sun-shutters, still present since the 1890s of photograph 1 (page 127). My uncle's Setter is, alas, now nameless.

Photographer uncertain,
perhaps my nanny Elcock?

istered morphine. Shortly beforehand, he had arranged for me to be re-homed with a brother as legal guardian, until reaching my Majority in 1953 when enabled to happily escape! Upon that pivotal date I inherited my mother's one-quarter share from the Maesmawr Estate sale in 1947, allowing me freedom and independence, thanks to my grandfather's Will.

He died at Maesmawr in June 1937, aged eighty-three, a month after my fifth birthday. He had been severely incapacitated by stroke some years before. Nevertheless the earlier photograph overleaf reminds me of him, and the daily visit that I made to his bedroom in the front of the house, accompanied by my mother or grandmother, or both of them.

By that time, grandfather was permanently confined to bed and I cannot re-member whether he could speak. He always liked me to stand close to him, so

25

My taid, Edward Jones, J.P. At his Llandinam funeral in 1937, amongst many floral tributes, one was inscribed, 'In sweet and loving re-membrance of our dear kind Master, from the staff at Maesmawr Hall'. Montgomeryshire Express & Radnor Times

Courtesy: Lib Rowlands-Hughes

that he might hold my little hand beneath the cosy quilt that covered him, gently supported by voluminous soft pillows, whilst I told him all I had been doing in and around the house, gardens and farmyard. Although visits to grandfather were brief, I believe he took pleasure in listening to his little grandson's 'Maesmawr enthusiasms'. I recall his fine white hair and bushy white moustache, whose colour matched the plumage of a beautiful crested cockatoo's very lifelike, but lifeless, stuffed presence perched within a large domed display case which stood on a table by the front window, light from which illumined its soft feathers.

Grandfather was tended by 'nurse Frances', who stayed at Maesmawr to care for him. Whilst nearly seventy years have passed since then, I can still remember her stately presence and kind nature. Everyone at Maesmawr, and those who

My nain, Mary Jones, her devoted household's 'dearest Missus'. The same armchair is seen beside the far corner door in the dining room, where the photograph was taken in the early 1930s.

Photographer: Miss Compton Collier, London

visited or came to stay, fondly called her 'nurse Frances', for she was a professional hospital Sister, many of whom imperiously 'reigned' in the wards of those days and terrified nursing teams under their strict regimes. Frances was not that sort – which is why she was chosen! Always clothed in a starched and spotlessly white linen dress and apron, around her ample waist she wore a dark blue woven belt with silver-plated clasp, signifying her status. Over her grey hair, Frances wore a similarly starched white linen cap, with a wide flap that lay flat behind, and reached almost to her shoulders. Her 'entirety' crisply rustled as she quietly moved to-and-fro about the house.

My grandmother died at Maesmawr in April 1947 aged eighty-four, and her son Emrys, who had spent his whole life lovingly with her – and ran the

Maesmawr Estate after his father's death – died suddenly, aged only fifty, eight months later. He collapsed while rough-shooting in his beloved Trewythen Woods with Lord Davies' head-keeper on 12ᵗʰ December. His recent sale of Maesmawr, its contents, and the three tenant farms, shortly after his mother's death, and the thirty-seven years he had spent taking care of Maesmawr since his arrival there with the family in 1910, were surely too great a strain. My uncle's tragedy was heightened by his having married, a mere six weeks before his death, his wife-to-be having come to Maesmawr to tend his mother in her last illness. After their marriage in Aberystwyth, they went to live in Llandinam, with the intention of eventually purchasing the little Georgian, wooded Bronfelen House Estate which nestles on the slope of gentle hills across the Severn valley, almost opposite Maesmawr.

I left Maesmawr in 1945 to live on the east Sussex coast with my future guardian's family – as it happened, a few months before my father's sudden death in Gloucestershire. At that time, I was still at Gordonstoun School after its very recent return to Scotland, following Wartime evacuation to Llandinam at the invitation and through the generosity of 1ˢᵗ Baron David Davies, who lent the school his three houses there: his own home, Plas Dinam, together with the Italianate mansion of Broneirion, built by his grandfather, and the late Georgian residence of Berth-ddu, two miles up the valley towards Llanidloes.

My next chapter details the nineteenth-century intermarriages of two successive generations of Lord Davies' paternal antecedents with those of my maternal family, the Jones'. Upon my mother's death, Lord Davies, who paid for my school education, agreed with my widowed father and my maternal family that it would be best for me to attend a school as close as possible to my beloved Maesmawr. Thus Gordonstoun was chosen. In any case, Lord Davies admired its unique character, and his two sons by his second marriage (who were several years older than I) were pupils at the same time. The eldest, the Hon. Edward Davies, became a Gordonstoun head boy, called the 'Guardian', at Llandinam.

The dreaded day for finally leaving Maesmawr, my cherished home, ultimately came, presageing my future home life with the previously unknown members of my father's family. After only a few weeks with them it was obvious to me that my guardian's wife was an unkind, cynical and taunting person; her only daughter, a few years older than I, felt the same way about her mother. My 'new' life in such circumstances lasted for the next five years during most of Eastbourne College's holidays – for I was sent by my guardian to that Alma Mater in 1946 rather than remaining at Gordonstoun.

I endured that unhappy 'home' life until I was able largely to escape from it and, leaving Eastbourne, embark on a five-year course of training in architecture at London's Architectural Association School; after that I lived and worked in London for the next decade, until my marriage in 1959.

Of course, I never envisaged all of that – except the fact of my imminent re-homing – as I sadly went up to my grandmother's bedroom to bid her goodbye. My cherished wish, as I climbed up the old stair, was to return during the next summer's school holidays for more weeks of happiness.

On the morning of our parting, my young senses deeply felt the enduring permanence of beloved Maesmawr; I knew that although it would cease to be my home from that day onwards, it would surely remain to await my next joyful return and those that would follow in the years ahead.

I vividly remember my "Goodbye" to grandmother. The tall French windows of her large and peaceful bedroom opened onto the white painted, balustered balcony that crowned the drawing room's bay window beneath. Below lay the wide west lawn bounded by evergreen shrubbery, and the great beech tree,

Plovers

Agnes Miller Parker, 1936

29

with its smooth silver-grey trunk. Beyond stood the tall oak, ash and sycamore trees of the orchard rookery. In the distance lay the river pasture with contentedly grazing cattle, its ancient Roman Road's raised agger heading towards Caersws. Before it, at shimmering Severn's edge, but now unseen beneath the myriad flat pebbles which were so perfect for skimming *ducks-and-drakes*, lay traces of the Romans' timber bridge, which had carried cohorts and supplies from distant Viroconium to the fort.

Waiting ominously for me on the gravel forecourt in front of Maesmawr stood the dear old Vauxhall car in which my uncle Emrys would shortly drive me to Moat Lane Junction. There I was to board the Paddington-bound train which would take me to begin my new, unimagined, life on the Sussex coast.

On either side, Maesmawr's beautiful gardens basked in that September morning's warmth; butterflies fluttered and bees hummed over herbaceous border flowers. Woodpigeons and doves cooed in the drive's ancient trees, and the neat boxwood hedges gave of their strange, sweet scent in sheltered corners. The BLACKSTONE oil-engine *chunked* the morning's run in her shed behind the garages, half-hidden by the east garden's trellis and arbour, which were smothered in roses and honeysuckle. Away in the orchard rookery, the dear black acrobats circled ever over, and seemed to caw to me a sad farewell – but also the promise of their exultant welcome at my return.

On still September mornings, the rooks fly in a long black thread across the uplands to the stubble fields, and the

sense of tranquillity is deepened by their erratic cawing. Some of the harshest tones of nature bring the deepest rest. Few things are so unmusical as the voices of rooks, yet a home with a rookery is a very peaceful place. Perhaps the continual cawing, like the ticking of a clock in a quiet room, emphasizes the surrounding hush; perhaps it is the associations of childhood and calm days; or is it something deep and old as earth that lurks in the harsh voices and comes poignantly to our hearts? Hear them on a windless evening, winging homeward heavily through rain, with desultory cawing! Listen as they settle clamorously for the night and you will know how well they fill the pauses made by departing sweetness. Autumn is full of leave-taking.

Mary Webb

"Goodbye, dear Nain, goodbye, Gwen and Gretta, goodbye, Evan, Walter and Brown; goodbye, *Miaow*, *Sooty* and *Nell*; farewell, *Dandy*, little *Seren* and docile cows *Ayrshire* and *Ty-Mawr* – I'll see you all again – very soon."

"Goodbye, dearest, safe journey to your new life – we'll all be here when you come back to see us again."

THERE WOULD BE NO COMING BACK – **NONE** – until all were gone, and until after all had changed, changed utterly and irrevocably at my remembered and beloved Maesmawr.

I NEVER SAW NAIN (MY GRANDMOTHER), OR MY UNCLE, EVER AGAIN.

She died, two years later, in her peaceful bedroom that had been the scene of our parting, which we then thought was only temporary. My uncle sold the Maesmawr Estate in late September of that same year, only to die himself that very December, as I found it necessary to mention earlier.

If those with whom my father had arranged my remaining boyhood's future been kindly disposed to Maesmawr, I might have returned there for at least one further holiday before my nain's death – which was to me entirely unexpected. Alas, although I must have asked them to arrange it, nothing transpired.

I was not present at my mother's funeral, for some reason of my elders which will always remain unknown to me. Neither was I present at my nain's funeral – again for reasons I was never told. My recent researches at the National Library have provided a contemporary newspaper report upon each, the latter stating that, amongst many others, a wreath was given saying, 'To dear Nain, from her loving grandchildren' (and upon the card was also written 'Michael' and the names of my three maternal cousins, who were present).

Inevitably, my young but deep roots at Maesmawr were torn up, almost entirely, at the tragic and drastic change of circumstance which overtook me at my parting from it in 1945. I did not visit the house again for nearly twenty years, whilst it passed through a succession of (to me and my family) unknown private hands for most of that period. Then Maesmawr became an hotel, and thus I was free to visit, and very briefly did so, but I was so distressed at first to see the drastic internal and external changes made to it that I felt I never wished to see the poor old place again.

However, almost a year to the day as I write, I happened to be in Maesmawr's close vicinity with my wife and two friends. So strong was my instinctive impulse to take them there immediately, that it overcame my fears of finding it even more tragically changed than I had remembered. Thus we had tea at Maesmawr, kindly given to us by the hotel's owner. As I poured the tea out, many vivid memories of the house and its surroundings, as they had been over sixty years ago, poured into my mind. "You must write all these things down," the trio said, listening intently to my detailed recollections. Within a few days I had begun to act on their suggestion, and it has taken me almost two years to complete.

On that visit, and after so many years' absence, I sensed that Maesmawr 'spoke' to me: *'Dearest Michael – WELCOME! After many years of depredations, on serene and moonlit nights, I weep both for all that has been taken from me and done to me since you were here, and for remembrance of my past with you and your dear family, whom my ancient walls once lovingly enfolded. I have suffered drastic change, as you have, and as many have to do, to a greater or lesser extent, at one time or another, in this ever-changing world. Nevertheless, I am still here, and shall remain so at your eventual return, and keep you for always.'*

I felt then, at heart, that a 'snippet' of my young roots had survived the cataclysm of former years, although I felt a twinge of remorse at having abandoned Maesmawr for far too long. Moreover, despite the Passing of all those whom I fondly remember to have lived and worked there during my boyhood, I knew that this root would henceforth once again prosper.

Thus do I still deeply love, and contentedly accept, a greatly changed Maesmawr. As an hotel, the dear old house awaits visitors and guests, thus continuing her long tradition of hospitality, albeit private in centuries past. Beneath her weathered roofs, Maesmawr's 'soul' lives on, and within an ever-open door, the Highway's weary traveller seeks sustenance and rest.

When the suggestion was made that I write my Maesmawr Recollections, I realised that to do so would, unavoidably, entail remembering the sudden orphan's pain and loneliness of that time, which I was loath to do, sixty-two years later; but I have been glad to find that memories of great *JOY* and amusement at Maesmawr have been even stronger.

But the sorrow is still there – even after such a long passage of time. I can only hope that occasional inference to it, intentional or otherwise, in no way intrudes. Be assured that I write from the heart.

I have been an architect by profession, and am neither a trained nor a naturally talented writer with the skills of concise narrative, neat syntax and perhaps some semblance of style – or at least an attempt at it – which are so desirable for the reader's enjoyment. What I have written, and the extent to which I have succeeded or failed – in whole or in part – I leave to the reader's generous judgement.

My maternal family lived at Maesmawr Hall for thirty-seven years, 1910–1947. Whilst it was my home, I experienced there a rural, domestic way of life, and a kind of small-scale farming practice, which has long since disappeared. In hindsight, and with increasing age, I view such past personal experience as a privilege, and, I most humbly venture, I feel a responsibility to Posterity not to allow that experience to pass out of living memory – insofar as it relates to Maesmawr Hall, as one example of the *genre*. The house itself, its gardens, out-buildings and equipment, have either been radically altered, within and with-out, or else demolished, in whole or in part, by successive owners across the past fifty-six years. The visitor today cannot but notice the disappearance of the gar-dens from their depiction in 1939, when so beautifully portrayed by Mr W.M. Harris in his pen-and-ink drawing of Maesmawr as I remember it. Already keen on sketching myself, I enviously watched him make it with professional skill and ease. The original, much larger drawing is my precious possession.

I hope these Recollections, as free of inaccuracy as possible, given the time that has passed since the original experiences, will pleasurably inform and occa-sionally amuse. Maesmawr thus remembered will always remain an innermost and indestructible part of me. I venture to believe that my readers will appreci-ate why.

M. E-J
September 2005

Fickle of choice is Memory:
But hidden in her secret deeps
She guards whatever in life may be
Vivid and sweet perpetually;
And of the love strict treasury keeps.

There childhood's flowers bloom for aye;
There, in a quiet grave, profound,
Those whom dark death hath lured away
Live on, with peace unchanging crowned,
Immune from Time's decay.

Walter de la Mare (1873–1956)

SOME MATERNAL ANCESTORS

THE MAESMAWR FAMILY,
THE DAVIES FAMILY OF LLANDINAM

Edward and Mary Jones, my maternal Welsh grandfather and grandmother, whom I shall refer to in Welsh as Taid and Nain (pronounced *Tide* and *Nine*), had forebears in both Montgomeryshire and Merionethshire.

Taid's great-grandfather, Griffith Jones of Rhosaflo farm, barely two miles due west of Llanfair Caereinion, was born in about 1740–1750, perhaps at Rhosaflo? I am guessing that this was the approximate date of his birth because his son, Edward Jones, was born in 1776 when his father was probably in his mid-twenties or early thirties; this seems a reasonable supposition. Edward, who lived to eighty-seven, may perhaps also have been born at Rhosaflo, but at some time he must have removed, perhaps temporarily, to Llanuwchllyn at the south-west end of Llyn Tegid (Lake Bala), with which he is associated. However, he later returned to the Llanfair Caereinion locality, where he became tenant of the Wern farm, which was on the extensive estate of Sir Watkin Williams Wynn, about two miles north-west of the town.

Elizabeth Jones (née Jones) (1814–1899) of Henblas Farm, Llanwnog, near Caersws, wife of the Reverend Evan Jones, my great-taid. They and their family of one son, Edward (my taid) and four daughters went to live at Trewythen-fawr, Llandinam, in 1864, at the gift of Evan's brother-in-law, 'Top Sawyer' Davies. 11 in LLWYNDERW photograph (page 44).

Courtesy: Lib Rowlands-Hughes

Edward Jones' son Evan (my great-taid), born in 1808 at the Wern, later went with his family to the nearby farm of Glanbanw, which they had bought for themselves before losing the tenancy of the Wern upon its being sold out of the Williams Wynn estate.

Evan Jones married an Elizabeth Jones of Henblas Farm, near Llanwnog, two miles west of Caersws, in 1847, and almost certainly at 'Zion' Chapel, Llanwnog. That was a first step towards his much later, and permanent, residence in the Llandinam locality, and his family's subsequent intermarriage with the Davies family of Llandinam. In 1851, four years after his own marriage to Elizabeth, Evan's sister, Margaret, married David Davies of Llandinam (1818–1890). The latter became popularly known as 'Top Sawyer', for reasons shortly to be explained. I shall also mention the very extensive contracting and coal-mining achievements of David Davies' subsequent years.

In 1848, the year following Evan Jones' marriage, he became ordained, at Machynlleth, in the Welsh

The Reverend Evan Jones, my great-taid. 3 in LLWYNDERW photograph (page 44).

Courtesy: Lady Davies

Calvinistic Methodist Church. Upon their marriage, Evan and Elizabeth became tenants of Llawrycwm farm on the Watkin Williams Wynn estate, three miles south-west of Llanfyllin.

In 1859, eleven years after commencing his tenancy of Llawrycwm, a General Election took place in which Evan Jones, now the Reverend Jones, voted with his conscience in support of the Liberal candidate, and not for Watkin Williams Wynn, his Conservative landlord of Llawrycwm. The ballot box was not confidential until 1872. When Wynn discovered how his tenant had voted, he immediately and drastically raised Evan's rent. Furthermore, several other tenants of his were evicted, and the deacons of

Margaret Davies (1814–1894), wife of 'Top Sawyer' David Davies, sister of the Reverend Evan Jones, my great-taid, from the Wern, Llanfair Caereinion. 10 in LLWYNDERW photograph (page 44).

Courtesy: Lady Davies

I, Martin Williams Esquire, one of Her Majesty's Justices of the Peace in and for the County of Montgomery, Do hereby certify that Evan Jones of Llawrycwm in the parish of Llanfyllin in the County of Montgomery Minister of the Gospel Did this day appear before me and did make and take and subscribed the several Oaths and Declaration specified in an Act made in the fifty second year of the Reign of King George the third instituted An Act to repeal other Acts and Amend other Acts relating to religious Worship and Assemblies and persons teaching or Preaching therein

    Witness my hand this fourth
    day of April
    One Thousand eight hundred and fifty one
                M Williams

The licence to preach of the Reverend Evan Jones, my great-taid, issued in 1851, when his home was Llawrycwm Farm, Llanfyllin, Montgomeryshire. He was ordained (at Machynlleth) in 1848, after marriage the previous year, and rented Llawrycwm until 1864, at which date he resigned the tenancy as a result of the Conservative landlord's viciously raising its rent. That was occasioned by the General Election five years previously, when Evan voted with his conscience for the Liberal candidate and not Llawrycwm's Conservative landlord – the ballot box not being confidential.

Courtesy: Lib Rowlands-Hughes

Trewython-fawr today. The Birthplace of my mother, her elder brother and two younger sisters. In 1910, my taid and his family travelled the foreground lane, then probably a dirt track, to begin their life at Maesmawr Hall, barely three miles away.

Photograph: Ellis-Jones

'Soar' chapel, near Llanfair Caereinion, with which Evan was most probably associated as a minister, were asked to surrender its deeds.

After five years of resultant and increasing unhappiness at Llawrycwm, Evan Jones resigned its tenancy in 1864. He was principally enabled to do this through the great generosity of his brother-in-law, 'Top Sawyer', David Davies, who, besides holding Evan in close affection, was also very sympathetic to his large young family's predicament of having to leave their home. It so happened that only the year before, David Davies had bought the farm of Trewythen-fawr, overlooking the beautiful fertile valley of Trefeglwys, between Llandinam and Caersws. Upon learning that Evan and his family were about to be homeless, Davies immediately made them an outright gift of Trewythen-fawr; they must have accepted his loving gesture with profound gratitude. Thus the Reverend Evan Jones commenced, when aged fifty-six, very many happy and fruitful years in the Llandinam locality.

Cynlas Farm, Cefn-ddwysarn, Bala, Merioneth; birthplace of Thomas Edward ('Tom') Ellis, M.P., my great-uncle, and his five sisters, Catherine, Mary Ellen (my nain), Wenofred, Jane and Winifrid Anna. Tom's very promising political career was tragically cut short by his early death, aged forty; his grave, with its Circle-of-Eternity headstone, is at Cefn-ddwysarn.

Courtesy: David
Owen Owen

When they moved to Trewythen-fawr in 1864, Evan and Elizabeth brought their children with them; Mary (1850–88) aged fourteen, Elizabeth (1852–1942) aged twelve, Edward (1854–1937) aged ten (my taid), Annie (1857–1940) aged seven, and little Margaret (1860–1923) aged four. As well as having this secure home for them, Elizabeth must have been delighted to be living a mere five miles from her own family's old home of Henblas, Llanwnog.

After many happy years farming Trewythen-fawr, for the first sixteen of which Evan, as minister, had spiritual oversight of the Llandinam and Caersws chapels, he retired to nearby Brynhafren, Llandinam. He was then aged at least seventy-two, but had seventeen or so years still before him. After his father's retirement, Edward continued farming Trewythen-fawr until he and his family moved down the valley to Maesmawr Hall in 1910.

My nain Mary Jones' maiden name was Ellis, and her paternal and maternal family trees abound with antecedents, the majority of whom lived in hill farms around Bala, Merionethshire, mostly within four or five miles of the town, and included on the latest Ordnance Survey map.

Mary's father, Thomas (1825–1912), married an Elizabeth Williams (1827–1917). Where, I do not know, but his family 'tree' attributes him to the farm of Cynlas, pronounced 'Cunlas', at Cefn-ddwysarn, two miles north-east of Bala and overlooking the road to Chester. Thomas and Elizabeth's six children were all born at Cynlas. They were: Thomas Edward (1859–1899), Catherine (1861–1888), Mary Ellen (1863–1947) – my nain, Wenofred (1865–1868), Jane (1867–1921) and Winifred Anna (1870–1959). Thomas was known as 'Tom', Catherine as 'Kate', Jane as 'Jinnie' and Winifred, 'Winnie'.

Thomas Ellis rose to become Liberal M.P. for Merioneth at the General Elections of 1886, 1892 and 1895. He was Chief Whip in Lord Rosebery's Government and, at home in Wales, famously became the Welsh farmers' political champion by fighting, on their behalf, against the Conservative landlords' widespread and vicious evictions. A magnificent bronze statue of Thomas Ellis stands in the centre of Bala town, erected by his many admirers in gratitude for his active and successful support of the farmers' cause. He died in 1899 aged only forty, after having had typhoid in Egypt some years before.

Thomas Edward Ellis, 'Tom', (1859–1899) of Cynlas Farm, Bala, Merionethshire, my nain's elder brother, thus my great-uncle. He became M.P. for that County, Chief Whip in Lord Rosebery's Government and political champion for the Welsh farmers' Liberal struggle against Conservative landlords' evictions of many. His fine statue, erected with the farmers' gratitude, stands at Bala.

Courtesy: Lib Rowlands-Hughes

I surmise that Edward Jones and Mary Ellen (née) Ellis, my taid and nain, married in about 1895, as their eldest child, their son Evan Emrys, was born in 1897. He had three sisters: my mother Elizabeth Beryl (1898–1942), Margaret Glyn (1901–1986) and Mari Elena (1904–1988). They were all born at Trewythen-fawr, and later moved to Maesmawr Hall, commencing the family's thirty-seven year association with the house and its Estate.

The Maesmawr that greeted their arrival in 1910 stayed virtually unaltered until it was sold in 1947, so its entire character was the same during my boyhood years there; thus the house, gardens, farm and outbuildings, which I remember so acutely, were as they would have been at the outbreak of the 1914–18 Great

The eloquent bronze figure of Thomas Edward Ellis, M.P. (1859–99), my great-uncle, in the centre of Bala.

W. Goscombe John, A.R.A., sculptor, 1925.
Photograph: Ellis-Jones

War – four years after taid's tenancy of Maesmawr began. The late Mr E.H.C. Davies, whose family had previously owned Maesmawr for generations, as its ownership 'tree' illustrates, informatively wrote in 2001 concerning several aspects of Maesmawr just prior to the Great War. He states that the house's 'service wing', which included the kitchen, back kitchen, dairy and laundry above, was built in 1908, the stable block in 1910 and the drive Lodge in 1912. Mr Davies does not mention the installation of the BLACKSTONE oil engine, but I assume that it must have been at about the same time.

Before describing the Maesmawr of my mother's childhood and early adult years, prior to her very premature death, I feel it necessary to digress a little. Firstly, I need to record my certainty that the Reverend Evan Jones, my great-taid, must have been profoundly grateful to his brother-in-law, David Davies, for the latter's outright gift of Trewython-fawr. Moreover, Edward Jones, my taid, whilst only a ten-year-old at that time, must have felt, in his youth and even more so in his old age, a keen sense of David Davies' great generosity to his own father. Had that gift not been given, my family's long association with Maesmawr Hall would surely never have transpired.

Therefore, I take this opportunity to record David Davies' exceptional generosity, so that its truth be acknowledged. The marriage between the giver and the receiver's sister in 1851 was followed, in the next generation, by a further marriage between the Davies and Jones families, and that affection for one another happily continues up to the present day.

My second so-called digression is to make more than a passing reference to David Davies of Llandinam. His was a pioneering career; he was the builder of Barry Docks in south Wales, the founder of the Ocean Coal Company, and an active participant in the sinking of its several profusely productive pits. He was the successful contractor for three Welsh principal railroads, the Vale of Clwyd, the Newtown & Llanidloes Railway and finally, in triumph, the Newtown to Machynlleth Railway. These are fully documented in the book *Top Sawyer* by Ivor Bulmer Thomas, first published in 1938. Its title is derived from the name popularly given to David Davies, originating from his very first local employment as the man who stood on top of the saw-pit in Llandinam's timber yard. That position indicated superiority over his luckless colleague below, who could not avoid being showered in sawdust from the tree-trunk or baulk above, which they were both engaged in cutting. In recent years, the book *Railway through Talerddig* by Gwyn Briwnant-Jones, published by the Gomer Press, provides a very detailed and lucid account of David Davies' railroad contracts, including the difficult but ultimately successful feat of making the deep cutting through rock at the hamlet of Talerddig in Montgomeryshire, through which passes his single track railway to Machynlleth, terminating at Aberystwyth.

David Davies' only son, Edward (1852–1898), shortly following the early

41

The purposeful bronze figure of David Davies, 'Top Sawyer', at Llandinam's bridge across the River Severn; it portrays him studying his plans for building Barry Docks. The original, by Alfred Gilbert, stands at the Docks' entrance.

Photograph: Ellis-Jones

'Aunt Bess', Elizabeth Davies (née) Jones (1852–1942), my taid's second eldest sister, second wife of Edward Davies, the only son of David 'Top Sawyer' Davies. She commissioned the translation into English of the biography of her father, the Reverend Evan Jones of The Wern (from *Y Drysorfa* magazine). I describe meeting aunt Bess in her chauffeur-driven motor car at the Penstrowed railway bridge.

Photograph: Harrison, Onslow Place, London SW1
Courtesy: Lib Rowlands-Hughes

death of his first wife – my taid's sister Mary (1850–1888), married my taid's younger sister Elizabeth (1852–1942). Their wedding took place in Canada because at that time English and Welsh church laws of Kindred and Affinity forbade marriage between a widower and his deceased wife's sister. My taid's second youngest sister Annie (1857–1940) married the Reverend David Lloyd Jones of Fron-haul, Llandinam, who succeeded Evan Jones, my great-taid, as minister of the Llandinam and Caersws Calvinistic Methodist churches. My taid's youngest sister Margaret (1860–1923) married John Owens of Chester, but had no children.

I have already touched on 'Top Sawyer' David Davies' marriage to Margaret, the sister of my great-taid. To conclude my dissertation on the Davies and Jones families' inter-marriage, I must mention David Davies' son Edward's first marriage to Mary (née) Jones (1850–1888), my taid's eldest sister. Their children featured in my boyhood years at Maesmawr Hall. They were David (1880–1944), Gwendoline (1882–1951) and Margaret (1884–1963), the latter called 'Daisy' by both families. David was raised to the Peerage in 1932 as 1st Baron Davies of Llandinam in recognition of his untiring international activities promoting world peace and, with others, advocating the League of Nations. Through it, Lord Davies came to know Dr. Kurt Hahn, headmaster of Gordonstoun School. I was a pupil at Gordonstoun from 1943 to 1945.

Lord Davies' sisters, Gwendoline and Margaret, bought Gregynog Hall, near Newtown, from their brother in 1924, when aged forty-two and forty respectively. The huge Black-and-White mansion – predominantly far younger than its outward appearance suggests – is situated in mature and beautiful parkland which was the creation of past centuries, surrounding a very much older house. Several erudite accounts have been published about the sisters' artistic achievements at Gregynog from 1924 until a few years before their deaths – Gwendoline's in 1951 and Margaret's in 1963. Among these achievements were their Collections of French Impressionist, Post-Impressionist and later paintings, which they began to form in 1924. Outstanding amongst Gwendoline's Collection were Renoir's *La Parisienne*, Cezanne's *Montagnes, L'Estaque* and Van Gogh's *La Pluie, Auvers*, purchased by her in 1913, 1918 and 1920 respectively. Margaret's Collection was more eclectic, comprising, amongst others, paintings by Boudin, Pissarro, Manet, Sisley, Vlaminck and Utrillo. Together, in 1917, amongst many works of that period, the sisters purchased one of Monet's surviving paintings of the 'Rouen Cathedral' series.

Gwendoline founded her Gregynog Press at the Hall after the First World War. During that cataclysmic struggle, the sisters created and personally attended a near-front-line canteen for French troops fighting in Flanders, a fact which I feel is most worthy of mention. The Gregynog Press issued its first prospectus in 1925, only a year after Gwendoline and Margaret had bought the Hall. The

THE DAVIES, JONES and LLOYD JONES FAMILIES at LLWYNDERW, LLANDINAM, MONT. in 1885

Photograph courtesy: Lord Davies

1 David Davies, 'Top Sawyer'; married 10, who was the sister of 3.

2 Edward Davies, son of 1; successively married 8 and 9, who were the sisters of 4.

3 Reverend Evan Jones, my great-taid; married Elizabeth Jones, 11, of Llanwnog near Caersws.

4 Edward Jones, son of 3, my maternal taid; brother of 7, 8, 9 and 15.

5 Reverend David Lloyd Jones, Llandinam minister; married 7, who was the third sister of 4.

6 David Davies, son of 2, grandson of 1; created 1st Baron Davies in 1932.

7 Annie Jones, third sister of 4; married 5.

8 Mary Jones, first wife of 2; eldest sister of 4.

9 Elizabeth Jones, second wife of 2; second sister of 4.

10 Margaret Jones, wife of 1; sister of 3.

11 Elizabeth Jones, wife of 3.

12 Gwendoline Davies, elder daughter of 2; ultimately of Gregynog Hall, Newtown, Mont.

13 John Lloyd Jones, son of 5 and 7.

14 Margaret Davies, younger daughter of 2; ultimately of Gregynog Hall, Newtown, Mont.

15 Margaret 'Maggie' Jones, youngest, fourth sister of 4.

The Reverend David Lloyd Jones, M.A., (1843–1905), of Fron-haul, Llandinam. Married to my taid's sister, Annie. Minister of the Llandinam and Caersws Calvinistic Methodist Chapels, and there succeeded the Reverend Evan Jones, my great-taid.

Photograph: Maclardy of Oswestry

'Aunt Maggie'; Margaret Owens (née) Jones (1860–1923), my taid's youngest sister, who married John Owens of Chester. Her epitaph in St. Llonio's churchyard at Llandinam reads: "I know whom I have believed and am persuaded that He is able to keep that which I have committed unto Him against that Day."

Photograph: Maclardy of Oswestry
Courtesy: Lib Rowlands-Hughes

Press produced books of exquisite quality in Limited Editions that far exceeded the artistic content and technical merit of the output of the commercial printers of those days. The Gregynog Editions were illustrated with wood engravings by Blair Hughes-Stanton, Agnes Miller Parker and Gertrude Hermes, and the books' sumptuous leather bindings were made and decorated in gold leaf by George Fisher.

The beneficent philanthropy of Gwendoline and Margaret Davies was principally expressed towards their beloved Wales, through the University of Wales, the National Library at Aberystwyth and the National Museum of Wales in Cardiff. To the latter they bequeathed their Collections of paintings for the Principality's cultural enrichment, and for Posterity. Nowadays, these are permanently displayed in the Museum's 'DAVIES GALLERIES'.

Margaret founded her Gregynog Festival of Music in 1933. It was held each summer in the mansion's Music Room, which was built especially to display the sisters' Collections of paintings, and as the venue for the Festival's concerts and recitals. The Festival flourished until 1938, shortly before the outbreak of the Second World War. Those who were invited to come there and conduct the Gregynog Choir and orchestra, to play solo instruments and give song recitals, included Adrian (later Sir Adrian) Boult, the soprano Elsie Suddaby, the oboist Evelyn Rothwell (the wife of Sir John Barbirolli), Sir Walford Davies, organist of London's Temple Church, and many others.

My immaturity – I was a mere five or six-year-old when the Gregynog Music Festival was in its prime – meant that I was too young to attend. My 'Maesmawr' uncle Emrys, possessing a fine bass voice, sang in the Gregynog Choir, and my mother, when able to visit Maesmawr in the summer, enjoyed the music greatly, as did

David Davies (1st Baron Davies of Llandinam) 1880–1944. 6 in LLWYNDERW photograph (page 44).

Courtesy: 3rd Baron Davies

her two sisters, the elder of whom, by happy circumstance, spent her entire and long life in Montgomeryshire. Her sister's long life was equally divided between that county and an adjacent corner of Shropshire.

To return, briefly, to my great-taid Evan Jones, I have been most fortunate to glean his biographical details through being loaned the little book whose front cover is here illustrated in reduced facsimile (page 53). This book was originally published in *Y Drysorfa* of September and October 1897. *Y Drysorfa* is Welsh for 'The Treasury', and it was a Welsh language periodical published by J. Parry of Caerlleon, which flourished between 1831 and its termination in 1968. Llyfrgell Genedlaethol Cymru, the National Library of Wales, holds a deposit copy of every issue between those dates. The Evan Jones article was later translated from the original Welsh by David Thomas of Caersws in 1938. The book's Foreword says: ***This translation has been prepared at the request of Mrs Edward Davies, Ll.D., J.P., of Broneirion, Llandinam. Except for omission of a few irrelevant passages and the re-writing of one or two paragraphs, I have tried to make it as faithful a reproduction of the original as possible. David Thomas, Caersws, Dec 1938.*** Mr Thomas' aspiration to translate accurately into English must have been entirely successful, as it obviously satisfied its commissioner, Mrs Edward Davies, whose own father was the book's principal subject. At Maesmawr she was called 'aunt Bess' and she lived in the Italianate mansion of Broneirion which was built by 'Top Sawyer' for himself in later life. After his death in 1890, his son Edward inherited Broneirion, although he lived there for a mere eight years until his own early death in 1898, aged forty-six. His widow ('aunt Bess') continued to live at Broneirion for the ensuing

Margaret ('Daisy') Davies, 1884–1963 (standing) with sister Gwendoline, 1882–1951 (seated far right), posing with friends at Plas Dinam, Llandinam, their father Edward's home, in about 1898. Edward died at Plas Dinam that very year. He was the only son of 'Top Sawyer' David Davies.

Courtesy: Lord Davies

forty-four years, until her death in 1942, aged ninety.

I can only recall meeting aunt Bess once, in around 1939, the unexpected venue being on the main road between Maesmawr and Newtown, close to the old bridge that crossed the railway at the hamlet of Penstrowed. Due to a tortuous approach from both directions, the old brick bridge was demolished many years ago and a replacement with straight approaches built in its place. Why I and a companion, whose identity I cannot now remember, were walking along the road remains a mystery, but suddenly, over the old bridge from the Newtown direction, came a large, black and sedately driven motor car. It halted beside us, and the chauffeur got out and came round to open the nearside rear door,

Gwendoline and Margaret Davies of Gregynog Hall, granddaughters of 'Top Sawyer' David Davies.

Photographs from *Spiritual Pilgrims* by Professor Ian Parrott
Courtesy: Lord Davies

revealing a very elderly lady dressed entirely in black, imperiously perched upon voluminous beige-coloured cushions, perhaps of velvet? The roadside meeting was brief; just sufficient for the small and nervous seven-year-old to be proffered a pale and cold handshake that was returned with a piping "Hallo – hallo, aunt Bess," once it had been hurriedly whispered to him who the 'black lady' was. After she had had a brief word with whoever was with me, the door was closed, and aunt Bess's Rolls-Royce silently glided away towards Llandinam and her 'palace' of Broneirion, and was gone. We returned to Maesmawr, whereupon I excitedly rushed to find my nain: "Nain! Nain! We've just met aunt Bess on the road. Why was she all black?"

I now return to the 'Maesmawr of old' that I so acutely remember from boyhood and, in my imagination, bring with me my taid and nain, my mother, my uncle Emrys and my aunts Megan and Mari, as they were upon leaving Trewythen-fawr in 1910 and coming down the short distance to Maesmawr Hall to begin the family's long association with the beloved old house.

50

JONES and LLOYD JONES FAMILIES at DOLWYDDELAN
near Betws-y-Coed, North Wales, in 1908

Photograph Courtesy: Lib Rowlands-Hughes, David Owen Owen

(The Jones family had driven up from Trewythen-fawr, Llandinam, in a car similar to the one illustrated! See page 112.)

M.E·J.

1 Edward Jones of Trewythen-fawr, Llandinam, my maternal taid; he and his family moved to Maesmawr Hall in 1910.
2 Mary Jones, wife of 1; my nain.
3 Elizabeth Beryl Jones, my mother; eldest daughter of 1 and 2.
4 Evan Emrys Jones, son of 1 and 2; my uncle Emrys.
5 Megan Glyn Jones, second daughter of 1 and 2; my aunt Megan.
6 Mari Eleanor Jones, third daughter of 1 and 2; my aunt Mari.
7 Mrs Ellis, mother of 2; my great-nain, of Cynlas, Cefn-ddwysarn, Bala.
8 Ivor Lloyd Jones, son of 5 and 7 in the 1885 LLWYNDERW photograph (page 44). Fell in First World War.

9 John Lloyd Jones (as 8 above). Died at Jerusalem.
10 Ieuan Lloyd Jones (as 8 above).
11 Dafydd Lloyd Jones, son of 5 in the 1885 LLWYNDERW photograph (page 44) and his first wife Sophia, who died in 1877, aged 29.
12 Edward Lloyd Jones (as 8). Fell in First World War.
13 John Davies, Liverpool tea merchant, family friend.
14 Gwen Davies, wife of 13.
15 Jane Ellis, sister of 2; my great-aunt.
16 Annie Lloyd Jones, sister of 1, mother of 8, 9, 10, 12. (7 in LLWYNDERW 1885 photograph on page 44).
17 Terrier's name not known, presumed a Lloyd Jones!

51

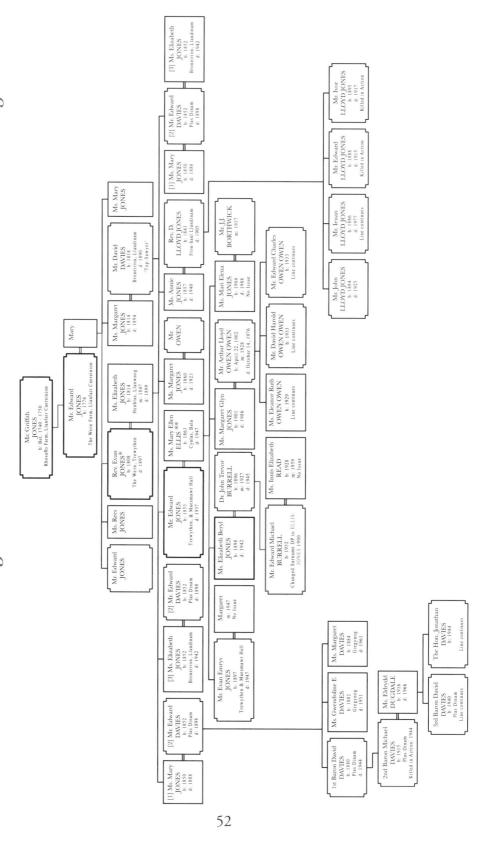

Mr. Griffith
JONES
b: Bef. 1740 - 1750
Rhosafio Farm, Llanfair Caereinion

Mr. Edward
JONES
b: 1776
The Wern Farm, Llanfair Caereinion

Mary

Mr. Edward
JONES

Ms. Rees
JONES

Rev. Evan
JONES*
b: 1808
The Wern, Trewythen
d: 1897

Ms. Elizabeth
JONES
b: 1814
Henblas, Llanwnog
m: 1847
d: 1899

Ms. Margaret
JONES
b: 1814
d: 1894

Mr. David
DAVIES
b: 1818
Broneirion, Llandinam
d: 1890
'Top Sawyer'

Ms. Mary
JONES

Mr. Edward
JONES
b: 1853
Trewythen, & Maesmawr Hall
d: 1937

Ms. Mary Ellen
ELLIS**
b: 1863
Cynlas, Bala
d: 1947

Mr.
OWEN

Ms. Annie
JONES
b: 1857
d: 1940

Rev. D.
LLOYD JONES
b: 1843
Fron-haul, Llandinam
d: 1905

[1] Ms. Mary
JONES
b: 1850
d: 1888

[2] Mr. Edward
DAVIES
b: 1852
Plas Dinam
d: 1898

[3] Ms. Elizabeth
JONES
b: 1852
Broneirion, Llandinam
d: 1942

Ms. Elizabeth Beryl
JONES
b: 1898
d: 1942

Dr. John Trevor
BURRELL
b: 1896
m: 1927
d: 1945

Ms. Margaret Glyn
JONES
b: 1901
d: 1986

Mr. Arthur Lloyd
OWEN OWEN
b: April 22, 1902
m: 1928
d: October 14, 1976

Ms. Mari Elena
JONES
b: 1904
d: 1988
No Issue

Mr. J.J.
BORTHWICK
m: 1937

Margaret
m: 1947
No Issue

Mr. Evan Emrys
JONES
b: 1897
Trewythen & Maesmawr Hall
d: 1947

[3] Ms. Elizabeth
JONES
b: 1852
Broneirion, Llandinam
d: 1942

[2] Mr. Edward
DAVIES
b: 1852
Plas Dinam
d: 1898

[1] Ms. Mary
JONES
b: 1850
d: 1888

Mr. Edward Michael
BURRELL
b: 1932
Changed Surname DP to ELLIS
JONES 1990

Ms. Innis Elizabeth
READ
b: 1928
m: 1959
No Issue

Ms. Eleanor Ruth
OWEN OWEN
b: 1929
Line continues

Mr. David Harold
OWEN OWEN
b: 1933
Line continues

Mr. Edward Charles
OWEN OWEN
b: 1933
Line continues

Mr. John
LLOYD JONES
b: 1884
d: 1925

Mr. Ieuan
LLOYD JONES
b: 1886
d: 1977
Line continues

Mr. Edward
LLOYD JONES
b: 1888
d: 1915
Killed in Action

Mr. Ivor
LLOYD JONES
b: 1895
d: 1917
Killed in Action

[1] Ms. Mary
JONES
b: 1850
d: 1888

[2] Mr. Edward
DAVIES
b: 1852
Plas Dinam
d: 1898

[3] Ms. Elizabeth
JONES
b: 1852
Broneirion, Llandinam
d: 1942

1st Baron David
DAVIES
b: 1880
Plas Dinam
d: 1944

Ms. Gwendoline E
DAVIES
b: 1882
Gregynog
d: 1951

Ms. Margaret
DAVIES
b: 1884
Gregynog
d: 1963

2nd Baron Michael
DAVIES
b: 1915
Plas Dinam
Killed in Action 1944

Ms. Eldrydd
DUGDALE
b: 1916
d: 1966

3rd Baron David
DAVIES
b: 1940
Plas Dinam
Line continues

The Hon. Jonathan
DAVIES
b: 1944
Line continues

52

Ellis family and friends at Cynlas, Cefn-ddwysarn, Bala, circa 1892 (page 38)
Seated: **Mr and Mrs Thomas Ellis**, daughter 'Winnie' between them, (page 62 and 63),
Standing from left: friend, friend, daughter **Mary Ellen****, my **Nain Maesmawr** to-be (page
87 and 27), friend, daughter '**Jinnie**', son **Thomas Edward** M.P.(page 39, 40).

Courtesy: my cousin David Owen Owen

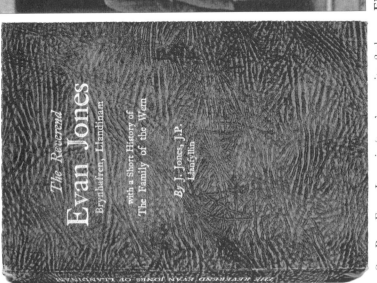

See Rev. Evan Jones in 'tree' opposite, 3rd from left *

Loan of the book. Courtesy: Lady Davies

53

A group of plovers

C.F. Tunnicliffe

THE MAESMAWR HALL OF MY BOYHOOD

THE BEAUTIFUL HOUSE

A large house, a fair house, fragrant, wide and high,
The lord of life has given us. Oh, hear the plovers cry!
Down upon the speedwell floor, beneath the speedwell sky
Come and see the multitude of living things go by.

Hung about with may-bloom, sweet and white to see;
Full of silver songs and little wings in every tree;
Crossed by beast and bird, discreet in merry company –
This is but His anchor-hold. What must His castle be?

Mary Webb, FIFTY-ONE POEMS

Maesmawr Hall by W.M. Harris, July 1939.
Original pen-and-ink Drawing, 9 x 14 inches.

In 1876, to the existing eighteenth-century Maesmawr farmhouse was added the major brick-built two-storey extension designed by the Victorian architect W.E. Nesfield, then a partner of the eminent London architect E. Norman Shaw. The book *Powys* in *The Buildings of Wales series* (Advisory Editor: Professor Nikolaus Pevsner) states that the house (Maesmawr Hall) was once burned and rebuilt. It is referred to as a 'regional-cum-Renaissance house of T-plan' onto whose north-facing wall, or gable, architect Nesfield built his extensive addition. An informative document about Maesmawr maintains that, prior to the Nesfield extension, an ancient kitchen-cum-service room of single-storey height, and with a single-sloped roof, abutted onto the house's north face. This was known as the 'Aisle', which is mentioned in the 'MAES-MAWR' article (pages 16 to 19).

This earliest photograph of old Maesmawr shows the front of the house and the gable-end of a weather-boarded wooden barn. The entirely bare foreground later became part of the house's Victorian and Edwardian gravelled approach

The earliest known photograph of the half-timber Maesmawr Hall. Its date must remain very uncertain, but it is most likely to have been before the 1876 Nesfield extension. The old house has an undisturbed appearance that implies that it had yet to be the subject of an architect's impressive Victorian design. Whatever the photograph's date, note the heavy stone chimney stack on the west (l.-h) gable. This needed a masonry gable to support it, which proves that the original half-timber gable was, for an unknown reason, superseded by masonry at some indeterminate date. Note also a glimpse (r.-h) of the 'MAES-MAWR' article's 'Dairy', the total absence of garden in the undeveloped foreground and the wicket fence across the house front, perhaps to protect its walls from free-roaming farm animals?

Myself, aged nine, with packed fishing rod beside the sundial in my nain's Rose Garden in 1941, the year before my mother's death.

Photographer: the late Janet Jones, a Maesmawr housemaid at that time. Courtesy: Tim Lewis, who found it!

Drive with gardens on either side. In the left-hand middle distance can just be seen the silhouette of a medium-sized, dome-shaped tree. This must be the beech tree, then young, which in my boyhood towered over the great west tennis lawn. In due season, the base of its mighty and silver-grey trunk was thickly surrounded with crocus and mauve cyclamen. The tree was an intrinsic feature of the wide view towards the orchard rookery, seen from the imposing bay-window of Nesfield's drawing room. There is just a glimpse of some outer branches on the extreme left of Mr Harris' drawing. My uncle Emrys was Commanding Officer of the combined Llandinam and Caersws Home Guard (the original of 'Dad's Army') during the 1939–1945 War. They kindly gave me unlimited and unused packs of rifle target cards, at whose challenging 'bull's eyes', at the centre of concentric circles, I aimed hopefully with my air-gun. The beech tree's trunk, onto which I pinned the targets, became peppered with tiny lead pellets, some having punctured the target centres – perhaps with unseen help from the 'Goddess of the Hunt' herself, whose name, 'Diana', my little weapon proudly bore. Alas, the great beech tree became irretrievably decayed after my time, and was felled – but not, I'm sure, as a result of my targetry.

A visit to that 'Aladdin's Cave' was always part of a Newtown shopping day. Note the BLACKSTONE agency; Maesmawr's oil-engine was probably supplied by them.

From: *1928 Montgomeryshire Express & Radnor Times*
Courtesy: *Powys County Times*

All changed, changed utterly:

W.B. Yeats (1865–1939)

Maesmawr's front door was prefaced by a little porch, just visible in Mr Harris' drawing, of framed and hooped iron rods which arched up and over, from low wooden sides, with a pair of wicket-gates to enclose them, all painted Black-and-White. Every summer a Jackmanii species of clematis scrambled up and over the dainty little structure, forming a leafy tunnel before the door. An inspired effect was created by the pale lavender wisteria, the deep purple of the clematis, and the Black-and-White of the old front gable. The entrance lobby behind has been drastically altered since my time, with the entire extraction of the hazardously steep ancient oak stair, which was removed by an unknown Maesmawr owner,

Maesmawr's lost treasure, the erstwhile and precious little ancient oak stair in the front entrance lobby. It was taken out shortly after my family's sale of the house in 1947, either with or without the knowledge and consent of the Local Authority of the day. Its fate remains unknown, as does the nature of its extraction: by careful means or – probably – not?

subsequent to the sale of the house in 1947. To deter the young, such as myself, or indeed anyone, from using the stairs – so slippery were the polished steps that no-one dared – there stood upon the (square) fourth a heavy glass display-case containing a fine example of taxidermy, a magnificent cock capercaillie (large wood-grouse) that my uncle Emrys had shot in his youth – and perhaps in the youth of the poor capercaillie also? – in the Scottish Highlands.

Additional alterations to the entrance lobby at some time after 1947 included the repositioning of its door, one step down into the Hall, and the closing-off of the door that had previously opened directly into the dining room, now called the 'Wainscot Parlour'. The low head-height, lathe-turned wooden spindle rail, seen in the photograph, over where the antique stair had previously been, was extended. The original portion of spindle rail would admittedly be a head-hazard, if the now closed-off door into the 'Wainscot Parlour' should ever be reused. Unfortunately, the extended portion of spindle rail directly crosses over the repositioned door leading down, by one step, into the now renamed (hotel) bar – originally the Hall. The potential head-hazard is thus perpetuated – as I have frequently experienced since my re-acquaintance with Maesmawr! Before leaving the lobby, mention must be made of the present front door, now placed centrally in the front gable. In my boyhood, a pretty square-paned window was there, and the front door was to one side (this is clearly seen in photographs 2, 3 and 5 on pages 128, 129 and 131), making the little lobby behind a much more attractive and useable space.

The Hall, as known by us of old, had always been the principal room in the house, remaining so in my family's time despite Nesfield's large and adjacent drawing room, which lay unused during the whole of the Second World War. Alterations to the old Hall, now a part of the hotel, include the bar-counter hatchway, the pair of glass-panelled doors leading out towards the reception desk, cloakrooms, and the now door-less approach to the staircase. In my time, a single door (replaced by the bar-counter) led into a small ante-room which in turn opened into the drawing room, nowadays the hotel dining room. The aforementioned glass-panelled doors have replaced the previous single wood-panelled door into what was called the lobby in my boyhood. A similar single door separated the Hall from the foot of the staircase, itself now greatly altered since 1947; I will attempt to describe it clearly in due course. The three wood-panelled doors had an incised diamond motif which can still be seen in the bed-room doors in the old part of the house. The little ante-room that once existed between the Hall and the drawing room, where the hotel two-way bar is now situated, was always a puzzle in my early childhood. I would think to myself: "If it's the ante-room, where are the aunties?" Mine at Maesmawr never entered it, nor did anyone else except for the purpose of occasional dusting. Against the wall, where nowadays the bar-counter opens, there stood – midway between the wood-panelled doors – a beautiful Welsh oak dresser, which had delicate drawers with elegantly moulded brass drop-handles at about table height. Beneath ran an open arcade with a deep shelf several inches above the floor. The dresser's crowning glory was the long series of polished shelves, supported by end-frames, upon which were displayed magnificent pewter plates of several sizes and Welsh antique china.

In a window corner of the Hall stood a tall wooden pedestal, on which was placed a bust of Nain's brother, Tom Ellis, M.P., to whom I have previously referred. Elsewhere in the room stood a second pedestal on which, throughout summer and autumn, was placed a large bowl of herbaceous flowers, the pleasure of gathering and arranging them being one of my mother's special delights whenever she and I – and she was very seldom without me – came to Maesmawr in those seasons during the 1930s. In winter, the old Hall was imbued with the sweet smell of wood-smoke, which lingered on into the spring and summer, when it combined with the perfume of fragrant and profuse flowers.

The old Hall was the scene for so many happy family gatherings and visits and stays by friends of Nain and my uncle Emrys; and my late Taid must have loved the visitors too, in former days, before his long illness. The Hall has also been a room of sorrow; it was the scene of my mother's and my nain's funeral services, only five years apart. However, it is with its remembered association of joy and laughter that I recall the Hall, at times of others' visits and on quiet Sunday afternoons in summer and winter.

After lunch in the dining room, the four of us – Nain, her companion Gwen, my uncle and myself – retired to the cosy Hall, there to suck digestion-promoting, transparent *Glacier* mints, whose crackly cellophane wrapping, when unwound by finger and thumb, revealed the embossed image of a polar bear balanced on a miniature ice floe – the floe being a *Glacier* mint! In winter, chairs were pulled up towards the old fireplace, where home-cut logs full of flame warmly glowed beneath the burnished brass hood.

Drastic alterations to the Hall since the 1947 sale include the hideous attempt by an unknown subsequent owner to simulate wood framing on its interior wall surfaces – including the fireplace – with some compound akin to congealed molasses, (the present hotel proprietorship happily intends to remove it all). I remember the walls lined with a hessian-like fabric painted in matt dark blue-grey distemper, which enhanced the pure white plaster ceiling panels, the polished oak furniture, and the pale tones of the William Morris fabric on the armchairs and high-back *settle*.

No-one's stay at Maesmawr was more cherished by my nain than when her greatly beloved younger sister Winnie and her husband Harry came up from their Carmarthenshire home. Harry Jones-Davies was a fortunate farmer who owned very productive land on the banks of the River Towy at Nantgaredig, a few miles upstream from Carmarthen town. Their home was the large old white-painted farmhouse of Glyneidden, and they were regular visitors to Maesmawr in their ancient pale green Austin car, which managed, with Winnie always driving it, to surmount the hilly route through southern Montgomeryshire without any break-downs. Upon arrival, the old motor was entrusted to the knowledgeable and capable hands of Walter, Nain's and Taid's trusty chauffeur, Estate

My nain's sister Winifred (1870–1959), 'Auntie Winnie', the wife of Henry Jones-Davies, CBE. Photographed about 1925.

Courtesy: Henry Jones-Davies

mechanic and carpenter of many years' employ, of whom I shall write in detail in due course. Walter would ensure that the car's four-cylinder and ageing 'heart' was checked with his mechanical 'stethoscope' and pronounced fit for the rigours of the steep ascents on the homeward journey.

Winnie and Harry had a daughter, Morfudd, and two sons, Tom and Glyn. Tom, who was a physician in Carmarthen, lived with his wife Nesta and son in the village of Nantgaredig. In his twenties Tom had played rugby for Llanelli, and was capped as a member of the International Welsh team in 1931. A large black-and-white framed photograph hung proudly at old Glyneidden, recording Tom at the very moment he scored a try for Wales at Twickenham in that year. He it was who so kindly gave me the charming photograph of my mother and her sister Mari on their handsome horses in front of Maesmawr. Tom suddenly produced it when we were gathered at Glyneidden for his mother's funeral in 1959, and it remains a treasured possession. (See page 120)

'Uncle Harry', as he was known to all the family, was short in stature and always dressed in a smartly cut suit of soft, medium-grey worsted. He wore light-weight black ankle-high boots, of a kind which were much favoured by his generation. I loved uncle Harry – as everyone did. He spoke very quickly, with a delightful 'sing-song' manner deriving from the strongly Welsh lilt that

Right: Henry Jones-Davies, CBE (1870–1955), uncle Harry, husband of Winifred, née Ellis, my nain's youngest sister.

Courtesy: Henry Jones-Davies, their grandson.

Below: 'Winnie' Jones-Davies, with her daughter Morfudd and sons Tom and Glyn, in front of Maesmawr Hall in about 1918. Tom (right), who became a physician, played rugby for Llanelli, and for Wales in the 1931 International season. Note the black-and-white wicket gate and canopied porch covered with clematis, which still existed in my days, as I specially describe herein.

Courtesy: Henry Jones-Davies, the late Dr. Tom Jones-Davies' son.

enhanced his way of talking. His voice was deep, and his conversation was quite hard to grasp, as the words had to find their way under his large and bushy walrus moustache. His kindly eyes had a humorous twinkle, and he always called me "My boy!" both before and after any conversation, however brief. He delighted in hearing all about my daily doings in and around Maesmawr. Winnie, who adored Harry, could almost have been taken for her sister's twin, although she was seven years younger than my nain. When they were together, they revelled in the sense of humour they shared, and would laugh about this-or-that until tears of amusement ran down their beautifully complexioned, pink and ageing cheeks. When death ultimately parted them, Winnie, the survivor, must have been grief-stricken.

Amongst the family friends of old who came to stay at Maesmawr during my boyhood, I vaguely recall a kindly, ageing, gentleman known as 'Hoppy' – his surname was Hopkirk, or perhaps Hopkiss? 'Hoppy' was a very long-time friend of both Taid and Nain, and his whole demeanour expressed his utter 'at- homeness' in the old house, its memories and its welcome love. Like Taid, he possessed a wonderful head of snow-white hair, but Hoppy's was much more luxuriant and bushy. I do not know – I never did know – whence he came, but nain frequently spoke about Hoppy to my uncle and my aunts, who were all so fond of him. A tall personage, a Dr. Fitzgerald-Clarke, a retired physician of a quiet nature, was also a fondly welcomed visitor. Nain called him 'Fitz', which seemed natural enough. I vaguely remember that Fitz, like Nain, loved and was very adept at word games, which were very much part of Maesmawr's indoor leisure hours. A third regular guest was my uncle Emrys' great fishing friend, 'Rumney' Evans. Rumney lived and worked in London, and he possessed a beard of great luxuriance. When a small boy, I always thought – though I never said so – that Rumney's beard would be an ideal place for him to keep his fishing flies, gently impaled by their barbs during piscatory expeditions with my uncle to local Llyn Du. Perhaps – but, thought I, the arrangement wouldn't have been so convenient at bedtime! Rumney was a truly jolly man, whereas my uncle Emrys was shy and retiring by nature and did not have close local friends in any number. He loved Rumney for his natural exuberance and enthusiasm for the 'wind through the heather, and the wave upon the lake', there for them both to enjoy Nature's beauty and a shared pursuit.

ON THE HILLS

Buffet on sweet buffet, the wildwood came,
Like a green wave or a green flame,
With melodies
And delicate fragrances
And the secret souls of the watching trees.

Colour on grave colour sleeps the ancient moor,
With its blue roof and its purple floor –
Where small birds fly
With merry, pencilled eye,
And like great gods the stately clouds go by.

Mary Webb, FIFTY-ONE POEMS

Llyn Du and its companions, Llyn y Tarw and Llyn Mawr, are natural lakes set as a group high on the hills above Carno. In my boyhood and before, Llyn Du belonged to Maesmawr. The other pair – certainly Llyn Mawr, if not also Tarw – were owned by Lord Davies. The largest of the trio, Llyn y Tarw, was at that time – and perhaps is to this day? – a favourite nesting site for seagulls. Hundreds of their nests – mere shallow depressions made by the birds amongst the small stones which formed the lake's shore – lay underfoot. In the nesting season, the Dinam Estate gamekeepers took large wicker baskets up the mountain track and from there to the lake, where they filled them with the eggs. These were taken back to Llandinam, packed into sturdy hampers, and put on the morning train for Moat Lane Junction, from there bound for London markets – most probably Harrods and Fortnum & Mason's Stores.

Reverting to my detailed descriptions of the Hall at Maesmawr, the quartered coat of arms above the fireplace is not what it purports to be, although my family probably had no idea that this was so. The following is an unabridged extract from an informative article by the late Mr E.H.C. Davies on several aspects of Maesmawr and his family's very long ownership of it, from approximately 1650 until 1920:

Above the brass-hooded oak fireplace in the main parlour is a quartered coat of arms. This presents a modern day puzzle to the Davies family. It was suddenly brought into use on a seal of 1701 and continued in use for generations, though the present carving is a Victorian installation only. The arms are pretentious and wholly bogus, and why they were suddenly introduced when perfectly respectable and much older arms had been recognized up until then is a total mystery. One can only assume that it was a folie-de-grandeur of some sort. The sons of the Reverend Herbert Davies obtained, in 1971, an exemplification (i.e. confirmation) of their entitlement to the original arms of 1569, and the family have now brought these back into use.

E.H.C.D. 2001

Maesmawr's west gable and roof under major repair at unknown date; the former's considerable thickness on slope shows, of interest, its (by then) masonry construction that superseded an earlier half-timber framed gable. See photograph and caption, page 56; did the (there shown) stone chimney exist before the roof repairs (above), thus temporarily dismantled for them (?), or was it first built at the time of these repairs? It will never be known. Note also the 'weeping' willow tree, at right. Was it the one I later often sat within (page 133), or a predecessor?!

Both windows of the original Hall have been radically – and, I feel, very unsuitably – altered at some time since 1947. Photographs 1, 3 and 5 (pages 127, 129 and 131) clearly show them as they were, when the smaller south-facing window was sashed with generously-sized rectangular panes, the frames being enclosed by a wide wooden surround and the whole painted white. Whilst being of a slimmer proportion than the south-facing window of the dining room, both were of similar design, as was the entrance lobby window, central on the front gable, but with smaller and square panes. The Hall's previous and original west-facing tall window reflected the elegant glazing proportions of its larger neighbour, the drawing room's bay window. The Hall window was obviously designed by Nesfield to balance his great bay window aesthetically, the latter being the ground floor's central feature. It should be noted that the previous west-facing window of the morning room was of similar design and size to the west Hall window. Thus Nesfield created a perfect aesthetic balance with the three windows. Although the opportunity to plead for the retention of the trio as an architectural entity, for its own sake and in the context of the building preservation Laws and Listed Building legal constraints, has been gone for many years, I feel that it was a degree of architectural vandalism that, presumably, permitted it at some time after 1947. The removal of architect Nesfield's elegant and balustered balcony, which crowned his dignified drawing room's bay window, was a further aesthetic tragedy for the west face of the house.

My personal judgement is that Maesmawr's present replacement ground floor windows are an aesthetic disaster; their quasi-antique 'diamond' leaded panes are alien to the former character of the house. As for the extraction of the previous entrance lobby window, and its substitution by the present front door, central about the gable, that was – tragically – the ignorant whim of one or another of Maesmawr's succession of owners since my family departed in 1947. Moreover, I maintain that if Planning consent was given for that alteration to a Listed building, it should not have been given. Neither should it have been given, if it ever was, for the extraction of the entrance lobby's antique stair.

My comment on the Hall windows, past and present, has drawn me into a digression upon other windows and allied characteristics. Before I proceed into further rooms, it is here convenient to consider the old staircase out of the Hall.

The lower flight of the original and elaborate staircase has been much widened since my time. Then, a single door, similar to those already described, gave immediate access onto a small platform before the flight of steps commenced. The present wide and door-less opening thus contained the single door, and a short length of blank wall, on the fireplace side. This allowed the end of a high-backed and upholstered *settle* – which was the length of three generous seats – to extend into the room at a right-angle. The *settle* gave very effective protection against the cold winter draughts which dropped down the staircase and around

The Hall at Maesmawr in 1947, shortly after the death of my nain; her favourite high-back chair stands poignantly alone in its former accustomed place. Far left; the single door which then enclosed the old stairs.

Clearer photograph found by my cousin, David Owen Owen, since 1st edition.

its thin enclosing door. It also formed a cosy corner close to the fireplace, and was upholstered in a bluey-greeny-grey William Morris fabric, as were all the armchairs in the room. My nain's special place beside the fire was on the opposite side of the hearth, in a deeply cushioned upright ladder-back chair, protected from draughts through the entrance lobby door by a tall *zig-zag* three-leaf screen. Beside her chair was a green baize covered card table on which stood a little brass table-lamp with a glass shade – pale green outside and white within. There she happily spent many hours in summer and winter, chatting and laughing with the family, visitors or staying guests, reading, resting from her daily involvement in much kitchen and back kitchen activity, playing solo card games and games with others – especially word games, writing letters, and sometimes just peacefully dozing.

The now precious and nostalgic photograph of the Hall as it was up to 1947, taken especially for the Maesmawr Estate's sale particulars that same year, is invaluable for reminding those of us who were then children of its past beauty, even if only dimly perceived. Happily, several principal features have chanced to remain unaltered, whilst others, including all the pieces of furniture, have, alas, long gone. Of the former, the fine ceiling beams with the early-eighteenth century plaster panels are paramount, and the fireplace's brass smoke-hood, with its Prince of Wales' triple feather emblem, survives, as does the (sadly bogus) crested overmantel above it. Two regrettable victims of subsequent alterations were the pair of single oak-panelled doors with their double-diamond incised motif, one opening from the Hall into the passage lobby, the other closing off the foot of the old staircase. The latter door can be seen on the extreme left of the photograph, partly behind the high-back upholstered three-seat *settle* that faced across the fireplace. The bold foliate pattern of the Morris fabric covering the *settle* and the armchairs greatly contributed to the character of the Hall.

Most worthy of mention, albeit barely visible, is the three-tiered Welsh oak *tridarn* whose antique and polished presence graced the wall corner close to the (here brightly lit) doorway into the front entrance lobby. Above the *tridarn's* lower

Myself beside the Hall's fireplace in September 2004, standing exactly where my nain used to sit in her favourite high-back chair.

Photograph: Vanessa Woodcock

and centre cupboards, its upper shelf displayed large circular pewter chargers and lidded flagons; a pair of each is visible by the light reflected from the tall window facing the west lawn.

On the wall between the left-hand end of the fireplace overmantel and the door to the stair hung a plaque bust, in pewter as I recall, of a generously moustached personage – perhaps Tom Ellis M.P. In my memory's hindsight, the bust had an Edwardian similarity to the composer Sir Edward Elgar, of whom I, aged ten, had yet to learn of, and his music to love. Whoever's bust it was, it is just visible beneath the end of the beam.

The old staircase is now much wider than it used to be, and a significant portion that formed a half-landing leading to the first floor was also taken out, presumably at the same time. When in due course I describe the many alterations that have taken place upstairs since my boyhood, I include the now absent half-landing on my way through it. (See page 95)

I well remember the balustered black antiquity of the old staircase up which family and guests would eventually ascend to bed, I to my little room, whose window is the right-hand one in the front gable as one faces it. There I would lie in the deepening summer night, aware of the old house's creaking timbers as they relaxed in the cool after a hot day, but slowly lulled to sleep by the hooting of Tawny and Little owls in the velvet dark, amidst the ancient trees along the drive; then I awoke next morning to the many doves' and woodpigeons' fluty cooing, and the occasional sharp short whistle from a shunting engine at Moat Lane Junction beneath the far soft hills. Another early morning sound was the steady *CHUNK-chunk-CHUNK-chunk* of Maesmawr's mighty BLACKSTONE oil-engine in her shed beyond the east garden. She drove a dynamo, charging batteries which supplied low-voltage electricity for the house, and also drew water for it from a nearby well.

Continuing my voyage of memory, I move out of the little ante-room into the drawing room, Nesfield's principal creation for the house in 1876, and nowadays the hotel dining room. I was baptised here during the summer of 1932, having been born in Aylesbury, Buckinghamshire in May of that year. The ceremony doubtless took place within the bay window, as affording the best natural light for that occasion. It was performed by the Reverend Dr. Richard Jones, D.D., the minister of Llandinam Presbyterian Church from 1907 to 1947. I shall recall him again when remembering the Sunday morning service at Llandinam, which was always mandatory for the Maesmawr party, of all ages, that happened to be assembled. I mentioned earlier that my taid died at Maesmawr when I was very young. In the decade of Nain's widowhood that followed, and also when she and taid were together, I remember the mutual close affection between nain and Dr. Richard Jones, whom she held in very high regard, as Taid surely must also have done.

70

Doves.

Agnes Miller Parker, 1936

Despite their similar age, Dr. Jones always referred to Nain as "Mrs Jones", when in conversation with her or anyone else, and she, likewise, always addressed him as "Dr. Jones" in similar circumstances. Occasionally I visit his, and his beloved wife's, grave in St. Llonio's Churchyard, Llandinam, and I muse that he it was whose hand once sprinkled my infant brow with the Water of Baptism. Whilst Dr. Jones was of a generation of ministers that pertained, in many instances, to the 'Old School' of thought, and may therefore have extemporised part of the ceremony, I am told that it is most likely that he would have spoken the following Baptismal Supplication. Its words are derived from the Book of Exodus, and were widely adopted by the (Welsh) Nonconformist Church in the 1920s and 1930s.

"In the Name of the Lord Jesus Christ, I now receive this child into the Christian Church and, as a token of that, I baptise him with water. Edward Michael, I baptise thee in the Name of the Father, Son and Holy Ghost. May the Lord bless thee and keep thee, and cause His Face to shine upon thee, through Jesus Christ, our Lord. Amen."

Surely a most beautiful wish within which to embrace the heart of the ceremony, and one that I feel blessed to receive throughout life, as wished for me by those present at beloved Maesmawr that day. Years later I was told that a paternal aunt had dropped me at some point in the ceremony, but no mention was

71

made of how far I fell or the nature of my landing, whether hard or soft. Suffice it to say that I must have bounced back, or up, as the case may be – unharmed, or relatively so, in that first, but not last, of Life's 'bumps' during my present *Three-score-and-twelve*.

During the Second World War, the drawing room's furniture included a magnificent highly-polished black grand piano – a Bechstein or Bluthner. I often wonder who was lucky enough to obtain it at the contents sale of 1947. The furniture was covered with white dust-sheets, and linen blinds were pulled fully down to the floor, across the bay window. No fresh air and barely any sunlight filtered into the room, which smelt stale and musty. Occasionally I would tiptoe in, lift up the piano's keyboard lid, and gently press the very white ivory keys with my little forefinger, one by one, out of curiosity. A door at the far end of the drawing room opened directly into the morning room, now a principal part of the hotel kitchen. Occupied daily, the morning room was usually entered through a second door at the far end of the central passage, which in my time extended the full length of the Nesfield extension, terminating with the side-door, which opened adjacent to the vegetable gardens and the apple, plum and nut-tree orchard beyond. Today, that long passage is interrupted mid-way by a hotel fire-door.

I will shortly describe the other openings off the central passage, but meanwhile will return to the morning room, which was the principal room that did so. In hindsight its name is puzzling, as it was not the scene of breakfast unless guests or additional family members were staying, when a large table became necessary. Excepting such occasions, breakfast was held in the servants' hall across the way, which I will describe separately. Newspapers, including the *Montgomeryshire Express & Radnor Times*, were perused in the morning room, where my uncle Emrys typed his letters concerning the Maesmawr Estate and the County Council committees of which he was a member. The morning room was especially associated with tea and supper, the latter being taken in the dining room only at my nain's discretion.

I vividly recall afternoon tea in the morning room in summers long ago. A large bowl of fragrant sweet-pea flowers stood at the centre of the table, at whose head my nain was seated before the large silver teapot, a silver jug of hot water to replenish it, and a smaller one containing cream – always cream! The semi-translucent bone china had a pretty floral pattern, and it was arranged upon a starched, brilliant white damask tablecloth with a crochet-adorned border. Home-made butter and varieties of jam and home-produced honeycomb were liberally spread on traditional Welsh *leices* (lightcakes). These were little flat discs, about three inches in diameter, made from a batter of flour, buttermilk, sugar and a pinch of salt and bicarbonate of soda. A spoonful of batter was dropped onto a very hot iron plate called a bakestone and allowed to bake until bubbles appeared on the top surface and the underside was cooked to a golden brown. The discs were then turned over and baked on the other side. They were served warm, and had a smooth but clammy texture on the tongue. They were all heaped high upon a plate, probably reminding those who knew of it of the Leaning Tower of Pisa. Home-made lemon sponge cakes and scones, together with plentiful and very thin slices of bread, all made by Nain, competed for my and others' attention. Her farmhouse teas were archetypal and eagerly consumed, whilst in the distance there circled and cawed the innumerable Maesmawr rooks returning to roost in the nearby tall trees of the orchard rookery, beyond the tennis lawn. As each evening drew near, summer and winter, so the dear birds came home to their

Maesmawr, the swirling flock's excited chatter being one of my most enduring memories.

Teatime often coincided with the fowls' 'teatime'. When sufficiently sated with her confectionery, I would say to Nain: "Please, Nain, may I 'get down' to collect the eggs and feed the hens?" She would smile and her eyes would say, 'You do love them so much, don't you?'; then she would say, "Yes, dearest, you may." "Thank you, Nain," and off I would rush to find a basket to fill with the speckled offerings – some of them still warm in the hay-filled nesting boxes – and scatter grain in the farmyard for their scurrying and fluttering providers.

The morning room was occupied in the evening, generally more so in the summer than in the winter, when the old Hall's cosy fireplace became the focus of family and guests' gatherings. Whichever of them was chosen, the morning room's coal fire or the Hall's of scented logs, the mode of leisure never changed. Some of us chatted, some read, and others would play at cards or at word-games. 'Scrabble' was very popular, and my nain was very adept at it, frequently producing unheard-of words – at least so we thought, until the faithful dictionary always proved her correct, at which tears of amusement would well up in her kind and ageing eyes. Whichever venue was chosen for the evening, everyone gathered first in the morning room, where in its corner on a table sat the elderly battery wireless. This was turned on just before the full nine sonorous strokes of Big Ben at Westminster, which boomed out to maintain the Nation's wartime morale and preceded the main news bulletin of the day. Worthy of mention in today's world of instantaneous electrical equipment is that Yesteryear's valve-circuit and battery wirelesses needed a few minutes for their valves to glow and thereby warm up – literally! The micro-printed radio circuit of today was then unimagined.

As the ninth stroke of Big Ben died away, the BBC's newsreader confidently announced: "This is London and here is the nine o'clock news read by (Bruce Belfrage)." He it was who, on the occasion when a wartime German bomb fell at the rear of Broadcasting House, continued to read the News as though nothing untoward had happened. Alvar Liddell – with the accent on the 'dell' – was also a newsreader at the time; although I believe he was a Scandinavian, he spoke English with immaculate enunciation, and his name became a byword for elegant delivery. Frank Phillips was a third reader of distinction, possessing a most beautiful *microphone voice*. The trio were the pride of Sir John Reith, at that time Director-General of the BBC. It was customary for the newsreader to confirm his identity before commencing the bulletin. This continues today as broadcasting practice, but the custom originated at the outbreak of the Second World War, to reassure listeners that their wireless was tuned to the BBC in London – information received thus being the Truth. Moreover, unknown to listeners at home, some phrase in a bulletin, which seemed innocuous, might conceal a coded message for a pro-Allied Resistance group in, say, France or Holland. They had to be reassured that the message was being broadcast by the BBC from London and not by an enemy radio station.

On the subject of wartime wireless, the following details may be of interest. The 'receiver', as it was often called, had a capacious wooden cabinet to accommodate the two separate power units needed. The larger of the two was the high-tension battery, comprising about fifty separate cells of 1.5 volts each, packed close together to form an oblong which was enclosed in stout cardboard. The centre of each cell was printed on the cardboard top as a series of dots. A positive wire led from the wireless circuits and terminated with a red push-in plug. The plug was inserted into the first cell by being pushed through the first dot printed on the cardboard; this effected electrical contact.

Depending on how much the wireless was used, each high-tension cell might last a week, or perhaps less; but eventually fading volume would indicate a need to obtain the next cell's power. The battery was then withdrawn from the back of the case, the plug inserted through the next unpierced dot and hey presto! – full power was restored.

The second battery, the low-tension one, also needed to be in a well-charged condition. It was a toughened glass jar about four inches square and six inches high, within which were a series of lead cells submerged in acid. The jar was leak-proof and had a sealed lid with a screw-down central terminal, and into it was offered, and tightened, a two-prong spade terminal which had a connecting lead from the wireless circuitry. This battery did not have an extensive working life either, and when it was exhausted, it was returned, by means of its drop-down carrying handle, to the ubiquitous wireless shop of those days for recharging, a fresh battery being loaned in the meantime. Low-tension batteries at Maesmawr were recharged in the battery room in the oil-engine's shed.

I also retain fond memories of the morning room for the pair of bronze figurines placed at either end of the fireplace's mantelshelf – two rearing horses being restrained from charging towards each other across the mantelshelf by their respective ostlers, bare-chested and bare-footed stalwarts clad in swirling skirts-cum-kilts, gazing upwards and grasping their chargers' flying reins with raised arms. The figurines were about fourteen inches high, including their heavy bases. So realistic were they, and so 'frozen' in their movement, that I would gaze at them intently for minutes on-end, hopeful of inducing a miraculous re-animation. It never happened, and a mid-shelf collision was thus avoided. I hope they galloped off to someone's kind 'stable' when bought at the 1947 contents sale.

Upon the leather-topped writing desk which stood in front of the morning room's north-facing window, overlooking the orchard, stood a 1919 First Edition set of hardback, green, cloth-covered volumes entitled *Birds of the British Isles and their Eggs*. The author was T.A. Coward, and this work of his is regarded as one of the finest of its *genre*. The set was kept upright by a pair of small but heavy mottled green marble bookends, on each of which crouched a most beautiful depiction of a snipe, fashioned in matt silver. Their feathers were so realistically articulated that one might have expected the little brace to take instant flight. My uncle Emrys was a keen amateur ornithologist. He was also a first-class shot with a 12-bore gun, a splendid example of which he kept in a corner rack behind his desk. In my boy-

hood, a very tall Scots pine-tree stood on the orchard boundary between the house and the river pasture. (This was surely the 'big fir tree' mentioned in the 'MAES-MAWR' article on pages 16-19.) Its topmost branches are clear to see in Mr Harris'

Snipe: wood-engraving
Clare Leighton

drawing (page 55), rising up behind the roofs of Maesmawr. Troublesome cormorants loved to roost high in this tree. They preyed on trout in the river, but uncle Emrys, in his heart, appreciated that it was their natural instinct, and instead of shooting the rascals, let them be.

Across the Nesfield passage from the morning room was the door-less way through to the kitchen, beyond which was the back kitchen and adjacent small dairy. The kitchen itself was preceded by the servants' hall, which was to the left of the way through and partially screened from it by a *settle*. I have earlier referred to an upholstered *settle* in my description of the Hall. The one in the servants' hall was entirely made of polished pine; it was about six feet long and had three hinged lift-up seats, each concealing a boxed compartment beneath. The high and very upright back of the *settle* – it was not a comfortable specimen to sit upon – was made of tongued-and-grooved boards to about six feet above the floor. The compartments beneath the three seats were barely able to accommodate my uncle's plentiful collection of boots and shoes, which he liked to clean and polish carefully before he put them away. A coal-burning stove warmed the room in winter. A square table in the corner, to the left of the window, was the venue for family breakfast, as and when its members, together with one or more visiting guests, descended to eat at whatever hour suited them. My nain usually had her breakfast in her bedroom so that she could rise in a leisurely way, but every day she was in the kitchen by eleven o'clock to supervise the morning's cooking and make her personal contribution to it.

For breakfast, porridge had always been made well beforehand, ladled into pale, constantly soda-scrubbed ash wood bowls, whose rims could barely contain the flood of cream poured upon the oaten delicacy. Scrambled eggs, sausages, plentiful wild mushrooms from the lush Maesmawr pastures where the house-cows grazed, and home-grown bacon, all in silver-hued domed warming dishes upon an electric hotplate, awaited the hungry. In due course I shall write about Maesmawr's annual piggies who, while never asked to do so, contributed themselves as eventual rashers. These came to the table as stiff as boards, sliced from flitches – salted joints of bacon which were prepared in a room over the kitchen which was called the laundry! Here, after salting, the flitches were hung from the ceiling on sturdy iron hooks, to cure for months – some, to judge from their wizened appearance, perhaps for much longer.

On the servants' hall window sill reposed a sizeable antique musical box with a blackish hardwood case – perhaps of ebony? – whose top, front and end were finely edged with an inlaid border of *mother-of-pearl*. Within was a second brass-hinged lid of framed glass whose sides rested on a velvet-lined rebate to help exclude dust. This inner lid was opened and lifted with a little projecting tongue of soft leather, and lay back against the outer lid when both were raised. Inside, a folded-back brass winding handle at one end wound up the spring by a ratchet mechanism. A tiny brass lever – all the musical box's component parts being brass except for the long comb shortly to be described – set the horizontal drum in motion. This drum's entire circumferential surface possessed, seemingly haphazardly arranged, myriads of miniscule projecting steel pins. As the drum revolved, some of the steel pins plucked the prongs of the tempered steel comb which lay fractionally above and parallel with the drum. Some genius had invented this mechanical system of pins which, when set into the revolving drum at predetermined and very accurate points, plucked the comb's prongs. Each prong, being very slightly longer than its immediate neighbour across the entire length of the comb, represented a single note, so altogether there were several octaves of tones and semitones. The ultimate but essential refinement was a 'butterfly' governor, a pair of tiny wings whose revolving axle, connected to the drum's drive mechanism, controlled the number of revolutions per minute and thus the melody's musical metre.

I spent many happy hours with the musical box. I especially remember one day, when torrential rain fell for many hours during the Second World War's battle and siege of Leningrad, now St. Petersburg again. Although none of the musical box's repertoire was Russian, I wound up the mechanism all day and repeated its melodies time after time. To this day, exceptionally heavy rain can set my musical box of memories in motion and I see in my mind's eye the little 'butterfly' on the governor whizzing round in a blur, and in my imagination again hear the crystal-clear, rather melancholy tinkling tunes that I have long since forgotten. Occasionally, when I gazed intently at the clusters of pins being rotated into the inner depths of the case after plucking the prongs of the comb, a cold fear would arise that, if I touched a pin with my forefinger, it would become impaled and be drawn into the mechanism, with terrible consequences.

Sharing the servants' hall window sill with the musical box was a heavy goffering iron, or wheel-goffer, which I illustrate together with a laundry mangle, linen press, flat iron and washboard. The goffering iron had an interlocking pair of brass rollers which impressed a corrugated pattern into whatever flexible material was wound through them. This device was used especially to decorate the edges of the starched white linen coronet-style caps worn by all the housemaids from early afternoon until bed-time. They were also worn for their serving of lunch in the dining room when guests were staying, and always for the family's Sunday lunch, which was held there. The goffering iron also made an attractive pattern in thin card; this had no particular purpose, but I often liked doing it when in idle mood!

High up against the right-hand wall of the way through into the kitchen stood a capacious store cupboard-cum-dresser with wooden panelled doors at low level and framed glass-fronted doors above, behind which were tiers of shelves laden with Nain's annually made delights. Jams, marmalade, chutney and bottled fruit, together with comb honey from Maesmawr's bees, stood in shining, succulent ranks upon them. There were also special delicacies such as crystallised fruits and stem-ginger, obtained from Harrods, London's Knightsbridge stores. To reach the highest shelves required the use of a rather old, potentially unsafe stepladder up which my nain precariously climbed, usually wearing Edwardian-style shoes with a thin button-down strap across the instep which, although hazardous in the circumstances, mercifully never broke to cause her downfall.

Before describing the kitchen, my journey through almost the entire house returns up the central passage – thus back into the old part of Maesmawr. On the way, I pass the foot of the very steep back-stairs down which I excitedly scampered to separate the morning milk before breakfast. What, you may ask, had it to be separated from? The CREAM, I reply, and I will shortly describe how. Next to the back-stairs was the cellar dairy, so called because of the perilously steep stone steps that descended into its cool depths. They had no handrail; down-and-up, and up-and-down – how many times, I wonder, did my nain, in her prime and in her later years, survive the cellar dairy's narrow steps? I visualise her now, with fine naturally silver-grey hair, in petal-patterned, long-sleeved cotton smock, and wearing delicate pendant diamond earrings, making her stately way in those favourite Edwardian shoes of hers, an empty dish in hand ready to collect something or other. Very close behind her, their tails optimistically held high in expectation, softly followed the family cats, *Sooty* and *Miaow*. *Sooty* was of course black, and *Miaow* was a long-haired pale grey tabby – and frequently said so! The little trio would shortly emerge in the same order; Nain with the object of her choice safely in hand, *Sooty* and *Miaow* still expectant. *Miaow* had been my pet cat when I lived in north Wales from 1936, when I was four, until the outbreak of the War in 1939. My father's problem made our family life style chaotic and uncertain, and unsuitable for pets. When we went down to the south coast of Devon to live, for only two years before my mother's death, *Miaow* was re-homed at Maesmawr for the remainder of his long life, where, with *Sooty* as inseparable companion, he was very happy. My uncle Emrys adored cats, and I eagerly looked forward to my Maesmawr reunions with *Miaow*.

Next to the cellar dairy was the so-called butler's pantry, although my family had never employed one. Perhaps the previous Davies generation of the Victorian era had done so? The room was one step down from the central passage. In my boyhood it was fitted with a shallow stoneware sink and wooden draining-board. The splendid range of wooden-framed and panelled wall cupboards fortunately remain today, and were made by Walter Pryce, the Estate carpenter and joiner. I will write about him later in these Recollections. The butler's pantry was home to the knife-grinder. No, he was not a shut-away recluse haloed in sparks. The grinder was a heavy circular wooden machine that sat on the floor in a corner. A cranked metal handle projected from its centre. The drum was about fifteen inches in diameter and about five inches thick. Unseen within was a geared wheel of some kind which could be (by me!) progressively wound up to a tremendous speed. Such velocity was entirely unnecessary to fulfil the device's primary function, but it was a boyhood compulsion of mine to discover whether the maximum velocity so obtained would perhaps, by Isaac Newton's Laws of Gravitational and Centrifugal force, propel the knife-grinder on its independent way across the pantry floor. The hidden wheel within was fitted with a sharpening stone and polishing brushes. The blades of the non-stainless steel table knives were successively inserted into a pair of projecting orifices on the top of the drum. After several minutes the blade was withdrawn, glistening and as sharp as a razor. Incidentally, being non-stainless, they were apt to taint meat with an unpleasant metallic tang.

Nesfield's central passage, which was then an uninterrupted length extending from the old house's lobby down to the far distant so-called side door, provided an ideal location for further boyhood exuberance. I loved to use the twin-shelved wooden trolley with rubber-tyred castor wheels for this purpose. It was always kept in a corner of the lobby for taking food to and from the kitchen and the dining room. After discarding my shoes, and aligning the trolley on the imaginary 'starting-grid' at the lobby end of the central passage, with my elbows on the top shelf, I would lean upon it while my feet propelled both the trolley and its 'driver' to an exhilarating speed towards the closed side door at the far end of the central passage. At about mid-way down the 'race-track', the kinetic energy thus generated allowed me to cease further effort, whereupon the soles of my shoeless feet were deliciously tickled as they sped over the myriad narrow joints between the red clay floor tiles. The trolley had neither horn nor hooter to warn of its imminent approach, thus potentially endangering anyone unaware of what was hurtling towards them. Fortunately, no mishap ever occurred. The Victorian floor tiles remain today, but the beautiful William Morris wallpaper which at that time hung on both sides of the central passage for its full length above the dado rail has gone; it was his 'Grapevine' pattern of bluey-purple hue.

The lobby, into which the hotel reception desk opens, contained a grandmother clock whose dainty chime tinkled at the hour and the quarter; my uncle wound it daily. Immediately left of the glazed doors, opening out of the hotel bar, and near the wall which the bar-counter has replaced, stood a chest-of-drawers

The '**Maesmawr Nativity**'. An early-seventeenth century carved oak panel (perhaps Welsh); 13 x 10 inches, and happily in-situ within the house today.

Photograph: Ellis-Jones

whose top was a very suitable height upon which to stand Maesmawr's only telephone receiver. This was widely known as the 'daffodil' model, imaginatively
so-called because of its upright design, which comprised a heavy circular base
with a central stem terminating with a faintly daffodil-shaped mouthpiece into
which – or rather 'at' which – the caller spoke. Projecting at a right-angle from
the stem was the 'Y' shaped bracket upon which hung the separate earpiece at-

tached to a lead which conveniently enabled the user to
raise the earpiece to his or her ear. Lifting the earpiece
off its bracket made contact with the incoming call, and
replacing it after the conversation closed the line. The
earpiece's connecting lead, like those of practically all
electrical appliances of Yesteryear, was wrapped in a
sheath of purply-mauve-black silk. The telephone was
made from a pre-plastic material called 'Bakelite' because it was invented by a Mr Baakeland.

Maesmawr's telephone number, in those far-away,
pre-STD days, was Caersws 221, which signifies that
there were no more than a few hundred subscribers in
the Caersws exchange area. Each was connected to the village's exchange, this
being simply the house of a responsible Caersws resident with the General Post
Office's basic equipment for connection to the 'outside world'. This Welsh worthy seemingly sat all day – and presumably far into the night – at the console,
ready at a moment's notice, which occurred at the drop of a little call-disc on the
console, to answer a request for connection. These operators, in their homes all
over the country, were proverbially the custodians of much local and parochial
news and gossip. They were silently able to glean this by the flick of a finger
upon a little switch on the console, which enabled the conversation to be over-
heard without either participant knowing it.

In those days, long-distance telephone calls were called 'trunks'. Upon being
asked to put through a long-distance call – perhaps being raised from gentle
slumber to do so – the operator said "trunks" in reply, and inserted a plug on
the G.P.O.'s console to connect him, or her in Caersws' case, to the semi-principal
Ludlow exchange. Upon contact being made between these two, 'Caersws' said
"trunks" to Ludlow, who acknowledged understanding by replying "trunks"
in return. The latter then passed the Caersws call through to the principal exchange of perhaps Birmingham or Exeter, Bristol or London. At that point in
the patient subscriber's progress, the principal exchange reversed the foregoing
procedure, making contact with a semi-principal exchange down the line. That,
in turn, awoke 'Caersws" opposite number, someone similarly sitting at home in
some remote part of the country patiently doing the same job. If all the operators happened to leave the wires between them 'open', the call's gradual progress

could be heard from start to finish, culminating in the well-known 'brrp-brrp', 'brrp-brrp'. Then, of course, after seemingly endless minutes of ringing-out, there might be NO REPLY! As it was rather discourteous to replace the receiver at this point without thanking 'Caersws' for all her trouble, one had to wait politely whilst the obvious outcome of the call was relayed back down the wires. When experiencing that kind of minor frustration, those of one's parents' generation and earlier, might mutter that quaint old adage: **_Patience is a virtue, patience is a grace; Patience was the little girl who seldom washed her face_**.

Where the hotel reception desk now opens, there was once a long and old-fashioned hot water radiator upon which **_Sooty_** and **_Miaow_** contentedly shared a warming blanket in winter. Adjacent was a cloakroom where, each morning, my uncle Emrys sharpened his Rolls Razor prior to shaving. The Rolls was, in its day, a revolutionary concept in mechanical wizardry. The steel blade, which had only one cutting edge, was on its reverse much thickened and rounded, and this round edge enabled the blade to be held in the grip of a folding-away handle cleverly connected to a side ratchet which flicked the razor blade over and

Agnes Miller Parker (date?)

back, to-and-fro, its cutting edge thus being sharpened on both sides, alternately. Sharpening was effected by the cutting edge being pressed against a strip of smooth oil-impregnated leather called the *strop*. This had a sturdy loop of cord at one end, passed over a hook – usually screwed into the back of the door at a convenient height for the user. The other end of the *strop* was passed through a thin gap under the blade's cutting edge, the strip of leather being about fourteen inches long. Rapid and repeated up-and-down motion of the blade's edge, pressed close to the leather surface, produced – after several minutes – the desired effect. The longevity of a Rolls blade was extensive, and thus probably not productive for the manufacturer's profit margins. As is the fate of most gadgets, clever or not, it became a victim of 'Progress' in due course. I recently saw a complete Rolls Razor Company's outfit which had been presented to Hereford's city museum. It was just the same as my uncle's, and I instantly recalled its inimitable *click-clack-click-clack* coming from the Maesmawr cloakroom in the early morning. After about fifteen minutes my uncle's silk dressing-gowned figure was seen scurrying through the lobby into the Hall and up the old staircase to his bedroom at the front of the house. In his wake drifted the perfumed scent of an exotic shaving soap, probably bought from Messrs Crabtree and Evelyn, or another of London's West End shops specialising in similar refined toiletry. To end this dissertation on the Rolls, the clever assemblage was enclosed in an elegant chromium-plated case with a fluted pattern impressed on the lid, surrounding the maker's name, which was proudly embossed on it.

The lobby was also home to the dinner-gong, whose sound announced either lunch or supper in the dining room only, not in the morning room. The gong was a heavy brass disc eighteen inches or so in diameter, its edges circumferentially turned back about four inches for rigidity. Its surface had a 'hammered' finish, and the gong was suspended from stout cords hung from two hooks on the horizontal part of its sturdy mahogany floor stand. It was struck with a mahogany drumstick, whose head was about the size of a tennis ball, wrapped tightly in soft chamois leather and resting horizontally above the gong itself on a pair of small brackets. I eagerly awaited every opportunity to sound the gong, but my frequent over-enthusiasm with the drumstick had to be restrained by dear Gretta, Maesmawr's senior housemaid. In later years, whenever I saw the beginning of a Rank Organisation film, Maesmawr's gong came to mind. Rank's introductory 'live logo' featured a swarthy fellow, clad in a loincloth, striking an enormous semi-replica of the Maesmawr gong with a similar but much larger drumstick. His efforts were, however, silent, because they were not on the soundtrack. Nevertheless, although I was clad in considerably more than a loincloth while attending a Maesmawr formal lunch, Rank's muscular drummer used to bring to mind my zestful boyhood enthusiasm for summoning family and guests to the repast.

The dining room, with its fine seventeenth-century wood panelled walls, was recently renamed the 'Wainscot Parlour' by the hotel. That name was dropped before my time, and was probably last used by the Davies family before it vacated the house in 1910. The room remains predominantly as in former days, except for the now absent bolection-moulded, plain oak fire surround. This is shown in the photograph (page 84), with its metal side-panels having a formalised tree design in relief. The fireplace surround was extracted and, by some means, dispensed with by a (now unknown) Maesmawr owner in the years that followed the 1947 sale. It included an inscribed brass insert in Welsh: *Ti Arglwydd fuost yn Breswylfa i ni ym mhob Cenhedlaeth* ('Thou, O Lord, hast been our refuge in every generation.') The present replacement was brought to Maesmawr from a room on the upper floor of a house in Norwich, now destroyed. The seven linenfold panels came from the house of William Coo in Dial Yard. They bear his name, that of his wife Anne Coo (formerly Clarke), his merchant's mark and the crest of the Mercers' Company (a virgin's head). Beneath these panels is the top of a doorway from the house of Geoffrey Clarke (Anne's father), the spandrels of which contain the Arms of the city of Norwich and of the Merchants' Adventurers. The entire fireplace dates from about 1500.

The dining room in 1947, with the portrait in oils of my uncle Emrys aged fifteen, painted by Carey Morris of Llandeilo in 1912. See page 83 describing the photograph's fireplace surround, which was extracted at some time after 1947 and replaced by another of proven antiquity, as had been its predecessor, with its Welsh inscription.

A small white-painted wooden greenhouse, made by Walter Pryce in the 1930s, once stood attached to the dining room's east wall, central to the window. It was always full of brilliant scarlet pelargoniums – better known as geraniums – which flourished in ancient fire-clay pots upon slatted shelves. The plants were all raised from seed by the gardener, Noel Brown. His Estate staff colleagues at Maesmawr, Walter Pryce and Evan Owen, had been there since before my birth. I will shortly include my word portrait of each, as I fondly remember the trio during my boyhood years at Maesmawr.

A handsome mahogany table stood in the centre of the dining room, com-plemented by a set of chairs with high backs and upholstered soft leather seats. A Sheraton sideboard stood against the wall facing the front window, upon which dishes of food, brought some distance from the kitchen on my 'racing' trolley by careful hands, were kept as hot as possible under their shining domes of Sheffield Plate silver. Above the table hung a circular black iron ring, an electric light fit-ting holding three bulbs powered by the 110 volt, home-generated, electricity supply. A crimson skirt of silk, which hung from the ring, gave a warm sense of comfort, its glow gently illuminating the surrounding panelled walls and the white plaster ceiling. My nain sat facing the front window, in the high-back chair with arms which can be seen in the distance, adjacent to the corner door, whose steps led down into the central passage lobby. My uncle Emrys sat at the opposite end of the table, with his back to the window.

The photograph of my nain (page 27), with the dark background, was taken in the dining room, and shows her sitting in the aforementioned chair, the wainscot panelling just visible. The portrait painting of my uncle Emrys, seen hanging above the Sheraton sideboard, shows him aged fifteen and was painted by the artist Carey Morris of Llandeilo in 1912. Emrys wears a dark-blue blazer and grey trousers, the blazer having the embossed badge of the Leys School, Cambridge, on its breast pocket. This painting and the one of my mother (page 86), also painted by Carey Morris, have the dining room's wainscot panelling as an unobtrusive background. My mother's picture portrays her aged thirteen, wearing a little dark-green velvet dress with half-sleeves finished in creamy-white silk elbow-cuffs. An undergarment of similar material finishes with a slightly frilly high neck. In both lowered hands my mother holds a slim, partially open book, whose vivid cerulean-blue cloth cover entrancingly catches natural light from an unseen window. A delicate bow of creamy-white silk is set into the crown of her shoulder-length dark hair. I treasure her young portrait in my home, where it hangs in the oblique light from a window, thus viewed as the artist intended. I am grateful to my cousin Ruth for rescuing the painting from an attic some years ago, having it re-framed, and enabling me to possess it.

During my boyhood at Maesmawr, my mother's portrait hung high on the left-hand wall of the old staircase principal landing; it had probably done so since its completion in 1911. Beneath it, and parallel to that wall, stood a short flight of carpeted steps that ascended to meet the upper corridor of architect Nesfield's extension. That corridor, which in my time and before served as primary access to my nain's large bedroom and its adjacent dressing room, no longer exists, having been incorporated into both rooms to provide en-suite accommodation when Maesmawr was extensively altered at becoming an hotel. Nesfield provided a second but lower corridor parallel to, and of similar length to the higher one. The lower corridor is retained and approached by several steps leading off the principal landing. Design-wise, Nesfield had to create the higher of the two corridors to provide height in his large drawing room, which is immediately beneath.

Both upper and lower corridors continued for some distance beyond their respective access steps from the principal landing. The upper corridor did so by about six feet beyond my nain's bedroom door, and then stopped at the door to the orchard bedroom. On the other side of that door were several steps down to floor level, these being necessary because Nesfield's morning room, immediately below the orchard bedroom, was some feet lower in height than the

Oil painting of my mother, aged thirteen, in 1911, by Carey Morris of Llandeilo, the same year that she was photographed at Maesmawr Hall receiving tuition on her harp from Nansi Richards (Telynores Maldwyn), see page 96. Both the oil painting and the photograph (with Nansi) show my mother wearing a similar bow in her hair.

Photograph: Ellis-Jones

My nain, Mary Ellen, circa 1920, probably at Maesmawr Hall.

Photographer: unknown

adjacent drawing room. Directly opposite my nain's bedroom door was another door which, by means of yet more steps, three or four steep ones, conveniently interconnected the two corridors. Those steps remain today, directly opposite the second flight of the steep back stairs.

Off the principal landing was Nain's bathroom, which, in my boyhood, was known as that to everyone in the house. Nowadays it is an hotel bedroom with adjacent en-suite facilities in what used to be the servants' bathroom. That small room was entered directly off the half-landing of the steep back stairs. If guests were staying, I was relegated to using it, but as its old bath's enamel surface had become worn and scratchy over the years, in my view it was only a temporary alternative; it was Nain's bathroom that I coveted! Its door, now blocked up, was in the far corner of the principal landing, adjacent to the left-hand side of Nesfield's pretty lead-paned window. The present bedroom, which has replaced the bathroom, is entered by a new door just inside the lower corridor. I had the pleasurable occupation of Nain's bathroom between certain times, as did my mother when we came to stay. It had a warm and welcoming feeling, unlike the chilly and white-glazed tile interior of 'bathrooms I have known'! The room was always imbued with the refreshing scent of old-fashioned bath-crystals, enjoyed primarily for their perfume and not for their water-softening ability, since Maesmawr's well-water was soft already, and was circulated around the house in pure lead pipes! Walter Pryce was Maesmawr's mechanic, as the reader will learn in due course, and his many skills included plumbing. I used to watch him make the plumber's traditional 'wiped' joints for lead pipes with a little pad of real moleskin wiped over the blow-torch softened solder, which gave a smooth surface to the lozenge-shaped joint, hence its name.

After that brief digression to mention the lead pipe plumbing, I return to the white, pink and blue bath salts. They were kept in a large glass jar with a ground-glass lid which had a large round glass knob to lift it out. It stood on a white-painted wooden dressing-table, overlaid with a white damask cloth with dainty crocheted edge, and backed with a swivel mirror. The floor was covered with a warm-toned linoleum and several thick wool mats which were cosy to bare feet. The bathroom walls and ceiling were white and a dado of thick and prettily embossed paper, also painted white, extended around on three sides. On the fourth side, opposite the window, stood a capacious old-fashioned white fireclay bath with thick rounded edges and a shining brass assemblage of two huge taps. A white enamel disc was set into the top of each, respectively marked HOT and COLD in bold black letters. A heavy brass shower-fitting, with a white enamel handle, lay behind the taps on a pair of 'Y' shaped brass brackets. Bath waste-water was emptied away not by a mere chain and rubber plug, but by the lifting of a brass cylinder about two-and-a-half inches in diameter, whose lower end was slightly recessed to receive a thick rubber ring which effected a water-seal around the large waste outlet. The brass tube was enabled to slide upwards about an inch, through a pair of brass ring-brackets, neatly affixed to the end of the bath through the fireclay. A matching and generously-sized knob enabled the bather to pull up the waste-water device when desired. When it was lifted up, the bath-water ran out with a deeply menacing gurgling and sucking sound. If I felt brave enough to remain in the bath until all the water had drained out – thus leaving one nakedly 'high-and-dry' but yet not dry – I was careful to keep my feet away from the snarling vortex of the outlet, lest its suction grab a toe!

Returning briefly to the orchard bedroom of my boyhood, its considerable size in those days has been reduced since Maesmawr became an hotel, because an additional bedroom and its en-suite bathroom have been formed from approximately half the original orchard bedroom's overall size. This additional bedroom, whose floor level is the same as that of the large one – possibly the hotel's largest and my nain's bedroom in former years – includes the fireplace that used to serve the orchard bedroom of former times.

The orchard bedroom was where my mother and I always slept when she brought me to Maesmawr in the 1930s. Our pair of beds stood with their heads against the west wall, adjacent to the two small windows in Nesfield's gable. The left-hand one of the windows is now the en-suite bathroom window of the aforesaid additional bedroom. The orchard bedroom was decorated with pretty pale pink and white wallpaper with a tiny flower pattern. The fireplace, now incorporated into the aforementioned additional (hotel) bedroom, was used regularly in autumn and winter for the benefit of the room's occupant. It had a cast-iron, black-leaded surround and a grate which, on cold nights, held a glowing coal fire. As I became drowsy with approaching sleep, I loved to watch the dancing and flickering patterns made by the flames upon the high white ceiling, while the wind could be heard in the orchard rookery's trees, in which the swaying and roosting birds tightly gripped the topmost branches with their claws. On Saturdays, after I had been tucked up in bed by my mother, or by dear Gretta after my mother's death, I listened for the train whistle from faraway Moat Lane Junction, which features in one of my forthcoming stories in these Recollections. Early every morning I was awoken either by the cawing rooks – who were the earliest risers at Maesmawr, even earlier than the devoted housemaids – or by the BLACKSTONE oil-engine being started up, or by both together. My then well, but weary, mother liked to lie a-bed on some mornings after chatting far into the night with hers. Circumstances meant that our visits to Maesmawr were infrequent, and although they exchanged weekly letters, and the occasional 'trunks' conversation via the rather tedious means I have described, nothing surpassed a late night chat! I used to try to feign sleep whilst they exchanged all their news and probably some intriguing bits of Caersws gossip also. Long before the yawns of both spelled sleep, I had – in nursery talk – *gone to the land of Nod*. Sometimes their arising bed-wards would very briefly half-wake me and I would hear the words "Good night, Mummy dear", as my nain departed for her own bedroom. So ingrained was my mother's bidding to hers in my boyhood memory that upon making a recent explanatory tour of my 'remembered Maesmawr', my entry into the bedroom that was once part of the orchard bedroom of my childhood brought my mother's "Good night" to hers – of sixty-six years ago – instantly to mind.

I must briefly return to the aforementioned lower corridor to say that after it passes the well of the back stairs, it turns sharp right to give access firstly to a room facing north, which has always been a bedroom, and secondly, a (now) additional bedroom, formed out of the laundry room of my boyhood, which was immediately above the old kitchen. In due course I will describe in detail, and with relevant photographs and my own drawing, the old kitchen, back kitchen and dairy.

Meanwhile, my descriptive and partly comparative progress through Maesmawr, past and present, returns to the old part of the house, starting with the old stair leading out of the Hall, which I have touched on previously in passing. The 'MAES-MAWR' article, reproduced earlier in these Recollections (pages 16-19), mentions the small doorway leading to that stair. It was there in my boyhood, and can be seen in the Hall photograph (page 68). The drastic widening of the old staircase's first flight during the last fifty-eight years involved the entire removal (who knows where?) of its elaborately carved early-eighteenth century balustrade and handrail. Fortunately a short length of it remains in perfect condition, leading up to the attic rooms from the narrow corridor serving the first floor bedrooms.

Since my family sold Maesmawr in 1947, several very drastic alterations to it, tragically inexcusable and resulting from ignorance, incompetence and insensitivity, were (presumably) permitted and carried out. I unhesitatingly blame the local Planning Authority of the Day for allowing them to occur.

Further alterations were deemed essential when Maesmawr became an hotel. The necessary provision of a fire-door in several locations, and the need for providing means of speedy evacuation from the old house – especially from the first floor and attic bedrooms – have had regrettable results of both historic and aesthetic nature. The foremost of these was the entire extraction of the half-landing and the short flight of early-eighteenth century stair and balustered handrail which led from the principal landing of that date, across and up to the narrow corridor serving the first-floor bedrooms. A fire-door now connects the principal landing with the corridor, through a, once solid, wall.

In my boyhood there were two bedrooms here, whose doors opened off the right-hand side of that corridor. The one nearest the house front was my uncle Emrys' for the entire thirty-seven years that he lived at Maesmawr. Its front gable previously contained two first floor bedrooms, reached by the aforementioned corridor, which turned to the left at its far end. Both these small bedrooms had a paired casement window overlooking the front approach to the house. During my years at Maesmawr after my mother's death, my bedroom was the right-hand one of the two, as one faces the front of the house. My taid's bedroom was the large one in the east gable, immediately above what is now the 'Wainscot Parlour'. The pretty window of intricately patterned leaded panes at the corner of the principal landing was inserted by architect Nesfield during his 1876 extension to the house.

An interesting question, although hard to satisfy with conviction, concerns Maesmawr's eighteenth or nineteenth-century west gable, now built entirely of thick masonry. Without doubt the west gable was at one time similar to the east gable, which is an unaltered half-timber gable whose upper storey slightly projects (jetties) over the wall frame beneath. There remains no proven reason as to why the west gable's half-timber construction disappeared; perhaps it suffered major decay or was damaged beyond repair by fire? The date of its disappearance is also conjectural, but a possible clue may one day present itself if an accurate date can ever be placed upon the earliest known illustration of Maesmawr, which the reader will have noted on page 56. My study of it shows a substantial chimney stack at the west gable's apex, whose very existence indicates an essential degree of support which could not possibly be provided by a half-timber frame, but only by masonry. The tantalising question posed by this illustration is its date. Is the west gable and its chimney pre-Nesfield, i.e. before 1876, or part of his work of extension? The illustration's apparent 'antiquity' may mislead us to assume it is earlier than it is. However, the extensive wicket fence seen crossing the house front (whether of wood or metal is irrelevant to the question), together with the barn-like gabled roof on the extreme right, give the impression of a peaceful farmyard, not yet disturbed by the major constructional work of architect Nesfield's forthcoming extension.

The obvious inequality of the respective lengths of the east and west gable roof may have some unknown connection with the disappearance of the west's original half-timber frame. On the other hand, perhaps the unequal roof lengths indicate the room sizes when those east and west wings, either side of the front gable, were built; in practical terms, that meant that the domestic needs of the intending occupants took precedence over the architectural niceties of creating east and west gable roofs of equal length.

I have earlier expressed my assumption that the BLACKSTONE engine-shed was built, and the engine and dynamo installed, in about 1912, two years before the outbreak of the First World War. The manufacturer's advertisement, which I include, is of the largest, static model, similar to Maesmawr's. My recent photograph (page 155) shows her shed still standing, nowadays providing excellent

1. Penstrowed Hall, two miles east of Maesmawr Hall. A delightful black painted chevron pattern onto brickwork; oblique winter sunlight accentuates its texture, denying the (otherwise) pretence of half-timber framing.

2. Imitation half-timber patterning on brickwork at Kerry. The little modern window does its best to intrude into the 'frame' by being the width of two 'uprights'. Prior to the nineteenth-century's splendid finial and fretted barge-boards, a central projecting chimney extended up beyond the roof apex, now closed off by the sloping capstone.

3. A close and similarly brick-built neighbour displays an exuberance of imitation half-timber frame. The curvaceous 'timbers' in the gable are delightfully humorous.

4. 'Gothick' at Kerry; a perfect concept of the Style. The elegantly tall, gloss-black-painted brick arches, set proud of the matt-white brick walls, together with the slender black iron railings as horizontal contrast, present great character. The rectangular paned windows in the outer arches are modern replacements.

Photographs: Ellis-Jones

storage for a variety of garden implements and dry firewood. No longer are the shed's cladding boards painted Black-and-White, giving the then viewer a (mistaken) impression of sturdy half-timber framing.

A further point worthy of mention concerns the relatively recent painting out of the artificial Black-and-White simulation of half-timber frame across Maesmawr's entire west elevation. I am no purist in this context, and know other Montgomeryshire examples of this popular Victorian custom. I view it as being entirely acceptable; and the better it is done in practical terms, the better it looks. I recommend any doubters to visit the village of Kerry, a few miles east of Newtown. Kerry has some magnificent examples of the custom, further enhanced by fancily carved barge-boards.

Now I must admit to a misapprehension on the part, at least, of my late aunt Mari, my mother's sister, and I. It occurred many years after our family's sale of the house, when one of Maesmawr's succession of owners, in the decades that followed, painted the old house's west gable white, leaving the entirety of architect Nesfield's west elevation with its artificial Black-and-White pattern untouched. "Such a great pity", we would agree, when driving past on the main road up Long Length. "It was shameful that he was allowed to paint over the gable's old timbers." The simple fact, which neither of us had ever realized – my dear aunt over many more years than I in my youth – was that the west gable in question had been built of solid masonry for more years than our combined ages. Maesmawr's owner, for whatever reason, was merely reversing the Montgomeryshire custom of painting brickwork in Black-and-White stripes. The old house's west gable had been thus painted, in all probability, for the past eighty-four years, since the Nesfield work of 1876; the custom, which I happen to like, and is especially attractive at Kerry, had, up to then, been merely continued on Maesmawr's west gable. My uncle Emrys almost certainly knew that the gable was solid masonry, but he had died eighteen years before our misapprehension had materialised. Maesmawr's Estate carpenter and engineer, Walter Pryce, who was also dead by this time, would certainly have known that the west gable was masonry-built and not half-timber frame, because every ten years or so he mixed his own black paint – with powder, red-lead and linseed oil – and spent days on a ladder repainting the Black-and-White pattern on the gable's surface. Elsewhere in these Recollections I draw attention to photograph 3 (page 129) and a drawing, the latter (with the 'MAES-MAWR' article on page 16) clearly showing the thick masonry-built corner of the west gable.

Today, Maesmawr's entire west-facing wall is painted white, that major part of it comprising architect Nesfield's Victorian extension being, in recent years only, covered with a rough, gravelly-textured *Tyrolean* cement coating that conceals the previous Black-and-White pattern painted onto brickwork beneath. Its characteristic surface, however, forbids repetition of any painted pattern. In contrast, the old house's west gable, whilst also painted white, fortunately retains the, probably original and advantageously smooth, surface coating of lime putty and sand applied in the Victorian era onto brickwork. The RCAHMW'S Crown Copyright photograph below fully depicts the overall painted Black-and-White pattern (imitating half-timber frame) that entirely existed at least up until 1947, when my family sold Maesmawr Hall and its Estate.

Albeit that the *Tyrolean* wall coating must, for the aforesaid reason, remain permanently devoid of painted pattern, the smooth wall coating of the old house's west gable awaits as an ideal surface for its hitherto painted pattern once again. That must, ironically in context, still exist beneath a mere layer of permanently opaque wall paint, also applied in fairly recent years, by one or other of Maesmawr's many successive owners, after my family departed.

Fortunately, the very modern availability of computer design graphics promises an easy means whereby to very accurately here recreate, from photographs, the established Montgomeryshire tradition of painted Black-and-White,

Maesmawr's Walter Pryce, during his thirty-seven years' employment here, every-so-often maintained architect Nesfield's Black-and-White pattern over the latter's entire west wall, as illustrated, Walter made his own black paint with powder, red-lead and linseed oil thereby keeping the Victorian simulation in good repair. In my boyhood it was ever thus, (see page 160).

Crown Copyright: RCAHMW

The Hall staircase in 1947. When Maesmawr became an hotel in the 1950's, this suffered drastic alteration to fulfil Fire Safety Regulations. Its short lower landing (left) and similar flight up (at right-angle beyond) that accessed original Maesmawr's passage and bedrooms, were wholly extracted; replaced by direct fire-door through blank wall (right) to aforesaid passage behind. (see page 67 and 90)

(Photograph found by my cousin David Owen Owen after printing of the 1st edition).

as it previously existed. I hope that many interested observers of Maesmawr's presently overtly plain, white-painted entirity of lengthy west wall, will share my enthusiastic suggestion; that its, respectively, future areas thus painted, would provide a best possible balanced aesthetic, now that the original Victorian patterning cannot be entirely recreated.

CONFESSI(A)N TO OSIAN

Several years ago, I attended a recital by the great Welsh harpist Osian Ellis in a Herefordshire church. At its conclusion, emboldened by the pleasures of his artistry, from which had arisen the 'hiraeth' that every Welshman has in his heart, but nevertheless tentative about approaching him, I knocked on the vestry door behind which he had retired. After he had bid me enter, I sought to excuse

My mother having tuition on her *telyn deires* from Nansi Richards (Telynores Maldwyn) at Maesmawr Hall in 1911. Written in Nansi's hand on the back of the original photograph are the words: 'Beryl and I in the home of Mrs Ed. Jones, the sister of Tom Ellis, Cynlas'. The bust of Tom Ellis, M.P., is side-lit in the photograph. Cynlas (Farm), near Bala, was his and my nain's family home. I refer to Tom Ellis at the outset of these Recollections.

Courtesy: Rhiannon Jones

96

my approaching him without introduction and expressed my wish to thank him personally for his recital but also to 'make confession'. He was understandably taken aback, but when I quickly assured him that my confession concerned the Welsh harp (the *telyn deires*) and not morals, he relaxed to listen attentively to my tale. Firstly, I revealed to him that my mother had played the *telyn deires* in her girlhood. At hearing that, he expressed great pleasure, and added that its three independent sets of strings, the outer pair diatonic and the inner pair of intermediate semitones, are difficult to play. When the Master said this, I instantly realised that as my intended 'confessi(a)n' concerned one of those very strings, I had no alternative but to continue along my chosen path!

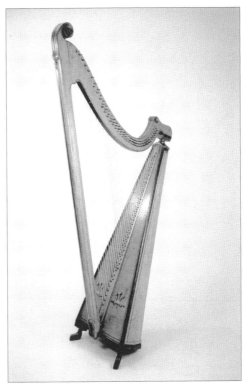

A beautiful ninteenth-century chromatic triple harp (Welsh: *telyn deires*) formerly owned by Lady Buckley of Dinas Mawddwy. Donated to AMGUEDDFA CYMRU (National Museum Wales) by Miss Ella C. King of Fronfeunol, Bala, in 1947.

Courtesy: Amgueddfa Cymru

I explained to Osian Ellis that in my boyhood my home for several years was Maesmawr Hall in Montgomeryshire, which was owned by my maternal nain. As soon as he realised that my surname indicated true Welshness, his attention quickened further as I continued. One day, I told him, when I was about ten years old, I went for the very first time to the topmost little room in Maesmawr's front gable. There, in a dark corner, stood a very dilapidated and lonely *telyn deires*. I was later to learn that it had been my mother's in her girlhood. I had never previously known that she had played the harp, but extracts from the *Montgomeryshire Express & Radnor Times* of March 7th, 1911 charmingly confirms that she did. I found them during research at the National Library of Wales.

At the time I discovered my mother's *telyn deires*, as I told the attentive Master harpist, I was keen on boyish archery, the ancient yew trees at Maesmawr providing supple branches for making bows. King Henry the Fifth's Welsh bowmen at the battle of Agincourt used yew for their bows, and I have sometimes fancied that Maesmawr's yew trees ('the Bower') perhaps provided some of that wood. The battle took place in 1415, on St. Crispin's Day – so long ago that even if the three yew trees forming Maesmawr's 'Bower' were growing in the

The 'MAES-MAWR' article's yew trees, 'the Bower', today, seemingly much taller than remembered from my boyhood.

Photograph: Ellis-Jones

first quarter of the fifteenth century, they might then have been too immature to have provided a Caersws bowman with the ideal wood for the famous longbow. However, as the yew is so long-lived, perhaps today's towering trio of trees did furnish the long and pliant branches used to make the famous, and also infamous, weapon?

My bow from 'the Bower', I told Osian Ellis, was relatively harmless compared with those used at Crécy and similar battles, but mine needed gut with which to string it … In a trice, he knew what I was about to say, which was: "The *telyn deires* appeared so pathetic and unloved in its dusty corner, and so broken, that I assumed it would never play again; and a conveniently long and thick length of gut hung down from a tuning-pin, ideal to string my bow with …" End of 'confessi(a)n'.

The Master remained silent for a moment – for me almost an eternity – and then, with an air of quasi-grandeur and a kindly twinkle in his eye, he pronounced my 'absolution' for the 'crime'. This he delivered in a very Welsh lilting voice: "Michael – you are forgiven," he decreed.

NANSI RICHARDS

Nansi Richards was born in 1888 at her family's farm in Penybont-fawr, close to Llangynog, which lies at the southerly feet of Montgomeryshire's Berwyn Mountains. Whilst of very tender age, she was musically attracted to the sound of the harp – and perhaps also to its graceful shape? Nansi first heard it played by some itinerant gypsies roaming Wales, who plucked its ethereal and evanescent tones whilst sheltering in her parents' farmyard barn for welcome rest, or else in hard weather. The harp played by the dusky wanderers was the *telyn deires*,

Nansi Richards
Brenhines Y Delyn

Nansi Richards at Llangynog in 1906.
Courtesy: Rhiannon Jones

Nansi Richards (Telynores Maldwyn) in 1911, the year she played to the Prince of Wales at his Caernarfon Investiture, and stayed at Maesmawr Hall to take part with Beryl (my mother) in harp duets at the local celebrations of St. David's Day. See *Montgomeryshire Express & Radnor Times* report of same (pages 234–235).

Courtesy: Dafydd Roberts,
SAIN, Caernarfon

Nansi Richards (Telynores Maldwyn) in about 1948.

Photographer: Alwyn Rosser
Courtesy: Amgueddfa Cymru

which is chromatic in compass, with three sets of strings, and becoming increasingly rare at that time.

At the age of twelve, Nansi first received tuition on the *telyn deires* from Tom Lloyd, a very tall quarryman from nearby Llangynog, himself an already renowned exponent on the instrument, and known therefore as 'Telynor Ceiriog'. The latter name may have been an allusion to the village of Llanarmon Dyffryn Ceiriog, some four miles to the northeast of Llangynog, as the hawk or raven flies, from whence Tom's forebears may have come?

His fame upon the harp was already international, and whilst touring and competing in America, on one occasion he was awarded a gold medal for his playing. In later years, Tom's young protégé Nansi herself toured America with performances on her harp, and lived there between 1923 and 1925. Nansi had also studied at London's Guildhall School of Music, and was often invited to entertain the then Prime Minister David Lloyd George and his family at 10 Downing Street, especially with Welsh melodies upon her beloved *telyn deires*.

101

Nansi also played to the Prince of Wales at the time of his Investiture in Caernarfon Castle in 1911.

On St. David's Day in that same year, Nansi was staying with my taid and nain at Maesmawr Hall, joining them in participation with the Caersws and Llandinam schools in their new freedom to celebrate 'Dewi Sant'. Hitherto, it had been forbidden by the English Board of Education but, probably in the context of the Prince of Wales' Investiture that summer, such authoritarian denial of Welsh children's patriotic enthusiasm was then and thereafter rescinded. I herein include extracts from the *Montgomeryshire Express & Radnor Times* of March 7th, 1911 (pages 234–235) which, in addition to my nain's address, entitled 'The Advice of a Lady', mention the (*telyn deires*) duets played by Nansi and my mother, both wearing Traditional Welsh costume. Nansi, then aged twenty-three, was ten years my mother's senior.

Nansi received an honorary Doctorate of Music from the University of Wales in 1977. She died in December 1979, aged ninety-one. Her grave, and that of her beloved husband, Cecil Jones, are in the tranquil churchyard of St. Melangell, Pennant Melangell, close to Penybont-fawr, her childhood home. (St. Monacella, whose very rare Romanesque shrine is in the chancel, is traditionally Patroness of the wild Brown Hare.) There, sheltered by the hills of her native Montgomeryshire, with the 'mew' of the soaring buzzard, the roaming raven's deep-dark 'croak' and the sighing of the Berwyn Mountains' winds, they Rest in an abiding peace.

Dürer's Brown Hare.

THE MAESMAWR HALL STAFF,
THE GARDENS

Tell of us – there dwelt or spent each day,
as how we served the Hall of old;
Served it, loved it – each's way,
in your tales so truly told.

M. E-J

Eight lovely people – Gretta, Ceridwen, Janet, Muriel and Nancy within the house and Walter, Evan and Noel without – comprised the Maesmawr staff of my very young years and later boyhood. There was also an agile fellow from Caersws, one Lewis Jones, who, while not at Maesmawr every day, as were the others, came to help whenever a tree needed to be lopped or felled. Lewis excelled at climbing trunks and high branches, just like a squirrel.

Maesmawr's happy housemaids in 1935: (l. to r.) Muriel, Nancy, Ceridwen and Gretta, with me, aged three, 'knee-high to a grasshopper'!

Courtesy of the recently late Ceridwen Bennett, and given me shortly before her Passing away.

Ceridwen herself, at Maesmawr in 1937, ready to attend upon tea.

The late Ceridwen Bennett

Gretta in the 1930s; very smartly dressed for her special 'day-off' and posing in front of my nain's dahlia bed. The splendid greenhouse in the background was Maesmawr's most recent loss in very recent years – gone.

The late Ceridwen Bennett

I must include Muriel and Nancy in this very happy company. Although they both left before the Second World War, perhaps to marry, they were nevertheless at Maesmawr in the year of my birth, 1932, and remained there until 1939. Janet then came to replace one or the other, joining Gretta and Ceridwen. Gretta remained at her beloved Maesmawr throughout the War years, devoted to my nain, who returned that devotion until, with Gretta present, she died at Maesmawr in 1947, as I mentioned earlier. Gretta married her darling Gerald Hamer, he from Caersws and she from nearby Trefeglwys. After my nain's death and Maesmawr's subsequent sale, the couple went down to live near Carmarthen. There, at the village of Nantgaredig, Gretta helped my nain's youngest sister, the aforementioned Winnie Jones-Davies and her husband, Harry, at their Glyneidden farmhouse. Gerald drove milk lorries for a local firm and they had a family of two boys.

Before she died, the late Ceridwen gave me these three delightful old photographs and gladly consented to their inclusion in this book. There I am, in 1935 and aged three, with those happy young women. Alas, because I was so young at the time, I have no clear recall of either Muriel or Nancy, although upon first seeing their photographs, a facial reminder flitted across my memory. Ceridwen and Janet remained, with Gretta, at Maesmawr, but both ultimately left for 'call-up', as it was known, into the womens' associated part of the Army and Air Force respectively, in about 1942. By that time, aged ten, my retentive memory of the 'Maesmawr scene', which was to become so acute in the years that followed, had developed, but in general terms I have no recall of the early or mid-1930s. My visits to my taid in his bedroom are the sole subject of recall from those earliest days; later, as I mention, I remember Mr Harris making his pen-and-ink drawing in the summer of 1939. From then on, as these Recollections prove, my boyhood memory garnered its profuse storehouse of events and personalities.

The individual people whose activities were part of the Maesmawr of those faraway days were an example of a phenomenon which has disappeared over the past sixty years. The outbreak of the Second World War in 1939 directly contributed to its decline and ultimate demise in a very short period of time. It was hastened, as in the case of Ceridwen and Janet, by 'call-up' into the Services, which was obligatory for healthy young men – and for women also (except those with dependant children) from 1941, although many women were informally allowed to continue in occupations such as teaching and nursing. Just as the First World War of 1914–1918 had spelled the end of the post-Edwardian 'Golden' era – 'Golden' only for the upper classes of society whose circumstances enabled them to enjoy its many fruits – so the Second World War added its own characteristic and forceful impetus for diverse social changes within all areas of society. Social, hence community, mores have metamorphosed to such a degree since the end of the Second World War that nowadays to use the term 'servant' to refer to a then universal mode of employment causes the speaker to hesitate – momentarily at least – at the inference such a term may denote in our equal-ity-oriented society, to whatever degree that sought Utopia may already exist, seem to exist, or be wished to exist.

Having defined the 'servant' as a class of individuals serving an employer in some way or other in an existing social and economic milieu, the term 'serving' must be appreciated for the values it held for both parties, the employer and the employed, in their own ways. That was certainly so in the great majority of cases, in which an opportunity to be part of the household of the 'Big House' – often far from big – was frequently valued both by the servants for their own self-regard and potential for promotion, and by their families, who regarded it, with justification and genuine pride, as being a significant rise in their own social and local status.

Maesmawr, in the several decades before my birth and the twelve or so years after it, was a typical example of the small landowner employing local men and women in his house and gardens, and additionally in his tenant farms (Maesmawr had three). While continuing my brief study of the subtle

105

and respected interpersonal relationships between employer and employed within such a typical community, I would use the phrase 'a natural formality within an informality' as existing amongst the parties involved. Those individual and personal relationships were interdependent, maintaining, at Maesmawr, for one, deep trust, great happiness, and utter contentment with that social code.

During my taid's twenty-seven years at Maesmawr, all his household and Estate staff would have addressed him personally as "Sir" and between themselves as "the Master". My nain was personally addressed by all the staff as "M'mm" and between themselves as "the Missus". My uncle Emrys, her eldest son, was personally addressed as "Mr Emrys", which was also how they referred to him amongst themselves. Prior to their respective marriages, all the staff would have addressed my mother and her two younger sisters as "Miss Beryl", "Miss Megan" and "Miss Mari". After marriage, they were each called by their married surname. In my boyhood years at Maesmawr, all the staff called me "Master Michael". I called each by his or her Christian name: "Gretta", "Ceridwen", "Janet", "Walter" and "Evan". The exception was dear Noel Brown, who, as I will seek to explain shortly, was just called "Brown" by everyone, and happily accepted being called by his surname.

The other quaintness of address concerned my nain's elderly companion, Miss Gwen Phillips, who came from an old Newtown family and had lived at Maesmawr with my nain and my uncle ever since the death of my taid. I think that Gwen was about ten or twelve years younger than my nain, who naturally called her "Gwen", as did my uncle. However, despite their long friendship, a relatively small disparity in age, and her role as Nain's permanent companion, Gwen called her "Mrs Jones" and my uncle "Mr Emrys", as the staff did. To the staff, Gwen was "Miss Phillips", both when addressed personally and between themselves; Gwen, however, called each by his or her Christian name. To conclude those charming habits, some of which I failed to understand when a child, Gwen always called me "Michael" – not "Master Michael" – and I called her "Gwen", personally and when referring to her when talking to anyone else at Maesmawr.

The team of housemaids always had a busy daily schedule, sometimes tedious in that Yesteryear of few and simple labour-saving machines, gadgets and devices to help ease the load, and without so many of the modern machines we take wholly for granted. Gretta, Ceridwen and Janet's sleeping quarters were in the topmost attic rooms of the old house, undeniably just beneath the roof, although its soffit was clad with white lime-washed plaster. The two rooms each had a window overlooking the gardens from a high vantage point. The only snag, apart from winter cold, which was countered with hot-water bottles, was the structural coming together of hefty roof and gabled timbers which were such a hazard for any tall person. Gretta, Ceridwen and Janet, unlike Muriel and Nancy, were all of quite short stature, so were not endangered by the low, head-knocking beams! By and large their rooms were attractive, although perhaps rather hot in exceptional summer weather.

A water closet was available on the floor below, entered by two steps ascending within the external wall's corner of the principal landing. I used to visit it daily, and recall the few steps up into the small space and the raised plinth-platform upon which the closet stood. However, it has long since disappeared, leaving me, the only person who now remembers it, with a permanent riddle as to exactly where, in relation to the inner corner of the bedroom (above the 'Wainscot Parlour'), it was situated. Today there is no explanation of how it could have been where I remember it to have been. In the context of an acutely accurate power of detailed recall for the 'Maesmawr-of-old', the closet, in hindsight, appears as a mirage; and I must leave it so!

The housemaids' – and Ceridwen the cook's – daily routine began early, with Gretta preparing a tray of early-morning tea and taking it to my nain, my uncle Emrys, Gwen, and whoever was staying as a guest. Meanwhile, Ceridwen prepared breakfast for everyone, while Janet attended to the lighting of winter's fires at that season, and every morning throughout the year received and separated the morning's buckets of milk. These were brought across from the cow-byre by Evan to the little dairy adjacent to the back kitchen, where the separation process was done – assisted by me at every opportunity. After the at-any-hour breakfast, and when family and guests had vacated their rooms, Gretta and Janet made up all the beds, and cleaned, brushed and dusted through the house as might be necessary. Meanwhile, Ceridwen, later joined by the others, did the breakfast washing-up in the butler's pantry – the scene of my 'Newtonian' experiments with the knife-grinder.

Clothes and bed-linen laundry day was undoubtedly the most onerous weekly task, and I will shortly and briefly describe it. After Ceridwen and Janet had left Maesmawr's employ to join the Forces, I think that my nain obtained 'casual' assistance from Caersws ladies on laundry day. The weekly days for butter-making and bread-baking saw her busy as expert 'commandress-in-chief' for both activities, while every morning Ceridwen received fresh vegetables from Noel's professionally-tended garden, washing them and preparing them for lunch and supper, or evening dinner in the dining room.

For their morning tasks, the housemaids dressed upon rising in their simple pale pink and white long-sleeved cotton dresses. Over the dress was worn an especially long white linen apron, extending up over the bosom and shoulders and tied around the waist with a matching tape. A little mini-coronet white linen cap, kept in place by black velvet elastic, often completed their mode of dress. The charming photograph of the four, with me, (page 103) almost certainly taken by my mother, with the kitchen window on the left, is a perfect illustration of Maesmawr's 'Morning Watch'. In the mid-afternoon, following their well-earned short nap in the servants' hall, they went up to their bedrooms to change into the formal attire required from tea-time until bed-time. The nostalgic photograph of Ceridwen (page 104), surely taken by my mother also, shows her ready to attend upon the morning room's tea-party or, with Gretta, similarly dressed, at evening dinner in the dining room. This formal dress comprised a long black dress of fine cotton with long sleeves, complemented by starched white cuffs. A little semi-starched white linen apron, tied around the waist, had its method of fixing at the bosom, concealed by a short gathered flap of black velvet. A wide collar of white linen, sometimes with a delicate crocheted edge for formal occasions, was matched by the semi-coronet cap, interlaced with a black velvet tape which was elasticated at the back and concealed by the wearer's hair.

At a meal in the dining room, Gretta, helped by Janet or Ceridwen, served and attended upon the family members, in order of seniority, and guests. Plates of meat or fish were accompanied by dishes of various home-grown vegetables, offered to each diner in turn upon the server's arm, which was draped with a brilliantly white damask napkin. Each dish was offered at the recipient's left shoulder, unless he or she was left-handed, as I was. So that I might more easily manipulate the large spoon, Gretta, with her sweet smile, offered me the various dishes at my right shoulder, lest the small boy should inadvertently shoot a roast potato onto the carpet beneath or, worse, spoon chocolate mousse into the lap of the lady sitting next to him. My uncle Emrys had a special fondness for cold baked apple and cream, which throughout the year was frequently specially prepared for him as an alternative to Nain's various puddings. Maesmawr's orchard trees, with their many varieties of cooking apple, together with the house-cows' milk separated into rich cream, (literally) 'full-filled' my uncle's dessert.

That reference to a principal meal at Maesmawr is timely, as I can here mention the custom of its being strictly teetotal for family and guests alike. The same was true of the 1st Baron Davies' home at nearby Plas Dinam in the village of Llandinam and his two sisters' home, the mansion of Gregynog. At the latter, only 'Robinson's Lemon and Barley Water' was on offer. Professional and frequently famous musicians at Gregynog's prestigious pre-War annual Music Festival were fully acquainted with the necessity of bringing their own alcoholic beverages and imbibing them from their bedroom's toothbrush glass. It was believed that Gwendoline and Margaret were aware of their musician guests' arrangements in that respect, but generously pretended not to know of them.

The absence of alcohol at Maesmawr in no way disadvantaged the humour of the happy gatherings that were an intrinsic part of the old house's atmosphere.

I feel sure that some of its guests imbibed in similar fashion to those musical guests at Gregynog, tactfully packing any empty bottles into their luggage before leaving. Calvinistic Methodism exerted a very strong influence in the locality, and Llandinam's minister, Dr. Richard Jones, D.D., was given a large and appreciative local audience in 1911 when he spoke upon the theme of 'Temperance and Purity'.

The housemaids' daily work was, in part, hard though never harsh. It was never finished until supper, or dinner, had been cleared off the table and all the dishes and glassware washed by hand. In winter, all the beds being occupied were provided with hot-water bottles, the kitchen range's fire was de-ashed and re-fuelled, and probably the breakfast table laid also, before the weary servants were

> **CAERSWS**
>
> LECTURE – An eloquent lecture was delivered at the Village Hall on Tuesday evening by the **Reverend Richard Jones, B.A.**, Calvinistic Methodist minister of Caersws and Llandinam, under the auspices of the Caersws United Temperance Society. His subject was "Temperance and Purity". **Mr. Edward Jones, J.P., Maesmawr Hall**, presided. There was a good attendance. The lecturer, who is an orator of the first order, made a telling effect upon his hearers which will long be remembered.
>
> *Montgomeryshire Express & Radnor Times* 1911

able to relax for a while in the warm cosiness of the servants' hall before retiring. The ubiquitous and constant television of today was, of course, unknown. Listening to the wireless, then often broadcasting some of the highest peaks of radio humour, was a welcome relaxation. What most people today would surely regard as mundane and boring occupations, such as knitting (socks for the fighting Forces and woollen 'Balaclava' helmets for those unfortunates in the War's cold climes), was almost a National spare-time activity. As mentioned earlier, reading, card-games and word-games, such as 'Canasta' and 'Scrabble', were very popular amongst everyone at Maesmawr, while doing nothing other than sitting in a comfortable chair in front of a winter fire, or taking a summer's evening stroll beside the River Severn's peaceful banks, in the utter quietude of those days, respectively rested tired feet and *restored the soul*. A half-day 'off' allowed the weekly treat of visiting family and friends in nearby homes, on the essential bicycle, or in the frequent green, smoky-exhaust-emitting, rattling old Crossville Co.'s motor-bus, which always stopped anywhere if requested. Those who patiently awaited it at the top of the Maesmawr Drive eagerly looked forward to being taken down to Newtown on a twenty-minute joy-ride, despite the conversation-preventing vibrations en route, to enjoy a shopping spree, somehow, despite the cheerlessness of Newtown's and Llanidloes' shops in those days of Wartime austerity. Those housemaids who were courting, as was Gretta with

The Maesmawr Hall household staff in about 1912.

Standing, with top hat, unknown (groom?), 3 horses kept.
Standing, with flat cap, Walter Pryce, chauffeur, his hand on his wife's shoulder.
Seated, Rose Pryce, cook, next to her sister.
Standing maids unknown; likewise the young lad sitting cross-legged in front.

Courtesy: Sharlene Jones

her beloved Gerald, stayed at Maesmawr on their 'off' afternoon for a cuddle and a chat, undisturbed – except perhaps unintentionally by "Master Michael", whom she loved. Not to be forgotten in my Recollections of happy days with the '*maids*', as we affectionately called them, was our playing of shuttlecock – with those little feathered and cork-nosed projectiles, hit with all the arm-power at our command, and even then only just reaching over the improvised net, which was merely a tightly stretched clothesline between a pair of poles pushed into the soft turf of the Maesmawr tennis-lawn. The cord was stretched tight so that light carpets, mats, curtains, blankets and suchlike could be hung over it. They were then beaten with cane beaters with a long handle and an interlaced face of openwork cane. With these implements, as well as enthusiastically beating the 'living-daylights' and accrued dust out of our suspended victims, we also propelled our little shuttlecocks towards a summer's azure sky. Up went the little boy's shrill challenge – "My 'advantage-in', Gretta!" – and sometimes the moths flew out!

Moorhens.
Close by the Roman Road, behind a hazel hedge running east from the stable-yard, once existed a tree-ringed, shaded, very deep pool. Moorhens always nested on a little central 'island' of rushes and twigs – the clutch of pure-white eggs thus tantalisingly beyond my boyhood reach and collection – of just one!

Agnes Miller Parker, 1936

THE ESTATE STAFF

Walter Pryce was Maesmawr's Estate carpenter and joiner, engineer and – before my time, except on a few occasions that I remember – the family chauffeur. I include photographs of the models of early motor cars in which Taid, Nain and their children travelled about, often up to Bala or thereabouts, where,

A replica of the early motor car that brought the Jones family from Trewythen-fawr to Dolwyddelan and back in 1908. Walter Pryce was chauffeur and everyone squeezed in somehow! Punctures in early pneumatic tyres were frequent, as Walter often recalled. Note the EP registration for Montgomeryshire; the letters continued to identify Montgomeryshire cars for decades.

Courtesy: Brian Demaus

as I have previously mentioned, their forebears had lived for many generations.

Walter lived at Caersws in a terraced house, No. 4 Dolwnog in Main Street, with his wife Rose, their son Glyn, who became a head teacher, and daughter Rose. 'Old Rose', as Walter's wife was affectionately called by my Maesmawr family – not due to her age but to differentiate her from her daughter, whom they called 'Little Rose' – had been cook and nursemaid at Trewythen-fawr in the years before she went with them to Maesmawr in 1910. There, she was the cook until the early 1930s. I believe 'Old Rose' had been an unofficial midwife

Left: Walter Pryce as chauffeur of Maesma-wr's car in about 1912, with my uncle Emrys, aunt Mari and governess. Note the car's curved brass 'Klaxon' horn and acetylene gas headlamp (lower right corner) with rear passengers' 'voice tube' fitted close to the driver's ear so that he could receive instructions! The dining room (now Wainscot Parlour) window can be seen in the background.

Courtesy: Sharlene Jones

Right: Walter Pryce and his wife Rose at their home, 4 Dolwnog, Caersws, Montgomeryshire, in about 1940.
Thus remembered by me as if it were yesterday!

Courtesy: Sharlene Jones, their granddaughter

Left: Walter and Rose Pryce: young husband and wife.

Courtesy: Sharlene Jones

at my birth in Aylesbury; she often told me that "I was the first to see you," so she must have been.

Walter had also been in my taid's employ at Trewythen-fawr, and the family's puncture-ridden motor car outings began at that time. Walter often told me about them, in hindsight, with much amusement. There were no emergency breakdown services in those now distant years, least of all in the mountainous regions of Montgomeryshire and Merionethshire. At the outbreak of the First World War, Walter became an army ambulance driver in France, returning to Caersws when the War ended and renewing his employment at Maesmawr. He was thus about sixty when it was my home.

Walter was tallish of stature, and walked with an ambling gait. He had a greying moustache, and wore gold-rimmed spectacles for reading. He dressed for daily work in a sagging old suit whose trousers were covered by dungarees, faded by frequent washing. The dungarees had a below-knee pocket in one leg that was never without a carpenter's traditional folding rule with little brass caps at both ends, which lay together when the rule was folded and protruded slightly from the top of the pocket. Walter wore an old and rather threadbare tweed jacket, beneath which an elderly waistcoat was visible, with a gold watch-chain securely held in a spare buttonhole. The gold timepiece itself sat snugly in its breast pocket and was consulted, sometimes with patient resignation, when he wished to check the relentless progress of 'Old Father Time'. A well-worn and rather oily tweed flat hat with a peak, and stout black boots, completed dear Walter's workaday dress. He spoke quite quickly in phrases that were frequently accompanied by short humorous chuckles, and with that 'sing-song' lilt so typical of Welshmen, whose fluent speech in their native tongue imbues their spoken English with that inimitable and endearing quality. Although Walter's voice was lighter than that of my uncle Harry Jones-Davies, it had a rather similar characteristic of gentle declamation expressed through concise and short phrases.

Walter bicycled the one-and-a-quarter miles between Caersws and Maesmawr four times each working day, in all weathers: down after breakfast, home for lunch, down again for the afternoon and back home in the evening, no matter whether it was pleasant summer or dark, wet winter. Even excluding all the years that he had thus bicycled before my birth, I have calculated that during the ensuing fifteen years, until Maesmawr was sold in 1947, Walter must have pedalled the staggering total of sixteen thousand miles – give or take a few hundred more when he visited the tenant farms for some small job or other, with his big carpenter's bag slung hazardously over the handlebars. How many tyres – indeed, how many bicycles – did he wear out in that time? In my boyhood Walter just came-and-went daily, and it never occurred to me then, or at any time later, to ask him. The bicycle I remember most clearly was quite elderly; it had a three-speed hub gear, and that particular rounded shape of handlebar possessed by bicycles of a *'certain age'*. Over the handlebars Walter hung his ex-First World War army-issue rain-cape, in case an inescapable Welsh downpour should suddenly fall.

His bicycle's front lamp (I think that a rear one was absent, Long Length's volume of traffic then being negligible compared to today's) was of the acetylene gas type. Those were still in popular use before and still after the Second World War. They were mounted on the front of some lorries, especially the SENTINEL steam-powered range, of which I include both an illustration and a detailed description. (A SENTINEL passed by Maesmawr every week, as I will relate.) That type of bright lamp – for the gas light was very bright – has been consigned to rural museums and such like for decades, but I feel that it is deserving of description here by one who remembers them in use.

Highly combustible acetylene gas (without the admixture of oxygen under pressure that feeds welding torches) is produced when calcium carbide meets water. This chemical was widely available from ironmongers and garages, for use in the road lamps of vehicles and bicycles. It was supplied in smallish, chalk-like pieces about one-quarter inch in average size, placed in an airtight container within the lamp's base. Above it was another container of plain water which, by means of a little on-and-off tap, allowed droplets to fall, by gravity,

The ROMAN ROAD'S raised agger, in nearly original condition, merely 100 yards east of Maesmawr Hall in Dôl-Hafren Farm's river pasture. The agger breaks off suddenly here, where a long-previous bend of the River Severn washed it away centuries ago.

Courtesy: Bill Putnam, photograph, and the Powysland Club, *Montgomeryshire Collections*, Volume 57, 1961–1962

onto the calcium carbide. The gas thus produced was piped to the centre of the lamp's chromium-plated reflector where, through a pinhole, a flame flourished after being lit with a match.

Opposite Red House Farm, the ROMAN ROAD's broad route runs west directly towards Maesmawr Hall, barely a mile away. Between the survey poles, a 12 feet wide strip of corn is stunted by the ROAD's foundation of stones and river gravel, the ground above it summer-scorched by lack of soil and moisture.

'And brings, in the untrampled wheat,
The tumult of a thousand feet'

(Mary Webb)

Courtesy: Bill Putnam, photograph, and the Powysland Club, *Montgomeryshire Collections* Volume 57, 1961–1962

Walter's carpentry workshop, which was the centre for his many skills, stood adjacent to the cow-byres at the eastern end of the Black-and-White painted stables, directly opposite what was then the Dutch hay-barn. Clearly visible from it was the old Roman Road from Viroconium – the Roman metropolis – to the important Roman fort at Caersws, via a ford or bridge, across the River Severn due west of Maesmawr. The agger, or raised causeway, which was the construction method used by the Romans for such roads, remains remarkably well preserved in the field today. From there, but no longer visible, it runs beneath the forecourt of the previous stables, thence continuing straight west under the front approach to Maesmawr, across the former orchard rookery and into the pasture beyond, where it meets the river bank. In summer drought conditions, a clear line of sun-scorched grass appears across the lawns either side of the house front, showing the route of the Roman Road beneath.

From: VIROCONIUM

Virocon – Virocon –
Still the ancient name rings on
And brings, in the untrampled wheat,
The tumult of a thousand feet.

The skulls of men who, right or wrong,
Still wore the splendour of the strong,
Are shepherds' lanterns now, and shield
Their candles in the lambing field.

Mary Webb (1881–1927)

I have here been conveniently 'waylaid' by the Road, to digress upon it with passing interest, as it was a mere 'slingshot' from Walter's wonderful old workshop, to which I will now return for a brief description. I spent happy hours in its oak or pine-scented interior, watching him at work making field-gates, the floor beneath him thick with wood-shavings.

The workshop was entered through a heavy, black-painted wooden door which was opened by pressing a small metal tongue in the centre of an iron ring-plate and thus lifting the interior latch. The nearby doors of the cow-byres and of the stables themselves were similar, except that they comprised two separate leaves, the lower one secured with a shoot-bolt and the upper opened by the kind of tongue-latch I have described. These doors are called 'stable-doors' for the obvious reason that the upper leaf can be opened separately to allow a horse to put its head out of the stable whilst remaining contained by the lower, closed leaf. The workshop had a long and very sturdily made workbench along the entire length of the inside wall. Fixed to the wall above it, and indeed all around the room, were wooden shelves, racks and metal hooks – with more hooks on the high plaster ceiling. These all held Walter's many and various hand-tools for the joinery and carpentry at which he was so adept. In those now distant days there were no electric power tools, and the mortice slots for field-gate construction, together with every type of cutting and sawing and chiselling, had to be done by hand. The revolving cutting bits of hand-drills, chisel blades, and especially the dozens of saw teeth, all required the skills of hand-sharpening. There were no 'use-until-blunt-and-then-throw-away'

saws in those days, and that included the huge circular-saw
blade in the heavy iron bench by
the BLACKSTONE engine-shed,
which cut logs 'like butter' after
Walter had sharpened it with his
files.

In a corner of the work-
shop stood a large sandstone
grinding-wheel about two feet
in diameter, turned by a crank
handle and revolving through a
water-filled trough. Axe-heads,
chopper-heads for splitting
firewood into kindling, curved
bill-hook blades for hedge-
trimming and the long straight
blades of haystack knives were
all sharpened to a keen edge by
the whetted stone. I was only
ten or eleven years old when
Walter first allowed me to use
his precious tools for my boyhood carpentry, but always
when he was near at hand, lest
I harm myself while doing so.

Mrs Rose Pryce, wife of the then late Walter Pryce,
upon her 90th anniversary at her home, 4 Dolwnog,
Caersws, Montgomeryshire, in 1976. "I was the first to
see you," she had said (of my birth in 1932).

Photograph: Ellis-Jones

Although very careful when using sharp chisels and saws, I was apt to be untidy
and was sometimes gently reproached by Walter for "not-returning-things-to-
where-you-found-them" – he was always patiently forgiving.

Behind and parallel to the workshop, separating it from the otherwise immediately adjacent stables, was the corn-bin store. This had two end doors directly opposite each other, one from the workshop and the other into the stables.
The corn-bin store contained large wooden barrels, with lids to exclude mice,
ranged along both its opposing walls. They contained a variety of proprietary
animal feeds, together with bran, sweet-corn and a wheat-with-oats mixture for
the several varieties of hen, and the pretty grey and white speckled guinea-fowl
who sauntered around the farmyard with their quaint gait and hunched shoulders. The corn-bin store was always imbued with the attractively sweet scent of
a corn-grinding mill. On its wall, beside the door into the stables, a pencilled
collection of short, horizontal lines, faded but still legible, had been pressed into
the white lime-wash of the soft plaster. Some of the lines were a mere quarter

inch apart, others more, the lowest being at about the height of a six-year-old. Each pencil line had a name and a date written beside it in a wobbly hand, starting with the year 1910 and rising, in approximately six-month increments, until about 1915. My reader will surely have guessed their significance; they were the recorded growth, from their early years, of my uncle Emrys, my mother, and their sisters. I am reminded that it was in 1910 that they came to live at Maesmawr from nearby Trewython-fawr, when my uncle Emrys was aged thirteen, my mother twelve, my aunt Megan nine and my aunt Mari six.

Walter also serviced and cleaned the house car. In my boyhood, it was a blue Standard '10' saloon with black wings, later superseded by a black Vauxhall '12'. In those days, the relative simplicity of most makes of motor car enabled their engines, brakes and chassis construction to be maintained by a competent 'all-round' mechanic such as Walter. The double garage at the west end of the stable-block had a pair of inspection and maintenance pits in the floor, the walls being hung with large and fully descriptive charts showing 'exploded' drawings of the vehicle's detailed anatomy; no uncertainty remained unexplained. On several occasions I recall Walter wearing his smart chauffeur's uniform of dark blue suit, black shoes, dark-blue full-length gabardine belted overcoat, flat-topped hat with a black and shiny peak, green on its underside, and dark brown calf-leather gloves. He must have been about to drive my nain to some important event.

The great BLACKSTONE oil-engine was Walter's pride and joy. In my most vivid and fond memories of him, I see him tending the engine almost daily, and making five-bar field gates from seasoned oak. Although it is now sixty years since he made his last, taking it to some field's edge, there for his fine handiwork to swing free for years to come, I like to think that some still swing there – '*In Memoriam*'.

Walter died in 1962 and Rests beside his beloved wife, 'Old Rose', in Llanwnog's peaceful burial field under the lea of Allt-Wnog's wooded hill. 'Old Rose' lived to be ninety-five. Her epitaph confidently says '*For ever with the Lord*' and Walter's, in trustful resignation, '*My times are in Thy Hand*'. Both are titles of their favourite hymns in the Church Hymnary.

As the stables were situated centrally between Walter's workshop at the east corner of the building and the double garage at the west corner, it is here convenient to describe them briefly. In my boyhood, horses were no longer kept there. The stables' hey-day had been the twenty or more years after they were built in 1910. During that time, my taid, my mother and her younger sister Mari each had a fine horse and probably rode the surrounding fields and the hills directly opposite Maesmawr during part of most days. In the years after 1937, in which year my taid died, my aunt Mari was married, and my mother had been married for the

My mother and her sister, Mari (facing r. and l.), in front of Maesmawr on their fine mares, circa 1920. The pretty *criss-cross* painted fence and gates now long-gone.

The late Dr. T. Jones-Davies, their cousin; his gift to me

past ten years, the stables remained intact but empty. Their spacious floor of hard, dark-blue engineering brick, with a *criss-cross* pattern to help prevent the horses' hooves from slipping in wet conditions, was divided into four enclosures. Three were open-ended for entry from the wide walkway which extended the entire length of the interior. Each stall had a wall manger for loose feed and a high-level hay rack, made of thin iron rods, fixed above it at a convenient height, enabling the horse to pull out tasty mouthfuls at will. The solid brick partitions that formed the horses' stalls were about six feet high, each topped with narrowly set, black iron bars to about eight feet or so above the floor. The fourth stall was enclosed by a stout door, provided for a mare with foal if need be. Adjacent to this end stall was a small door opening into the narrow but tall harness room, which had a second door directly from the partly cobbled forecourt in front of the stables. A steep and narrow stair on the harness room's left-hand wall rose to give access to the loft above through a ceiling trap-door. On the opposite wall there projected a series of iron brackets to support saddles, and smaller ones on which to hang harness and the straps of shiny steel stirrups. Most of the brackets no long held them – those soft pieces and lengths of leather, kept pliable and gleaming with leather soap and neatsfoot oil. (Neatsfoot oil is rendered and purified from the feet and shinbones

– not the hooves – of cattle, and remains liquid down to low temperature.) The little harness room always smelt of wood-smoke. No wonder, for Lewis Jones, Maesmawr's occasionally needed branch-lopper and expert tree-feller, boiled his blackened tea-kettle on handfuls of tinder-dry wood shavings from Walter's workshop floor. He stuffed the tiny fireplace's grate with them to overflowing; some smoke went up the chimney, but the rest 'stayed at home'!

Evan Owen, like Walter, had known me since my infancy. Happy were the hours of my boyhood spent in his ever jovial company, either watching him milk the docile cows or being his keen assistant when hedging in winter, and when we drove **Dandy** in the shafts of his two-wheeled wagon to collect dry bracken from above Bron-felen, as a traditional base for the stack of unthreshed corn. The tales that will follow –'SEREN ESCAPES', 'DANDY AND DAVIS', 'THE VANISHED COWS' and 'JUST GOING FOR A WALK' – all concern Evan and me in various circumstances.

He was born and raised at the little homestead of Tynllidiart, on a narrow lane between Trefeglwys and Caersws, and was one amongst a large family of children. Evan was stocky and of a strong constitution. For his daily work, he invariably wore a collarless cotton or wool shirt to suit the season, with a brass stud fastened into the topmost button-hole. An old waistcoat and grey trousers suited him on most days, and his stout leather boots were frequently encrusted with dried cow manure – especially after he had brushed and washed out the messy cow-byres. His headwear was a favourite flat cap with a short peak. When milking the three cows, he donned a long-sleeved pale brown linen coat to below the knee, his old flat hat, from which he was inseparable, turned back-to-front so that its peak did not stick into the cow's flank whilst he milked her.

The late Evan Owen, then retired from Maesmawr Hall.

Courtesy: Ieuan Owen

When I visited him in his retirement, Evan told me that he and his wife Elizabeth Anne lived for sixty-two years at White Cottage, beside Long Length, barely fifty yards from the Maesmawr Lodge gates, in the Caersws direction. There they raised their happy family of a daughter and three sons, Freda and Donald, Derek and Ieuan. After Elizabeth Anne died in 1962, Evan continued living there alone – except for frequent visits by Ieuan and

The Maesmawr housemaids' 'privy' lavatory; today, a determined tree-trunk is 'bent' on destroying it!

Photograph: Ellis-Jones

his wife Mair – until he was almost ninety years of age. Although he had remained contentedly independent, considering his advanced age, he then agreed to move to Caersws. He settled in happily, being nearer to his son and daughter-in-law, and spent his last two years in a little semi-detached one-storey dwelling, basically independent, but with qualified supervision always available if needed.

In his many active years at Maesmawr, in addition to the twice-daily milking of the house-cows, tending the annual pair of pigs and large flock of fowls, not forgetting the proud but fierce old Rhode Island Red rooster, his tasks were many and various in both summer and winter. Cutting the amount of hay needed every day from the old Dutch barn with the long two-handled 'T' shaped and razor-sharp stack-knife took much careful time. There was a lot of long grass on the extensive boundaries of the formal gardens that required regular summer scything, and bracken to be carted back for the base of the autumn-built corn stack. In winter, Evan patiently cut all the field hedges within hailing distance of the house, trimming them by hand with a long-handled billhook. There were ditches to clear, firewood to chop and split for the house, not forgetting (he never did!) to empty and dispose of the privy lavatories' relentlessly produced contents.

Evan was fond of singing – or sort of singing! – a small collection of memorised ditties, either to himself or to me as his sole audience, especially, and understandably, when tedious tasks were in hand. It was he who explained to me the cooing of the woodpigeon thus: 'coo-COO-coo-cuckoo --- coo-COO-coo-cuckoo-COO', interpreted as 'take-TWO-cows-David --- take-TWO-cows-David --- TWO', when the bird espied a thief.

During his last two years of retirement at Caersws, I visited him as often as possible, although I was living in Oxfordshire at that time. When I appeared, often unexpectedly, the first thing Evan would say was, "Lovely to see you – lovely to see you." What more of a dear friend's welcome could there be? He would repeat it several times, in that slow and Welsh lilting voice that I can vividly recall, especially when looking at his photograph. When, unknown to me, Evan sensed that he had not long to live, he asked me to be a bearer at his funeral. I immediately promised him that I would, but did not expect it to be so soon. However, on a cold but sunny day in March 1990, I was greatly saddened, yet also felt singularly privileged, to assist in laying him to Rest, beside his cherished wife, at the grand old age of ninety-two, in St. Llonio's Churchyard at Llandinam.

My most enduring memory of dear Evan will always be the sight of him ambling homeward from Maesmawr on a summer evening, carrying his full white-enamelled little milk-can by its swinging handle, the three house-cows quietly and slowly wending their way in front of him into the lush pastures after their milking; his loved little home of White Cottage in the distance, its white lime-washed walls reflecting the rays of the setting sun. Behind him, as he went, the great black chorus of cawing rooks in Maesmawr's orchard rookery bade him 'Good night' and gradually settled themselves to roost in the ever-fading light.

Noel Brown was a 'Breiddin Man' – the Breiddin being that rock bastion standing beyond Welshpool as the Gate of Wales; in other words, he was a born-and-bred Salopian. Moreover, he was a professional gardener, trained in the 'Old School', like his close contemporary, the late Percy Thrower of Shrewsbury fame. Those of their generation were thoroughly versed in all aspects of horticulture. In that era, gardeners had to make-do with a very sparse range of potions for combating the attacks by pest or spore upon flowers, vegetables, trees and bush fruit. The modern gardener's 'pharmacy' could not have been imagined by them or their predecessors. In those days, a few chemicals – chemicals of great potency, capable of inducing human

A young Noel Brown beside his beehive in Maesmawr's orchard, about 1941.

Courtesy: Norman Edwards

death in a few seconds if ingested, possibly if even smelt for more than a mere split second – were the professional gardener's cure-all.

Noel came to Maesmawr as sole gardener in about 1934, having previously been a member of the garden staff at Leighton Hall, the Victorian mansion situated on the River Severn's valley slope directly opposite Powis Castle. Noel, with his wife Winnie and daughter Sybil, lived at Maesmawr's gate Lodge, at the top of the Drive, for the entire period of his employment. They were a kindly family and, like Walter's and Evan's families, were held in high esteem and great personal affection by my taid and nain during those long-ago happy years.

Noel had a quiet manner, being a little shy but not without humour. Unlike Walter (Pryce) and Evan (Owen), whom

Noel Brown's potting-shed on the right; he deftly created dew-fresh tokens of Joy and Sorrow within its shaded and compost-scented interior.

Photograph: Ellis-Jones

everyone at Maesmawr knew by their Christian name, Noel was 'Brown' to them all. I have always believed that this quaint anachronism was in essence a transferred habit. Noel's predecessor as Maesmawr's gardener had been a Mr Humphreys, whose forename I never knew and who retired in 1934. During my boyhood, I recall that any reference to Mr Humphreys was as 'Humphreys', and thus the surname habit was transferred to 'Brown' upon his succession. Noel was not averse to it in any way. Further quaintness existed in how the Maesmawr family and the house staff always referred to, or personally addressed, the wife of a staff member. Thus Evan's wife was known as 'Mrs Owen', Noel's wife was 'Mrs Brown' and Walter's wife – 'Old Rose' to the family – was 'Mrs Pryce' to the others. That suited everyone!

Noel was a man of medium height, with receding black, rather sleek hair, with not much of it on top. He had very kind dark brown eyes (perhaps that was really why he was called 'Brown'!), somewhat olivaceous skin and a quiet voice. He always wore a hat, a weather-beaten old grey trilby in cool and winter weather, and a jaunty panama in summer's heat. Noel favoured a collared shirt and tie most days, but in summer, a white or cream shirt without a collar, but with a brass front stud, was evident. He was partial to an old waistcoat; from a top button-hole hung a gold watch-chain, its matching watch having a brilliantly white enamelled face, black Roman numerals and elegant hands that traversed his devoted gardening hours, safely snug in a breast pocket. A faded grey, heavy linen apron was worn for each and every job, and black rubber gumboots were Noel's preference over leather ankle-boots. The little brick potting-shed was the focal point of all his skilful activity.

Today, it is packed to the roof with dry firewood, as is the building next door, which was the men's privy lavatory. Opening the potting-shed door after sixty years had passed, I wondered what I would find within. Still there, sandwiched between the logs, was the stout work-bench, only its thick front edge visible. On the wall above it, where the topmost firewood had been used, a long shelf remaining from former days could be seen. Upon this shelf, Noel kept his 'armoury' – tins of fruit-tree grease, sulphur powder, Bordeaux-Mixture powder, Jeyes fluid disinfectant, nicotine and soft-soap. Several old hooks projected from the shelf's edge, from which he used to hang plant labels made from thin strips of soft lead, coils of galvanised wire of several thicknesses – none plastic-coated in those days. Upon the work-bench he filled little clay pots with his homemade recipe for sieved compost; how many hundreds, I wonder, during the fourteen years that Noel was Maesmawr's gardener? Now gone – he surely took it with him upon leaving – was a little wooden cabinet comprising a dozen or so pull-out drawers, standing at the work-bench's farthest corner, in which were kept innumerable seed-packets of flowers and vegetables, many proprietary – such as those from Messrs Suttons – and others, kept in small, labelled, brown envelopes, which were his own collection of especially favoured varieties, gleaned over the years.

The potting-shed was imbued with the scent of sweet compost. There Noel frequently and deftly made beautiful wreaths, some Seasonal but most for Sorrow. The latter he created, often at first light, with dew-fresh flowers from his herbaceous borders, having them in early readiness for their sad occasions. When he was making them, I would find him perched on a high stool, a jugful of the finest blooms awaiting his selection as, one by one, he deftly wound a short length of florist's pre-cut wire around each flower's stem. These were then gently pushed into the compressed natural moss bound onto the wire ring that formed the wreath's circumference.

Close to the potting-shed stood a magnificent white-painted Victorian greenhouse, which can be glimpsed in Mr Harris' drawing (page 55) and, more clearly, in the photograph of Gretta smartly posing in front of my nain's dahlia bed (page 104). The greenhouse remained there, and intact, until about five years ago, when it was either demolished or, hopefully, carefully dismantled and sold to be re-erected.

The greenhouse had a range of slatted wooden shelves along both long sides and a large galvanised water-tank by its door. Upon its tranquil surface, until disturbed by the filling of a watering-can, lay a film of some minutely-leaved aquatic plant whose myriads covered the water's surface. Overhead, and spreading across close under the glass roof, extended a magnificent white grapevine, whose heavy bunches of semi-transparent and bloomed fruit hung down in the humid heat in great profusion. The swelling bunches had previously been carefully thinned by Noel with his scissors, thus ensuring that the remaining grapes would develop to their greatest size. The vine was prone to seasonal attack by the red spider mite, but potential damage was hopefully prevented either by a nicotine-and-water spray or, much more drastic, by the entire removal of the vine's typically dry and self-peeling bark by scraping it with a sharp knife. Ranged along the slatted shelves were many large clay pots in which grew luxuriant tomato plants and varieties of indoor flowers, especially the brilliant scarlet pelargoniums, better known as geraniums. The greenhouse's hot and humid atmosphere had quite an impact on the unsuspecting senses as one entered it. Moreover, the humidity held that inimitable and pleasantly pungent scent, particularly of tomato plants, that only an old and seasoned greenhouse possesses! Several long and white-painted elderly hot-water radiators stood close to the mottled brick walls, which were a mere three feet high, and upon which the iron frame of the side windows and roof was built.

Wasps at Maesmawr, as elsewhere, were a problem amongst the plenteous tree-fruits in the orchard. The pests were effectively destroyed by Noel's application of the lethal potassium cyanide. In those days, that compound, perhaps one of the most poisonous chemicals known, was available to professional gardeners – perhaps farmers also? – upon their signing the chemist's 'Poison Book' – often the sole proviso for supply. The bona-fide entomologist was also able to obtain cyanide as an instantaneous killer of insects and butterflies; this method prevented them from damaging their delicate legs and wings when fruitlessly and pathetically flapping against the glass side of the *killing-bottle*. The chemical is so lethal that a quantity of it, less than can be contained in a small gelatine vitamin capsule, killed the German war criminals Hermann Goering, Heinrich Himmler and others, almost instantly. They were being tried at the Nuremberg War Trials in the late 1940s, following the end of hostilities. These prisoners somehow managed to obtain, or continue to keep, unbeknown to their captors, tiny glass phials of cyanide, which each crunched in their teeth at the chosen moment, and were dead in a few seconds. I recall that Noel once, and very quickly, passed the open top of a jar of potassium cyanide across my nostrils at a safe distance of several feet. I can still – in the mind, not the nose – recall the unmistakable odour of crushed almonds that cyanide possesses.

Over sixty years ago, Nature was so profuse at Maesmawr, as she was in the Welsh and other countryside, that my making and keeping a small boyish collection of common birds' eggs and butterflies did not threaten ecology. To kill the latter, I fortunately only had recourse to household ammonia on cotton wool – fortunate for me but not, alas, for the poor butterfly. I never sought, nor accidentally found, Noel's cyanide; I am certain that, knowing its terrible potential

Photograph 1. Maesmawr Hall after architect Nesfield's major extension of 1876. This west elevation comprised a beautifully balanced composition of gables, with half-timbered patterns painted on their masonry. The majestic bay window of his drawing room, with its elegant balcony balustrade and the similar proportions of the central gable's French windows above, together with those of the mini-gables and the two principal gables, combine to enhance the overall design. Alas, it has not survived unaltered. Photograph circa 1883, contemporaneous with the drawing dated 1883 – note the bare iron railings in both.

Crown Copyright: RCAHMW

if misused, he kept its storage place very safe and secret.

For a time, the gardens depicted in Mr Harris' 1939 drawing (page 55) all remained exactly as he recorded them with the skill of his pen. However, within a short period of my family's sale of Maesmawr, both the house and the gardens suffered grievous damage and change; this continued to occur over succeeding decades at the hands of several successive owners.

I now hope accurately to describe the gardens of my Maesmawr boyhood, some parts of which the very observant Mr Harris could not encompass in his drawing, due to his static vantage point. Comparison of the gardens up to 1947 and their much earlier characteristics, commencing after the Nesfield extension of 1876, is greatly helped by the following five photographs.

Photograph 1 is almost self-explanatory, showing the extensive area of wide gravel paths, bisecting areas of plain grass. I presume to date this photograph at about 1883; if this date is accurate, it was seven years after the completion of architect Nesfield's extension. I choose 1883, or thereabouts, from observing the

Photograph 2. The same viewpoint as the 1883-dated drawing (page 16), but a decade or so later. The great beech tree of my boyhood was here approaching its maturity.

wall-climbing plants, then approaching a height of about eight feet, growing on both sides of the tall central window in each of the principal west-facing gables. I believe that these plants could have grown to that height in as many years, assuming they were planted very soon after the extension was complete, and after the builders' scaffolding and associated rubbish was cleared away. A second point of interest concerns the bare, white-painted iron railings which run to the corner of the east and west gables. Both are bare of plant growth. (Compare that with photographs 2 and 3.) A third point concerns the several mature deciduous trees seen beyond the front gable. The nearest, whose topmost branches rise above the roof ridge, was then growing where, in an unknown number of later years, the formal east garden was created. The further distant trees were then growing on what subsequently became the farmyard.

Photographs 2 and 3, having been taken together, can thus be examined together. However, the first point of interest relates to the white-painted iron railings in photograph 1. Here, their shared direction, running to the outer corner

Photograph 3. The west gable's masonry corner is obvious here. Beyond it is a glimpse of architect Nesfield's great bay window to his Victorian drawing room, crowned by the elegant balustered balcony onto which the French windows of my nain's bedroom opened. The lady at Maesmawr's front door was probably its then owner, Jane Anne Pryce (1816–98). Date as photograph 2.

Crown Copyright: RCAHMW

of east and west gable respectively, is evident. However, in the interim between the taking of photographs 1 and of 2 and 3 together, mature hedges of clipped boxwood have completely enveloped the previously bare railings (of photograph 1) – except for two panels of (still bare) railing adjacent to the west gable's outside corner and a barely visible wicket-gate of similar material at the outside corner of the east gable. Boxwood being a very slow-growing plant, I conclude that photographs 2 and 3 are about ten years later than 1.

On that assumption, I date photographs 2 and 3 as being about 1893. Photograph 3 shows a (left-hand) glimpse towards the balconied bay-window of architect Nesfield's drawing room. On the photograph's far right, the thick foliage of the trees indicates that the formal east garden, of my boyhood and probably two decades beforehand, had yet to be created. I believe that the lady shyly posing at the front door with her attendant hound, surely a Great Dane, was Jane Anne Pryce (1816–1898), from whom the Reverend Herbert Davies inherited the Maesmawr Estate, which he rented to my taid from 1910 and sold to him in 1920.

Photograph 4. Maesmawr Hall in June 1947, following my nain's death there that April. Her Rose Garden glowed 'IN MEMORIAM'.

Courtesy: Tim Lewis

Thus the appearance of the house itself shown in photograph 1, taken in about 1893, was very probably much the same that welcomed my taid and his family seventeen years later, in 1910. The sole addition in the intervening years may have been the little clematis-covered hooped canopy with its pair of black-and-white wicket gates at the front door. Whether or not the boxwood hedges that enclosed the iron railings in about 1893, and the tree seen close to the east gable, were still there in 1910 is conjecture. The taller branches behind it are those of the yew tree which, in my boyhood, stood close by the kitchen door and sheltered the coal stack.

Photographs 4, 5 and 6 were taken in 1947, the year that my family sold Maesmawr. Photograph 4 is from a viewpoint a little forward of that chosen by Mr Harris for his drawing. Photograph 5 shows the aforementioned hooped canopy and wicket gates at the front door, and part of the kitchen wing. The latter, as previously stated, was built in 1908 – two years before my taid's renting of Maesmawr began. The elegant greenhouse mentioned earlier is clearly seen, and the yew tree's topmost branches shown in photograph 5 have been lopped level with the eaves of the 1908 wing.

Photographs 4, 5 and 6 thus illustrate the Maesmawr of my boyhood, and as

130

Photograph 5. Maesmawr as I remember it when it was my boyhood home, including Noel Brown's heavy wooden wheelbarrow, which I could not lift even when it was empty! Cormorants roosted high in the great pine tree; my uncle Emrys let them be; the tree was felled years ago.

it had remained – except for the growth of shrubs, hedges and trees – since long before my birth in 1932. With regard to all the gardens of my infancy and boyhood, their character remained exactly the same as illustrated by photographs 4, 5 and 6, and Mr Harris' drawing of 1939. My brief analysis of the illustrative information as to the extent and character of Maesmawr's gardens, beyond that perceived in photographs 4, 5 and 6, poses this question: What garden, or gardens, existed – or were laid out – in the years between 1893 (or thereabouts) and 1910, the year that my family went to live there? Did they find a garden already laid out and having developed during the previous twenty years, or did my taid and nain (perhaps with 'Humphrys') create that garden themselves from 1920, when they became Maesmawr's owners? During the preceding ten years, whilst renting it from the Reverend Herbert Davies, they would have had to obtain his consent to embark on any such undertaking. None of my relatives who, as children at Maesmawr from 1910, might perhaps have been able to answer the question are now alive. So it remains!

Photographs 4, 5 and 6 are of Maesmawr as I shall always remember it and before subsequent harmful hands destroyed so much there in the years after my nain had died and my uncle had sold the Estate.

131

I have, with sadness, already enumerated the many drastic changes meted upon Maesmawr's exterior and interior across the past fifty-eight years. I hope that some, at least, of my readers, upon visiting the house today, will take the opportunity of using what I have written to compare 'Yesterday with Today'. Some may, and some may not, share my view that many of those changes have not been aesthetically happy ones. Incidentally, the sixteenth-century date inscribed at the apex of the front gable is incorrect, and merely the ignorant whim of some unknown owner since my family sold Maesmawr.

I will now take pleasure in describing the former gardens, taking the view of Mr Harris' drawing (page 55) as my starting-point. In the central foreground is my nain's rose garden with its sundial, beside which Janet took my photograph in the summer of 1941. Close to the drawing's left-hand margin there extended a deep and lengthy herbaceous flower border, backed by shrubbery growing from a lower level, in whose leafy depths a retaining wall of large stones terminated. The southern end of the flower border was bounded by a small terrace with three steps down onto a wide grass path whose gate, into the orchard rookery, is just beyond the drawing's left-hand confines. The northern end of the flower border was partly enclosed by a right-angular length of clipped boxwood hedge which, with a similar and longer length opposite the path, gave entry onto the large lawn known as the tennis-lawn. That had been its principal use in the 1920s and 1930s, and it had also been the scene of a large and joyous garden fête in 1938. I recently found the *Montgomeryshire Express & Radnor Times'* full report of the occasion in the National Library of Wales, and obtained a copy. Included with the descriptions of many stalls and the names of the members of my family who attended and those of their friends who manned the attractions, the newspaper report also said: '*The marquees and tents were kindly lent for the occasion by Lord Davies, Mr David Thomas, headmaster of Caersws Council School, and Mr JG Nicholas; in addition, Lord Davies also provided the ponies for the children's pony rides*'. I wonder where 'D-D', as he was known, obtained the ponies? Surely not from amongst the wild herds of mountain ones that roamed above Llandinam – otherwise a lively outcome would have ensued! What a lovely day must have been had by all on Maesmawr's huge lawn. Alas, for some reason, my mother and I were not present, but I recall that on my subsequent visit with her, there remained in the house boxes of red, blue, yellow and white balloons whose inflated globes proclaimed: '*Maesmawr Hall Fête, July 23, 1938*'. (As I write this, I realise that tomorrow is July 23rd – there is much in Life that defies the rational.)

Photograph 6. Maesmawr's east garden, in 1947.

Courtesy: Tim Lewis

Returning to the tennis-lawn, now that all the adults at that fête have Departed and the children of my generation who were there are no longer young, I must again recall the mighty beech tree that towered over its western edge, whose venerable old trunk had, without complaint, suffered the lead pellets of a small boy's airgun. Beyond it, at the northern edge of the tennis-lawn, flourished a thick shrubbery containing a red-berried and very prickly Berberis bush. The shrubbery hid the yew-trees, 'the Bower', beyond, which was mentioned in the 'MAES-MAWR' article (pages 16-19), and of which I include a photograph to show its height today (page 98).

The right-hand portion of Mr Harris' drawing, being so accurate in its depictions, naturally agrees with the frontal view, in photographs 4 and 5, of Maesmawr as it then was. I used to love sitting – for no particular reason – deep within the old weeping willow, on the right. Within, it was very roomy, and the pendulous and breeze-swaying branches created an open dome spacious enough to contain a twin-seat wooden bench. The willow was not very old, because in the photograph of my mother and my aunt Mari on horseback in front of the house in about circa 1920, (page 120) it cannot be seen. Its later location was, so to speak, 'between' the cheek-bone and the reins of my aunt's horse.

In contrast to the west garden, the smaller east garden was of a different character. Its lawn, whose curving front edge delineated that of the gravel forecourt, had a large central flower bed, behind which was a fine herbaceous border. This was both deep and lengthy, and was backed for its entire length by a *criss-cross* braced pergola made from many straight lengths of Scots Pine. This was then a very popular timber for such purposes, retaining its rough bark for many years after being cut and thus giving the structure a *rustic* look, which was complimentary to gardens; the drawback was that it was an ideal host to earwigs and other pests. The Maesmawr pergola stood about eight feet high, successfully screening the lower half of the stables, the BLACKSTONE engine-shed and the garages from both the house and the east garden. It is nowadays difficult accurately to describe from where, and to where, the pergola ran, because several nearby features have gone in the intervening years. However, photograph 6, taken in 1947, shows the character of the east garden, which I will attempt to describe.

Suffice it to say that the pergola was incorporated into a roofed and similarly *rustic* arbour, about half-way along its length. The arbour had a very uncomfortable bench seat along its back and side walls, made from the Scots pine timber whose bark had been preserved. The comparatively thin logs that formed the bench were set close together, and its front edges were made of long lengths of pine supporting the end of the logs, with similar struts from off the *crazy-paved* stone floor. The rough bench was unkind to the backs of legs in short trousers! The entire pergola and arbour – including its gently sloping roof, which was made of Scots pine also – was copiously covered in a wide variety of climbing and rambler roses, large-flowered clematis, and masses of sweet-scented honeysuckle. Along the edge of the east lawn, which bounded the semi-drive that curved into the garage forecourt from the main Drive, were set four Scots pine posts, equally spaced. Fixed to the top of each was an inverted bowl-shape made of stout galvanised wire, and up each post a large-flowered clematis scrambled, to spread its saucer-sized blooms upon, and cascade over, the wire support provided.

Innumerable butterflies of many varieties fluttered above, or sunned themselves upon, the magnificent herbaceous flowers. *Red Admirals, Peacocks, Painted Ladies, Tortoiseshells, Commas,* and some of the *Blues* were to be seen, often arguing determinedly with a honey-bee for a perch upon the stamens of an especially favoured flower. There were then, in the fruit-tree orchard, a number of hives which my uncle decided to install in about 1941. Noel was his bee-keeper, enveloped in protective white overalls, a wide-brimmed hat within an encircling fine mesh net, and long gauntlets, the latter awkward for gripping the bee-keeper's smoker and squeezing out some puffs every so often, to tell the bees who was 'boss'. Noel may have learned bee-keeping at Leighton Hall before coming to Maesmawr. However, that was six years before, and in the interim he had not done any, even if he had learned the craft at Leighton in his former years there.

At the northern end of the east garden, backed by the now absent Victorian greenhouse, there grew a row of equally spaced, dark green, upright juniper trees, then eight to nine feet high. In between and around each, profuse dahlias of many colours, both single and double, grew annually. My nain adored them as cut flowers in the house; she and Noel frequently held knowledgeable discussions on the dahlias' characteristics and merits, and he devotedly grew them from especially favourite seeds. The tall juniper trees and the dahlia plants – the latter before they flowered, as it happened – feature in the pre-autumn and pre-War photograph of Gretta in her smart suit and shoes (page 104).

My uncle Emrys cut the lawns with an ATCO cylinder motor-mower, painted dark green, whose grass-box displayed the Royal Arms to show that the machine was 'By Appointment to His Majesty King George VI'. The mower had a subdued engine-note, and its pale blue exhaust smoke imbued the warm summer evening air with a pleasant scent. The smoke almost matched my uncle's cotton shirt, which he wore with those elasticated and silver-plated armlet rings, just above the elbows, which prevented over-long sleeves from enveloping the wrists. He especially liked to mow of an evening, after the day's summer heat had abated. He and the ATCO went to-and-fro across the long and wide expanse of the tennis-lawn, making immaculate, alternately light and dark, stripes on the sward. I followed a short distance behind, eagerly hoping for his invitation to operate the mower. It never occurred – and for good reason; the clutch lever on an ATCO, operated solely by the thumb, had – alas for my hopes – a wide 'travel' which needed quick release to engage traction and an even quicker thumb action to disengage it. The small spread of my boyish hand was insufficient for my thumb to stretch and operate the clutch. That inability potentially promised a very prickly journey's-end into spines of a Berberis bush at the lawn's northern end!

Instead of driving 'King George VI's' motor-mower, I helped to empty the grass-box's profuse contents into Noel's capacious wooden wheelbarrow. It is seen in photograph 5 with its additional drop-in frame; this made it capable of holding more, and also made it very heavy – too much for me to lift, let alone push!

Summer evenings at Maesmawr held a special magic for me. After my uncle, his mowing completed, had put 'King George VI' away, although the swirling rooks continued their cawing, that dearly remembered sound contributed to, and never detracted from, the all-enveloping peace that fell upon me and my beloved surroundings. Being an only child, after the trauma of the early death of my mother, I soon learned to develop an inner self-sufficiency engendered through the security and love received from all whom I herein mention and depict. Nevertheless, there were many hours, in many days, when I had to – and did – amuse myself, in addition to the happy times spent in the company of the family, the housemaids, Walter, Evan and Noel, not forgetting my chum Ieuan

Owen, a few years younger than I. Such isolation was certainly not painful. On the contrary, being on my own enabled the gradual development of a spiritual independence, which, although perhaps I didn't consciously realise it at the time, flourished within the emotional and material security which Maesmawr gave me in abundance during those years. Its beauty, and the great love I received there, were gifts beyond measure, which enabled me gradually to surmount my deep personal loss. Moreover, Maesmawr, having been the beloved home of my mother's childhood and young womanhood, was to me imbued with a continuing 'presence' of her, which illumined my every waking hour.

Thus, when I recall those summer evenings of long-ago, the scene in my mind's eye is vivid: the old house's Black-and-White aglow in the setting sun as this sank over the river pasture and beyond distant Caersws, its deepening

orange-red intensity dazzling the unwary eye, should it for an inadvertent split-second have caught its glare between the shadowed trunks of the orchard rookery's trees. Dusk drew near. The rooks slowly ceased their clamour, and the owls began to hoot in the gloaming. Only the second-long *whoosh* of a solitary motor car on Long Length, as it passed the top of Maesmawr's Drive and the sound travelled down it, momentarily distracted. The rest was silence, and '***left the world to darkness and to me***'.

Today, the ancient rookery has gone, and all Noel's pride-and-joy is gone too: his lovely flower gardens, his vegetable plots, the soft-fruit cage, the glorious greenhouse, and almost the entire fruit-tree orchard. So have all the boxwood hedges which he patiently clipped with hand-shears (helped by a step-ladder); those thick and curved-top forms which, at dawn on an autumn morning, were decked with a myriad of gossamer cobwebs, glistening with silver dew. All that remains of Noel's devoted Maesmawr days is the great mauve-flowered wisteria, which embraces the front of the house, as though to offer comfort – comfort which is surely (in human sentiment's terms) accepted, as the climber seeks to compensate for the architectural spoilation which it witnessed in past decades, and the many and grievous changes that accompanied it.

I last saw Noel, Winnie and their daughter Sybil in 1982; that dear trio have now Departed, and Rest in Llandrinio's peaceful churchyard within close sight of the Breiddin. When they left Maesmawr after the Estate's sale, they were kept busy at a smallholding at Pool Quay, on the River Severn beyond Welshpool. However, after some successful but hard-won years, during which the severe river floods, in pre-Clywedog Dam days, were destructive, they moved several miles to safer Rhos Common, in close proximity to Noel's cherished native Breiddin. There he retired to grow his favourite alstroemaria flowers and graft old apple trees. I visited Noel and Winnie one day. "It's perfect weather for grafting," he said, and almost added "Master Michael". No book could fully explain that – but Noel knew.

Myself with Noel, his wife Winnie and daughter Sybil, in their flower and vegetable-filled garden at Rhos Common, Llandrinio, near Welshpool, in 1982. Noel Passed away in 1997, aged 86, and Winnie ten years beforehand, in 1987.

Courtesy: Norman Edwards

Winnie with one of her beloved pet cats.

Courtesy: Norman Edwards

137

THE KITCHEN, BACK KITCHEN
AND DAIRY

My nain was in her element here, spending part of every weekday – usually the morning – supervising the general cooking. Each week throughout the year she made the bread, the butter and, occasionally, soft cheese. In due course, I will explain the baking of bread and the making of butter by hand, as well as the mechanical means for obtaining the cream to make the butter. Firstly, I must briefly describe the kitchen of my boyhood, and then proceed into the back kitchen, which was adjacent to it, and into the small dairy next door.

The kitchen's principal feature was the old black iron, coal-fired range, containing the glowing fire behind its retaining bars, and a set of ovens of differing heats to suit individual cooking requirements. Every so often, the fire was allowed to die of its own accord, and the entire range to cool, so that it could be polished with black-lead paste. This was sparingly applied with a soft-ish bristle brush, and it dried in a few minutes. The entire range was then polished to a gleam by further and enthusiastic brushing which obtained the desired result. Coal for its fire was fetched in galvanised buckets from the huge 'cliff' of coal blocks, built close to the kitchen door, which had to be laboriously broken up into suitably-sized pieces to feed into the top of the grate. In my earlier comparison of the nineteenth and twentieth-century photographs of Maesmawr, I drew my readers' attention to a tall yew tree, then growing in front of the two-storey 1908 service wing, which included the individual rooms I now describe. Moreover, that tree, by then much reduced in height, is clear to see in the distance 'between' the heads of my mother's and her sister's horses, photographed in front of Maesmawr (page 120). In my years there, the old yew tree still flourished, annoyingly continuing to drip for hours after heavy rain, wetting anyone who stood at the kitchen door and making that rear corner of the house rather gloomy. Its topmost branches also denied north light – not the brightest at the best of times – into the back stairs' half-landing window.

I return to the kitchen and recall the long pinewood table that stood across the window. Its top was bleached white from years of weekly scrubbing with a hard bristle brush and washing-soda crystals. It had been scrubbed so much that the soft fibres between the hard annular rings had been worn away, leaving the latter as slightly projecting ridges along its entire length. A wooden cheese-press stood against the wall opposite the range, and beside it was a tall unpainted pine chest-of-drawers with glass-fronted cupboards and shelves behind. The large and very smooth blue slate flagstones remain today in as fine a condition as they were over sixty years ago. They continue into the back kitchen with similar excellence.

Just inside the door between the servants' hall and the kitchen, and on the right-hand side, there used to be a door giving immediate access to a steep flight of wooden stairs leading up to the laundry. It was the same size as the kitchen immediately beneath. I know only one person who visits Maesmawr today and remembers that stair of former years; she and I are the only ones. Both it and the lovingly polished old range, whose continuous and homely warmth once glowed with its welcoming coals, have been absent for many years, the range almost certainly taken out when Maesmawr became an hotel.

I will return briefly to the laundry in due course, but meanwhile will describe my young memories of the back kitchen's weekly scene of three essential activities, and the adjacent dairy's twice-daily procedure for separating 'milk from the cow' into skimmed milk and cream. After these descriptions, I shall return into the kitchen, in my mind's eye, and both illustrate and recall the scene of weekly ironing that followed 'wash-day' in the back kitchen, where bubbling and steaming fabrics created an atmosphere somewhat akin to that of a Turkish or Roman bath!

Early every morning, and each evening too, Evan brought a heavy bucket of warm, frothing cow's milk – sometimes two buckets, depending on the season – to the back kitchen. He had carried them, without need of a yoke, from the farm cow-byres at the rear corner of the stables, across the yard, through the kissing gate near the potting shed, and up the brick-paved path to the back kitchen door. I can clearly remember the *click-clack-click-clack* of Evan's hobnail boots upon the slate-paved floor, as he took the heavy stainless-steel milk buckets into the adjacent dairy. Similarly echoing in my memory is the stridently harsh clank of their handles when dropped upon the rim, after Evan had emptied a portion of milk – at shoulder-height, be it noted – into the reservoir bowl, locked into the top of the separator.

As my drawing shows (page 140), this clever invention used centrifugal force to separate milk direct from the cow into skimmed milk and cream. Its designer was a Mr Gustaf De Laval, a Swede who founded the firm Alfa-Laval, closely associated with milk-separation technology and the manufacture of dairy equipment.

By this means, milk is separated into skimmed (milk) and cream as it flows through the ultra-fast revolving and multi-perforated cone at the machine's mechanical centre. After filling the reservoir and opening its flow-tap, the cranked handle was immediately turned at a requisite speed, indicated by the ringing of a bell. After about a minute, the skimmed milk began to flow out of the lower spout, shortly followed by the cream's lesser and more leisurely flow through the upper spout. The reservoir's slowly draining-away contents were topped-up as necessary.

The revolving cone comprised a heavy stainless-steel base with a central recessed slot on its underside which engaged with a vertical high-geared spigot activated by the cranked handle. The base also had a central and vertical spigot

139

A Lister milk separator at Acton Scott Farm Museum, near Craven Arms, Shropshire.

Photograph: Ellis-Jones

My diagrammatic illustration of how a milk separator works.

whose topmost half-inch was threaded to receive a stout brass nut. Over this spigot were stacked, one upon the other, about twenty-five stainless-steel multi-perforated and wafer-thin cones, held tightly together by the screwable brass nut on its top.

When the separation process was finished, the reservoir bowl was twisted slightly to release it from the lock-together flanges that secured it to the upper cream ring-spout. It and the skimmed milk ring spout were similarly secured together by locking flanges, the latter, in likewise fashion, locked onto the top of the machine's iron body. Removal of the ring spouts exposed the centrifugal cone, and then both spouts and cone were disassembled completely and sterilised. The cone's brass nut, which was circular and not faceted for a spanner, was loosened with a special tool which engaged its top and unscrewed it. The set of cones was lifted off the spigot and laid out in the old salt-glazed sink that stood in front of the back kitchen window. There, copious quantities of boiling water were poured over both cones and spouts; they were then allowed to dry naturally, which, being so hot from the boiling water, they did comparatively quickly. When dry, all was reassembled onto the separator's body, ready for the next occasion.

Milk separation took place every morning and every evening throughout the year; so the time taken to do it, including the assembly and disassembly of the separator's component parts, amounted to about three hundred and fifty hours a year.

140

I took every opportunity to turn the separator's handle, in my enthusiasm often erring on the hasty side until reminded by Gretta or Ceridwen or Janet that, "You MUST listen to the bell." A clever mechanism in the machine ensured that the bell only went *ting-ting* when the cone revolved at the requisite speed to produce a satisfactory end-product. On some mornings, whilst still in bed, I was awoken by the little bell's distant chime, which resulted in a pyjama-clad and steep scamper down the old back stairs to take over the separator's handle from whoever had pre-empted me.

After separation, the skimmed milk was taken and poured into the great oak cask of pig swill – the pigs' favourite delectation – which stood within a few yards of the iron kissing-gate, this in turn, beneath its sheltering holly tree – still growing and now much taller – being adjacent to Noel's potting shed.

The cream was allowed to settle and mature, with thickening consistency, in glazed clay bowls of about eighteen inches diameter, called *crocks*. They stood,

side by side, on the dairy's long slate shelf, each covered with a fine muslin net with little coloured beads sewn around its edge. There the cream awaited my nain's expert inspection and approval that it was ready for making into butter. The seasons, and the often changeable weather within each, largely dictated the time that the cream needed to reach maturity – but it was usually ready within a week of its separation. I found the thick slate shelf that supported the separator in the (now disused) dairy still undisturbed after sixty years. My photograph shows the four holes through which the old machine was bolted. Remaining also is the fine copper-mesh fly-screen fixed to the window!

Earlier in these Recollections, I included the poetic and poignant line of W.B. Yeats: '*All changed – changed utterly*.' 'My' Maesmawr has since been changed in so many ways – but once in a while I un-

The old dairy's wide slate shelf remains today, after sixty years; the Alfa-Laval milk separator was bolted onto it through the four visible holes. Even the window's copper-mesh fly-screen survives!

Photograph: Ellis-Jones

expectedly come across some little very tangible reminder of those distant days.

BUTTER-MAKING

The butter-churn and the butter-table at Maesmawr were very similar to those at the Acton Scott Farm Museum, which I photographed at the end of its open season in 2004. The churn is shown hooked upside-down; it was always kept in this position – with its lid separate – when not in use. Thus, although the lid is not shown, one of the several hinged, clamp-and-screw metal brackets that press the lid's circumference into a stout rubber gasket around the churn's rim can be seen hanging down. Also visible is the removable wooden bung close to the bottom of the churn, through which the residual buttermilk and the subsequently copious cold churn-rinsing water is drawn off. Buttermilk, as its name loosely implies, is the residual, thin and whitish liquid that slops about in the bottom of the churn,

A typical butter churn at Acton Scott Museum. Note that it is hooked upside-down whilst not in use.

Photograph: Ellis-Jones

from that sudden moment when the original cream turns to a consistency closely resembling scrambled-egg. That amazing semi-metamorphosis occurs after the churn has been steadily revolved for about ten to fifteen minutes. The churn has a small circular spy-hole of toughened clear glass in the lid, through which the turner can readily assess the gradual and then sudden change into a semi-solid consistency. Both the right speed and steadiness of revolving the churn with the cranked handle are essential requirements of successful butter-making.

As soon as the 'scrambled-egg' has developed and is half-floating in the buttermilk, the churn is hooked upright, the lid unclamped, and a sterilised bucket placed under the wooden bung. The bung is extracted by several taps sideways with a mallet to release it, and the buttermilk poured out into the bucket. The butter-to-be has then to be thoroughly rinsed with cold fresh water. The wood bung is reinserted, a bucket of water is poured in, and the lid is replaced and clamped tight. The churn is then rotated for about half-a-minute, hooked upright, and the first of the rinsing water drained out through the bung-hole into a bucket, and disposed of. The bung is then re-inserted, further rinsing water poured in, the lid replaced, and the procedure repeated until the drained rinsing water is as clear as when first poured in. That stage indicates that the potential butter is as thoroughly rinsed as possible. If it were not, it would very soon become tainted when made up into brickette-sized packs for sale, or kept in cold storage.

After its final rinse, the butter-to-be is gathered up in an ash wood hand-scoop and placed on the butter-table. No resinous wood is used for any butter-making equipment. The loose consistency of the developing butter is spread out across and beneath the wooden multi-ridged roller which, by means of a cogged-wheel mechanism operated by the cranked handle, draws the revolving roller up-and-down over the table. This gradually spreads the butter into a ridged mass, the ridges being imprinted into it by the roller. The rolling action also squeezes out all traces of residual rinsing water, which is drained-off through a small bung-hole in the table's far corner. If the butter is to be salted, the desired quantity is sprinkled evenly over it and the rolling is repeated, to integrate it thoroughly. On com-

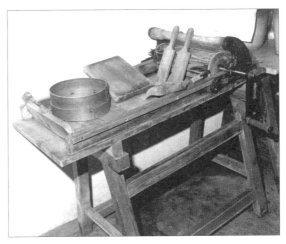

A typical butter-making table at Acton Scott Museum with essential accessories. Note the multi-ridged roller, wound up and down the table by cog-wheels and cranked handle. All the wood is non-resinous, and a pair of butter mitts can be seen, to 'knock it up'.

Photograph: Ellis-Jones

pletion, the butter is picked up in small heaps with a pair of ash wood mitts, one face of which is finely ridged so that, when wetted with cold water, butter does not adhere to it. By the deft manipulation of a pair of these tools, the butter is made-up into whatever size of brickette is required. For decorative effect, the completed brickettes are often impressed with the ridged pattern, or pressed into butter moulds, exquisitely carved depictions of, for example, corn *stooks* or cows. Often carved out of boxwood or holly, the design is cut in 'reverse', so that when impressed into the soft butter, a 'positive' image results.

The buttermilk was kept in the dairy as a valuable ingredient of Welsh baking. After maturing for several days, it developed its own special flavour, akin to full-cream milk in consistency, although entirely free of fat. It had a delicately acidic quality which caused a slight prickle on the palate. I was very fond of drinking a daily glass at mid-morning and, if not near the house at that hour, would be summoned for it by a hearty peal on the old bell, which still today hangs high on the north wall, its clapper silent with no rope to excite it. The buttermilk that remained, after my daily glass and its essential inclusion in my nain's Welsh-cakes and other delicacies, was given to the pigs – they loved it too!

At Maesmawr, very cold fresh water was drawn up through the old black iron hand-pump which was fixed to the wall close to the right-hand side of the back kitchen window. It drew a plentiful well, which lay beneath the slate-paved floor and was discharged through the pump into the stoneware sink that I have previously mentioned. Incidentally, the sink was ideal for scrubbing and rinsing the many varieties of vegetables brought to the kitchen by Noel from his bountiful plots in the nearby garden. The sink and, alas, the pump, have not survived Maesmawr's changes during the intervening years. Only my memory's 'ear' can still easily hear that long-ago, loose-limbed and heavy grease-lubricated rattle of the old pump, as its long, curving iron handle was lifted 'up-and-down', 'up-and-down', the crystal clear and icy cold water gushing forth from its generous spout, in rhythm with the handle. Such water has been called, somewhat Romantically, 'Nature's wine', and doubtless with good reason, especially when poured into cut-crystal glass upon Maesmawr's Time-honoured and plenteous dining table. Around it, conviviality flourished, although the 'presence' of Bacchus, God of Wine, was forbidden.

Mallard Drake.

Agnes Miller Parker, 1937

THE BREAD OVEN,
WEEKLY LAUNDRY DAY

The Maesmawr bread oven was similar in size and design to the one I have, though mine is now incomplete having lost the ash-slot of former years. This was a three-to-four inch wide gap, extending across the full width of the oven door immediately in front of it, with the top of the gap level with the sill of the door frame. This gap enabled residual wood ash from the oven-warming fire to be brushed out thoroughly before the bread dough was placed directly upon its brick floor. The ash fell to the floor, where it collected in a small recess for disposal. The ash-slot was formed with bricks. Directly above it, level with the curved top of the iron doorframe, but just outside it, a flue was formed that led directly into a nearby chimney. The fire was

My bread oven; beneath the stone sill, a vertical ash-slot in the brickwork (now blocked up) received brushed-out wood ash from the heating fire, which fell to the floor for disposal. Its flue once opened at the wall recess's top-right corner.

Photograph: Ellis-Jones

My oven's domed brick roof still retains soot deposit made by a not-hot-enough wood fire of long-ago.

Photograph: Ellis-Jones

burned with the door partly open, allowing most of its smoke to find egress into the oven's outside flue and thence up the chimney.

The oven's brick floor was about three feet above floor level and laid upon a sub-structure of brick-enclosing core of rubble or solid stone. Upright bricks formed a semi-circle at the back. When their bedding mortar had set, damp sand was shovelled in and made level with the tops of the rear upright bricks, and a piece of board of width similar to the height of the bricks was wedged across the

145

door-frame to contain the sand. More damp sand was heaped onto that already present, and formed into a dome, and then additional bricks-in-mortar were laid over the sand. When they had set, all the sand was shovelled and brushed out, and the internal shape of the bread oven was thus formed.

Early on the morning of Maesmawr's bread-making day, Evan brought a sackful of wood shavings from Walter's workshop floor and kindling wood from the hot water boiler's stokehole to the back kitchen. With them he laid and lit a lively fire on the bread oven's floor. Whilst this fire was making smoke, the domed bricks became blackened with its soot. However, when the fire's increasing heat no longer smoked and was a mass of fiery red embers, a miracle of science occurred, whereby that great residual heat cleared the black soot from the domed bricks. Furthermore, it had been discovered by the earliest builders and users of brick bread ovens that the heat clearance of the soot gave an infallible indication that the oven temperature was ready to bake the dough.

Well before the bread oven's fire was laid and lit, my nain made and thoroughly kneaded the dough in the warmth of the cooking kitchen and not the cooler back kitchen. Thus, when the oven reached ready heat, her dough was ready also to be placed within it. Evan remained nearby for this moment, whereupon he quickly brushed out the hot residual fire ash. The lumps of dough were brought on trays from the kitchen, and each lump of dough was, one at a time, inserted into the far end of the oven until all the lumps, slightly separated from each other, filled its floor. A long-handled wooden implement called a *peel* was used by my nain for that purpose. Its end was a wide and flat spade-cum-shovel onto which a lump of dough was placed and, by means of the long handle, inserted into the oven. This filling of the oven had to be done both quickly and calmly, so as not to lose valuable oven heat in the process. When it was done, the door was closed and the dough baked for the requisite time. The exciting moment, for me, and for the 'Master Baker' herself, no matter how many times she had done it, was when the oven door was ultimately opened and the golden brown, crusted fresh bread was revealed. In front of it were several rather over-baked and oddly-shaped loaflets which, as small lumps of the remaining dough, my nain had shown me how to knead as my contribution to her baking day!

On laundry day, there was no labour-saving device like the present-day washing machine. In those days washing had to be done by hand, with much wearisome tedium and regularity. The big hot-water cauldron was the first receptacle for the majority of articles awaiting the weekly wash. It stood in the back kitchen against the outside wall, between the (corner) bread oven and the kitchen's outside door. The cauldron was of iron, about thirty inches in diameter and twenty-four inches deep. It was raised and supported all around the rim by brickwork whose top edge, flush with the cauldron's rim, was about forty inches above the slate-paved floor. Beneath the cauldron, about one brick's thickness above the floor, was constructed a largish cavity for a wood fire. Its hearth comprised the single course of brick and the front opening had an iron door to close off the fire, similar to, but smaller than, the bread oven door. The cauldron's base was fitted with a pipe that led to a big brass draw-off tap fixed to the brickwork, several inches above bucket-height, so that the residual dirty water could be drawn off and disposed of.

The cauldron was, in effect, suspended within its enclosing brickwork by its wide and thick rim. The cavity thus created enabled the heat of the substantial wood fire to circulate all around the cauldron, which – eventually (!) – raised the water temperature needed for the initial washing of the soiled articles. The smoke from the fire was vented at the back of the brick cavity and rose into the chimney flue, which was shared by the bread oven's fire.

After the requisite pummelling and stirring of the articles, assisted by a stout wooden stick, which was bleached white-as-a-bone from constant immersion, the cauldron's very hot contents were lifted out of the water with wooden tongs.

The washing was done in batches which were transferred across to a pair of huge white glazed fireclay sinks which stood against the wall to the left-hand side of the window. One of the pair remains today and, I feel, warrants my photograph for having survived – although probably unused for almost sixty years – including its pair of brass taps. The sink's front edge is fitted with a rounded wooden rim that supported the *washboard*.

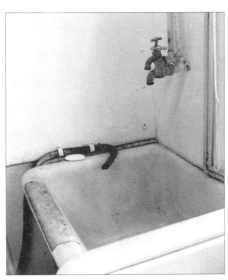

That heinous and primitive device, bruiser of the fingers, nails and knuckles of those then casually called 'washerwomen', was in common use as the best-known method of removing resistant grime from fabrics, whether tough or fragile. The *washboard* was a multi-ridged panel of either thick glass or, more frequently, zinc sheet, held within a stout wooden frame.

One of a pair of huge clothes-washing sinks still survives in the back kitchen – taps included!

Photograph: Ellis-Jones

The washing medium was a primitive soap jelly, made by shaving a large block of coarse soap, dissolving the shavings in boiling water, and leaving them to cool. The fabric, with some jelly, was vigorously rubbed to-and-fro over the *washboard's* ridges with bare hands; it was indeed harsh treatment of them, in the days when protective rubber gloves had yet to be invented. After the washed articles had been energetically agitated on the *washboard*, they were thoroughly rinsed in fresh hot, and then cold, water from the wall taps.

The washed fabrics were thereupon heaped into large wicker laundry baskets, with non-fast colours kept separate from 'whites'. The next stage was to wind them through the mangle, whose pair of inwardly rotating wooden rollers, turned by the cranked handle, very effectively squeezed out the residual water. The mangle would also unmercifully pinch – at the very least – any unwitting finger that carelessly came within its vicious grip. The water squeezed out by the mangle dripped into a galvanised bath beneath it.

The very popular 'blue bag' was immersed in every wash of 'whites'. They were (perhaps still are?) little cubes of a chemical made by the firm of Reckitt & Coleman, commonly known as 'Reckitt's Blue'. Each cube was about the size of a sugar lump and of a fabulous *lapis-lazuli* blue that would have delighted the painterly eye of Fra Angelico or Vincent van Gogh. The cube was tightly wrapped in a little white cotton bag, its neck tied with string, and one or more bags were put into the washing water of, especially, sheets, pillow-cases and other 'whites'. The 'blue bag' was also very effective in relieving the irritation of wasp stings. Reckitt & Coleman's claim that '*It makes whites whiter*' was true.

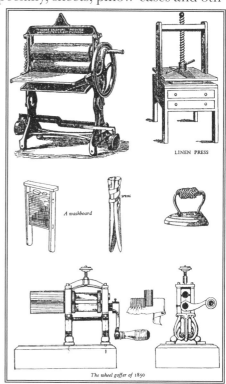

LINEN PRESS

A washboard

SPRING

The wheel goffer of 1850

After being put through the mangle, the washed articles were taken and hung out on the clotheslines in the drying-yard, near to the soft fruit cage. Then, when dry, the washing was taken up and aired in the laundry above the kitchen. The clothes pegs were of the only variety then available, but far from ideal, as they were apt to make little rust marks on the fabrics at the point where they pinched them onto the line. They were made by the gypsies roaming Wales, from little half-split lengths of hazel stick with the bark scraped off. Each peg had a narrow strip of metal, cut from the lids of sardine tins (!), one end inserted tightly into the semi-slit peg, the other wrapped around it and secured with a 'blued' tin-tack tapped into the wood. The gypsies sold them in dozens,

Various essentials on Maesmawr's weekly washing day.

Courtesy: Dorothy Hartley, from her
'WATER IN ENGLAND'

148

Maesmawr's typical kitchen scene on ironing day.

each dozen held, side by side, on a split length of slim hazel branch. Every so often, a dusky-complexioned, buxom and colourfully shawled figure would come and knock on the kitchen door, offering them for sale. They were always bought – as there was nothing else as an alternative.

On the weekly ironing day, and after breakfast, a flotilla of quite heavy little black hand-irons was set out upon the back of the hot oven range, with their prows all facing one way. They sat there absorbing heat for about twenty minutes, or until hot enough to be picked up, in strict rotation, and deployed upon the ironing-board. Each iron indicated its readiness, or otherwise, for use when finger-flicked with droplets of water onto its underside. If the droplet of water sizzled, this was an approximate guide to show that the iron was hot enough for use. However, unlike the modern electric iron with its wide temperature control, the old-fashioned flat-iron required experienced usage if scorches were to be avoided. A further disadvantage of the flat-iron was its brief heat-life – within a minute or so of being applied, most of the heat was absorbed by the fabric being ironed, and the iron needed replacement by another from off the hot range. The photograph on previous shows a typical ironing-day scene as was Maesmawr's.

I have earlier mentioned that dry washing from the outside clothes lines was taken up to the laundry above the kitchen to air, and then taken down into the kitchen for ironing. Apart from its use for airing, and for the annual breaking down of large blocks of white salt for salting the bacon, the laundry was largely unused. The exception was the weekly visit to Maesmawr of the Estate account-ant, Richard Morgan. He lived in Llandinam and, 'come-rain-or-shine', always bicycled the two-and-a-half miles there and back. Richard arrived soon after our breakfast, on an elderly machine, and never without his old brown raincoat, either worn or slung over the handlebars. He always wore a bowler hat. A simi-lar scene today, with the wearer upon an ancient bicycle, might appear eccen-tric, unless he was a serving officer of a Guards' Regiment, for whom the bowler hat is *de rigeur* when he is dressed in mufti, but sixty or more years ago, this hat was usually a social indication of professional standing – especially for lawyers and accountants. Poor old Richard – the laundry was a cheerless room in which to account for pounds, shillings and pence. He came down to the morning room for morning coffee and stayed for lunch. Afterwards, he was fond of distributing toffees, wrapped in noisily crackling cellophane of the type loathed by dedicated concert and theatre-goers. The ends of each wrapper were tightly twisted con-trariwise, and automatically unwound to release the sticky contents upon being pulled apart by two fingers and two thumbs. After the meal, and a final check on the week's accounts, on went his trouser clips, to protect his trousers from an oily chain, on went the old brown raincoat, if the view towards Llandinam from Maesmawr threatened rain, and, after bidding "Goodbye" to my nain or my uncle Emrys, or both together, on went the faithful bowler hat. It was hardly sufficient for cranial protection in the event of Richard's having an accident en-route. However, the risk of that was so remote on the very quiet main roads that nobody gave it a thought.

THE CHINA MENDER

He was a memorable character also, but his welcome visits to Maesmawr were much less frequent than Richard Morgan's weekly appearance. The china mender's travels, and his customers, were spread far and wide throughout Montgomeryshire and perhaps beyond. He came to Maesmawr about twice yearly, 'out-of-the-blue', as the old saying has it – and after announcing his arrival by a hearty knock on the kitchen door, set up his bicycle beneath the welcoming shade, if hot weather prevailed, of the old and spreading yew tree. If it was raining, he betook himself and his bicycle to shelter in the stables. The bicycle provided the simple motive power for his amazing skill: the brass riveting of cracked (but not broken) china and earthenware plates, dishes and bowls. Glass objects, even if only cracked, which was not commonplace, could not be repaired his way, but all other cracked ware offered the china mender the opportunity to deploy his skills of repair.

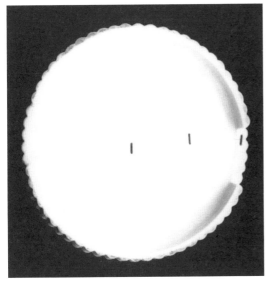

A china's mender's typical brass rivet repair on the underneath (always) of a cracked article.

Photograph: Ellis-Jones

A tiny and fast rotating drill was his principal tool, together with a pair of wire-cutting pincers with which he cut and bent the requisite short lengths of brass wire for making the rivets. The drill was mounted on his bicycle handlebars and rotated by means of a rudimentary drive-belt, made of stout cord, which passed over and within a grooved ring affixed to the bicycle's chain-wheel. The rear wheel was raised off the ground an inch or so by a retractable sprung metal strut. Thus the china mender sat upon his machine and, in effect, pedalled the drill in front of him.

My photograph shows a typical brass rivet repair to a piece of china of mine which, although it is similar to those of Maesmawr's skilful exponent, was done before I bought it. Considering the thinness of the china, it is a marvel of manual dexterity to drill miniscule holes in china, for the subsequent rivets, without the drill-hole penetrating through the china and being visible on the upper face. As to how the rivets remain inserted, alas, I never watched to find out, but never as yet have I seen a similar repair that has failed through the dropping out of a

151

rivet, or more than one. Such skill remains a mystery, but if its explanation never comes, I am content just to admire it, all the same.

The china mender was himself a mystery – no-one at Maesmawr either knew or sought his name – but he might have had Indian ancestors. He just came and then went. His valued skills were gladly paid for, and he gratefully accepted proffered tea and cakes. Then this quiet craftsman bade us "Goodbye" and slowly pedalled away up Maesmawr's Drive to disappear – eastwards or westwards we never knew, but we did know that he would visit us again – one day. Meanwhile, cracks would occur in the intervening months, for his hands happily to mend whenever he returned. I believe such skills as his emanated from the East (Near or Far?) – but I doubt he was pedalling that far after visiting Maesmawr!

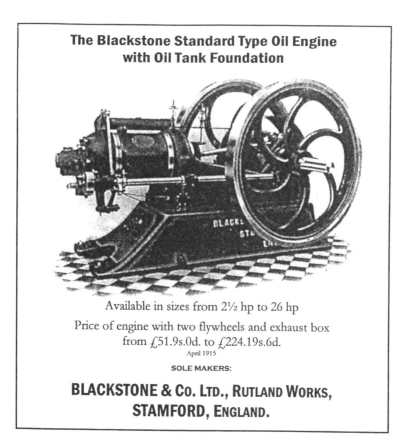

Engine exactly like Maesmawr's BLACKSTONE oil-engine. Note the central spigot on the flywheel for the drivebelt drum revolving the (external) circular saw. The pair of flywheels were 56 inches diameter x 5 ½ inches wide.

Courtesy: Michael Key

152

THE BLACKSTONE OIL-ENGINE

The engine was a constant attraction to me, and I affectionately refer to it as 'she' or 'her', as she was so personable – as all her mechanical ilk are felt to be. *CHUNK-chunk-CHUNK-chunk-CHUNK-chunk*: that is the closest onomatopoeic I can conjure to illustrate her deep exhaust note, reverberating up through heavy iron pipe. That sound, together with the rooks at early morning, was among Maesmawr's most characteristic ones. She has been gone for many years now – probably over fifty; to where and to what fate no-one knows, but perhaps working for someone who appreciates her worth or, perish the thought, broken up for scrap iron. I like to assume the former, and if I had her serial number would probably be able to find the 'old lady'.

A BLACKSTONE Registration and Serial number plate. Courtesy: Michael Key

Before I continue my reminiscence, the reader deserves to know why Maesmawr Hall needed its electrical independence, which was installed in about 1910. It was because at that time and, as it transpired, for the ensuing forty years, no public electricity supply extended along the Upper Severn valley beyond Newtown. Even where such existed in that locality, it must have been limited and somewhat primitive in its provision. Nowadays, that circumstance may seem almost incredible. I have always understood that, until 1949–1950, the inhabitants of Caersws, together with their near neighbours at Llandinam, including the outlying farms and cottages on the hills and in the valley, depended for light on the paraffin lamp with its brilliantly burning incandescent mantle, and candles. Thus there was no supply for the increasing, multifarious electrical equipment and gadgetry slowly becoming available to an increasingly affluent public after years of Wartime austerity. Such labour-saving commodities were the sole preserve of those living in areas where some sort of public electricity supply existed, and where the required 220-240 volt current powered the domestic and commercial equipment.

Whilst adequate for essential but limited needs, Maesmawr's BLACKSTONE dynamo merely generated 110 volts D.C., whereby the coiled elements of an old-fashioned electric fire could only dimly glow – though that was preferable to no fire at all! At Llandinam, by 1903, David (later 1st Baron) Davies had installed his independent water-powered set of turbine-driven dynamos, which provided, without storage batteries, a relatively low voltage but direct electrical current. This served his home, Plas Dinam, and his family's Italianate mansion, Broneirion, across the valley from the village. A few fortunates in Llandinam, naturally including the Dinam Estate office and its timber-yard workshops, availed themselves of the electricity. A few others, such as the Church of Wales rector of St. Llonio's Parish Church and the Presbyterian Church's minister, were also connected, but certainly not the 'Red Lion' public house. The Davies family had been teetotal since 'Top Sawyer' David Davies' time. Moreover, under the family's influence, the 'Red Lion' became a Temperance Hotel in 1911, only resuming an alcoholic licence in 1959. David Davies generously charged his several consumers the annual sum of one shilling for each electric bulb point they enjoyed!

A Llandinam story of old, its 'tallness' perhaps heightened over the years by many retellings, concerned David Davies' chauffeur, who had been appointed as electrical curator of the turbine house at Fynnant, Llandinam. The tale has it that during a banquet at Plas Dinam, the seated guests were suddenly plunged into total darkness. Next morning, there were some 'sparks' 'twixt host and his electrician, which resulted in the latter's being allowed to retain the chauffeur's seat but henceforth being relieved of his other 'dynamic' responsibilities – or so the story goes!

To return to the BLACKSTONE at Maesmawr, the engine-shed still stands, made of brick-and-board; the latter was once painted Black-and-White, simulating a half-timber frame, in similar fashion to Maesmawr's Victorian extension. Nowadays, the shed is a wood-store and repository of garden equipment. Shattered remnants of the concrete base upon which the mighty engine once stood are surrounded by vestiges of the Edwardian clay floor tiles. Long ago their slipperiness, from Walter's occasional oil spills, was potentially hazardous to a small boy in rubber boots, until Walter wiped the spills away.

The BLACKSTONE'S purpose was threefold: to drive dynamo-charged batteries for the house electricity supply, to pump water to the house from an adjacent well, and to drive a saw-bench for cutting logs and reducing baulks of timber into planks for Estate carpentry, especially field gates, and other items. The dynamo was situated at the far end of the engine-shed, eighteen feet from the centre of the BLACKSTONE'S pair of large-spoked flywheels. The inner one rotated an 'endless' drive-belt made of, I presume, thick canvas impregnated with some proprietary and flexible fabric-binding compound. The belt tapered down towards the dynamo, slightly flapping (an inch or two) up-and-down as it sped from off and back onto the five-inch-wide rim of the fifty-six-inch diameter flywheel. Today's legally empowered safety regulations would require the entire drive-belt to be enclosed within a protective mesh cage; but sixty-two years ago, such excellent precautionary measures did not exist, and potential accidents to life or limb were ever-present.

The former BLACKSTONE engine-shed today; its boarding was former-ly painted Black-and-White to simulate half-timber framing. (See photograph 6 of east garden on page 133.) On many a morning I would wake to hear her exhaust pipe's *CHUNK-chunk* and scamper downstairs to see my beloved engine in action. The sawdust-caked circular saw-bench stood directly outside the double doors, on rough farmyard ground.

Photograph: Ellis-Jones

The engine-room's entire length was divided, at about one-third of its width, by a floor-to-ceiling wood-framed partition, clad in vertical tongue-and-grooved pine boards. It formed the narrow battery-room, entered by a door just within the double doors of the shed itself. The latter were bolted fully open when the adjacent saw-bench was used.

The battery-room contained fifty-five thick glass tanks, each about eighteen inches square and high, ranged along both walls on a continuous wooden shelf. This supported the tanks at twelve inches above the floor, so as to be well above foot traffic. Each glass tank was a battery with a range of lead cells submerged in acid – probably hydrochloric – which received current from the dynamo. The batteries fizzed whilst being charged, at the same time producing acrid fumes from the acid. Indeed, the fumes from their open tops were so irritating to the eyes that I was only able to be in the battery-room for a few minutes before seek-ing the fresh air outside to relieve the irritation. A control panel on the room's end wall, just inside the door and opposite the engine, contained an array of switches and white dials behind glass, similar to ships' clocks. At their centre rotated and twitched the indicator needle showing the voltage and amperage being produced by the dynamo. All the dials and switches were neatly mounted on a panel of some black material which was a bad conductor of electricity, for protection in the very unlikely event of a circuit leakage. A thick rubber mat lay beneath the control panel as an additional precaution. The batteries required regular topping-up with acid, which was obtained from a supplier in spherical clear glass carboys. These were two feet in diameter, and had a short and straight neck with a cork stopper. The carboys were enclosed within stout wire-mesh spherical containers, with a flat base enabling them to stand upright independently, whether they were full of acid or empty. The wire containers' diameter was six inches greater than that of the carboy, the space between being packed with straw for protection and stability. In my time, the engine-shed's long side wall, with its three windows, overlooked part of the farmyard, and tall, rough grass grew along the base of the wall. Half-hidden in the grass were several wooden boxes full of glass tubes, which were about two feet in length, with an internal diameter of three-eighths of an inch – just the right size to 'fire' an average-sized dry pea when blown through the tube, whose perfect straightness made them ideal peashooters! I never asked Walter what purpose the glass tubes served, but I presume they were replacements for any that, frequently or otherwise, needed renewing within the batteries.

There were times of boyish exuberance when either Walter or Evan or Noel became my harmless peashooter's target. However, the projectile's slow velocity – due to the peas frequently being much smaller than the bore of the tube – meant that most of their shooter's 'puff' was wastefully expended at source!

The BLACKSTONE was run several days each week, depending on the strength of the electrical charge held by the batteries. In addition, the pumped water supply to the house had to be maintained, and the saw-bench was often used too. This had a large-diameter blade of about eighteen inches, with a removable weather-shield and additional sack wrapping to exclude rain and damp. I can vividly remember the high screaming note of the revolving blade before it was presented with timber for cutting, then the drop in sound frequency when the saw was actually cutting into the wood, followed by a ringing timbre immediately the teeth were free. That quickly resolved into the steady whirring note of the freely rotating blade, before again being put under load by the next piece of wood presented to it. The saw-bench, with its heavy iron supports,

BLACKSTONE static model oil-engine.

Courtesy: Michael Key

156

KEY TO LETTERS

A1	Bed Plate	J2	Exhaust Valve Guide	N3	Ignition Connecting Rod
A2	Bed Cap	J3	Exhaust Valve Spring	N4	Ignition Valve Lever
A3	Bearing Brass	J4	Exhaust Valve Spring Button	N5	Ignition Valve Guide (Bottom)
A4	Bearing Cap Bolt	J5	Exhaust Lever	N6	Ignition Valve Guide (Top)
B1	Cylinder Liner	J6	Exhaust Lever Roller	N7	Ignition Lever Pull Spring
B2	Cylinder Water Flange	J7	Exhaust Lever Roller Pin	N8	Ignition Lever Roller
B3	Cylinder Force Feed Lubricator	J8	Exhaust Roller Shifting Pin	O1	Vapour Valve
B4	Cylinder Rubber Joint	J9	Exhaust Lever Set Pin	O2	Vapour Valve Box
B6	Cylinder Sight Feed Lubricator	J10	Exhaust Lever Fulcrum Pin	O3	Vapour Valve Spring
C1	Combustion Chamber	J11	Air and Exhaust Cam	O4	Vapour Valve Spring Button
C2	Exhaust Flange	K1	Air Valve	O5	Vapour Valve Lever
D1	Crankshaft	K2	Air Valve Box	O6	Vapour and Ignition Lever Fulcrum Pin
D2	Balance Weight	K3	Air Valve Silencer		
D3	Crank Oiler Banjo	K4	Air Valve Spring	O7	Vapour Valve Lever Set Pin
D4	Crank Guard	K5	Air Valve Spring Sleeve	O8	Vapour Valve Lcvcr Roller
E1	Connecting Rod	K6	Air Valve Rocker lever	P1	Piston
E5	Small End Bearing	K7	Air Valve Rocker Lever Joint	P2	Crosshead Pin
E6	Small End Bolts	K8	Air Valve Lever Joint Pin	P3	Piston Rings
E7	Small End Plate	K9	Air Valve Push Rod	Q1	Insperator
F1	Flywheel	K10	Air Valve Cain lover	Q2	Induction Pipe
G1	Governor Case	K14	Throttle Valve Lever	Q3	Nipple Holder
G2	Governor Cain	L1	Camshaft	Q4	Fuel Nipple
G3	Speed Screw Lock Nut	L2	Camshaft Bracket	Q5	Overflow Nipple
G4	Speed Screw	M1	Vapouriser Body	R1	Water Drip Valve
H1	Fuel Oil Pump	M2	Vapouriser Case	R2	Water Drip Pipe
H2	Fuel Oil Pump Lever	M3	Vapouriser Top Cap	S1	Igniter Case
H3	Fuel Oil Pump Cam	M4	Vapouriser Shutter	S2	Igniter Coil
H4	Fuel Oil Delivery Pipe	M5	Vapouriser End Cap.	S3	Igniter Plug
H5	Fuel Oil Suction Pipe	M6	Vapouriser Bottom Plug	S4	Igniter Bumping Plug
H6	Fuel Oil Overflow Pipe	N1	Ignition Valve	S5	Igniter Bottom Coil
J1	Exhaust Valve	N2	Ignition Valve Knuckle Joint		

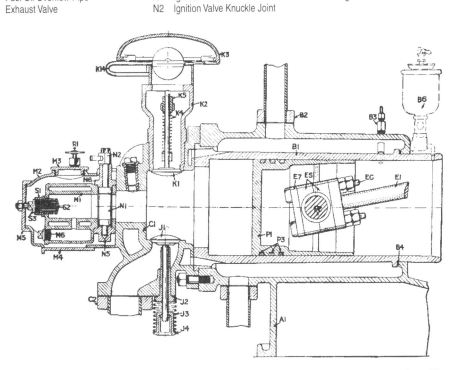

BLACKSTONE, longitudinal section through centre of Vapouriser, Combustion Chamber and Cylinder. Key to letters on both illustrations, see above list.

Courtesy: Michael Key

half-submerged in caked sawdust, was driven by a small 'endless belt', similar to the large one driving the dynamo which I have already described. The former had a belt-drum temporarily put onto the engine flywheel's hub spigot. (The spigot is visible in the illustration on page 156.)

The engine's principle of combustion is the compression of heated paraffin oil vapour mixed with air; I use the present tense as there are many BLACKSTONEs in fine working order today, either having been exceptionally well cared for all their lives, or else restored to that condition by worldwide engine enthusiasts, who possess extensive knowledge of the marque, and know the whereabouts of many working engines. (They would probably be able to locate Maesmawr's, if I knew her serial number.) One, in Australia, has an extensive website, and another, Michael Key of Didcot, provided me with these BLACKSTONE illustrations (except that of the trolley model).

There are many different models and sizes of BLACKSTONE engine, both static, as was Maesmawr's, and the trolley model. The static engine is mounted, integral with its own fuel tank, and driven by a single piston through a central crankshaft. This drives the pair of flywheels. I must, for the sake of easier description, revert to the past tense to explain the engine's starting-up procedure. Walter and Noel used to do it together, as a two-man team. Firstly, Walter lit his traditional painter/plumber's paraffin blowlamp, pointing its very hot blue flame at the engine's vaporising chamber. Its metal had become permanently

tinged pinky-red from many years of that mode of pre-heating. The blowlamp remained in position for about ten minutes, by the end of which the vaporising chamber was sufficiently hot for the paraffin-air mixture to be drawn into the chamber by initial slow rotation of the flywheels. The wheels were heavy, and their stationary inertia had to be overcome by the combined effort of both men, one at each wheel. Each placed his weight upon one foot, on the outside of the rim, at the base of a spoke. Then, with both hands grasping the top of the spoke at their feet, they applied their combined weight of twenty-four stone to overcome the wheels' inertia. That gradually increased their clockwise rotation

BLACKSTONE Dynamo

and, through the crankshaft, the to-and-fro travel of the piston. Within a very short time, the flywheels' rotation had increased beyond a speed that hands and feet could touch, and the engine was running on her own. By some means, when under-way, the necessary working temperature within her combustion chamber was self-maintained. However, in very cold starting conditions, the blow-lamp was used to assist further for about fifteen minutes.

The Maesmawr BLACKSTONE was water-cooled from a tall circular tank made of corrugated iron which stood against the shed's outer wall, about halfway between the engine and the dynamo. After the engine had been running for about twenty minutes, steam began to drift off the top of the tank and found its way out of the shed as best it could – I do not think any window was opened, summer or winter. I loved to watch the engine being started-up on every possible occasion, but was too young and too small to provide practical help. Occasionally, on early morn-

BLACKSTONE 7hp, 'JAV', trolley-model oil-engine.
Photograph: Ellis-Jones

ings, when I was still in bed, I would hear her distant *CHUNK-chunk*; then I knew I was too late!

Whenever Walter needed to attend to some situation on the far side of the engine, between her and the outside wall, rather than walk up the entire length of the shed and around beyond the dynamo, he invariably took a short cut. That was natural when the engine was stationary, but it was also his frequent habit whilst she was in motion. Walter would step nonchalantly between the upper and lower hurtling portions of the drive-belt, and ominously close to the flywheel, where space between the parts of the belt was greatest. Whilst passing through, he merely lowered his head a few inches, his old flat cap staying on whilst he did so. In hindsight, I have often recalled the dear man's potential folly. Moreover, Walter being my hero, I copied him on frequent occasions, although I am sure he must have remonstrated with me gently at the time. One slip on the tiled floor when ducking through the drive-belt, in adulatory pursuit of him, would have spelled my instantaneous downfall, if I had been caught in my worshipped engine's maw. In further hindsight across the intervening years, I like to feel that the dear old BLACKSTONE knew I adored her, and that her protective aura kept me safe on those occasions.

WALTER: A REFLECTIVE TRIBUTE

My predilection for turning the handles of Maesmawr's milk-separator, butter-churn, butter-table, knife-grinder and operating the old water pump, held a boyhood fascination that I took for granted. So also did the BLACKSTONE engine's multiplicity of moving parts – and watching railway engines, as I will relate. To others at the time, these enthusiasms might have suggested the possibility of my choosing mechanical engineering as a career. Instead, I became an architect, involved with static components, rather than an engineer addressing movement. Nevertheless, in hindsight, and across so many years, I know that my boyhood delight in the design and construction of devices has never deserted me. Its culmination was the making of a harpsichord, ten years ago.

I am certain that Walter's kindness and innate understanding in allowing me the unfettered freedom of his carpentry workshop, and the use of his precious tools, first awakened my young and intuitive inclination and ability to create and work with my hands.

THE 'LOST' AEROPLANE

One summer Sunday afternoon in 1943, we heard the unexpected sound of an aeroplane circling Maesmawr, descending lower and lower each time it did so. It may be helpful to those of my readers who were not then born to know that all aircraft of that era were piston-driven, the roar of the modern jet being then beyond imagination. After several minutes, the sound died away in the direction of the Long Length railway Crossing. 'Mrs Davies-the-Crossing', as its gatekeeper was known to all, was probably the first to watch the aeroplane land on the field adjacent and parallel to Long Length, which extended as far as the trees of Maesmawr's Drive.

All of us, except for Nain, who valued her afternoon's rest and was of an age that forbade pursuing aeroplanes, excitedly ran towards the Crossing, via the river bank and through the two pasture fields between it and Maesmawr. Together with my uncle Emrys' Welsh springer spaniel **Nell**, we arrived breathless at the top corner of the 'landing-field' opposite the railway Crossing. In those days, white-painted iron railings defined the field's corner, giving unrestricted vision to road users approaching from either direction. The railings were taken away many years ago, but each time I pass the corner, I vividly remember our excitement, and visualise the stationary aircraft facing towards distant Maesmawr.

It was a canary-yellow, twin-engined Avro ANSON, a non-combative aircraft used for reconnaissance and sea-convoy escort roles. Near the port wing stood the pilot and colleague – presumably his navigator – and upon it they had spread out a map.

An Avro ANSON reconnaissance and convoy-escort aircraft;
THE 'LOST' AEROPLANE(!)

Soon there appeared, approaching from Caersws, a group of the curious, including Police Constable Jones, regally pedalling his old bicycle and wearing carpet slippers. He, like my nain, valued his afternoon nap, which had been disturbed by an urgently expressed telephone call from Mrs Davies-the-Crossing saying that a yellow aeroplane – "Yes! A yellow AEROPLANE" – had landed in the field opposite her; would he "please come quickly to investigate it". Come he did, and after resolutely leaning his bicycle against the railings and clambering over them in as dignified a manner as his carpet slippers would permit, he strode over to the aircraft. After a mutually-acknowledged nod of greeting, Caersws' guardian of Law and Order got into a huddle with the aviators to ascertain their reasons for having descended into his domain. The map was rotated on the aircraft's wing to align it with true North, and the trio examined it with visible urgency for some minutes. The bystanders, in a watchful line along the hedge, exchanged opinions on the puzzling situation. Their conversations were inaudible to us, standing several yards away, but I like to imagine what one might have said to his neighbour, after some minutes of deliberation: "Could be Jerry's spies – funny to lose themselves if they're not – their map's as big as a hayfield. If they've got the right one, it shows Moat Lane and the river – you can't lose yourself with that – and from way up there too!" "You're right, Dai bach – he'll arrest them, you'll see."

PC Jones made no arrests, and no doubt hadn't even remembered to bring his handcuffs with him; back at home they did noble horticultural duty keeping his tomato canes together. The likelihood of two German spies flying about in a British aeroplane with the RAF's red-white-and-blue identification circles on fuselage and wings was inconceivable, even if it was possible that German spies might speak such impeccable English. The Law decided to 'release' them, and with a firm handshake of both, bade the aviators "safe journey" after telling them where they were! Their map was folded, pilot and navigator clambered on board, and within minutes the engines sprang to life. They then 'revved-up', having completed the pre-take-off safety checks.

Suddenly the long grass flattened, and the engines' roar increased until the yellow tip of each propeller blade became a blurred circle from their myriad revolutions. Spaniel **Nell** strained at the leash in a frantic attempt to chase after the yellow 'bird' – the more so as it began to move away from her, and the chances of retrieving it for her master dwindled, her floppy ears blown back by the aircraft's slipstream breeze. Every one of us watching held high hopes that it would become safely airborne in time to clear the distant trees along the Maesmawr Drive, towards which it was hurtling. Visual foreshortening made it impossible for us to tell whether there was any real danger, but suddenly the little yellow aircraft lifted herself up, well before the trees, and soon became a mere distant dot in the summer afternoon sky.

As far as all the locals were concerned, the where-from and where-to of the aeroplane's journey remained a mystery. Police Constable Jones kept his own counsel – understandably, if the aircraft's mission was a Wartime secret, as many were in those days. Like so much else in that faraway time, we who were then young recall such seemingly insignificant events with a great sense of nostalgia. PC Jones took his 'Last Flight' many years ago, and with it, perhaps, a well-kept secret?

Rook.

Agnes Miller Parker, 1937

Eiluned Lewis.
Courtesy: Katrina Burnett, her daughter.
Photographer: Howard Coster in 1934

EILUNED LEWIS

The Welsh novelist, writer and poet Eiluned Lewis (1900–1979), who wrote under that, her Maiden name, was a very close friend of my mother Beryl in their girlhood and young womanhood, Eiluned being the younger by two years. The Lewis family home was the warm mellowed brick Georgian house, Glan Hafren, situated directly beside the River Severn and nestling in its small private park, upstream of Newtown and just three miles below Maesmawr Hall.

Eiluned's professional career began as a young journalist in London's Fleet Street newspaper 'world' of the 1930s, where her instinctively natural, and seemingly effortless, style – later to imbue her intuitive and captivating creativity, was honed by journalistic demands for a concisely clear fluidity in expressive and descriptive writing. Whilst in Fleet Street, she worked upon the *Sunday Times* and the *Daily News*, (afterwards the *News Chronicle*), thereby knowing and collaborating with the latter's venerable literary editor Robert Lynd, the theatre critic James Agate, Ernest Rhys and a host of other newspaper figures and 'characters'.

Eiluned Lewis achieved 'overnight' literary acclaim with her first novel *Dew on the Grass*, it being an unspecified, but autobiographical, account of her beloved family childhood at Glan Hafren, with brother Peter and sisters Medina and May.

Dew on the Grass was first published in July 1934, accompanied by a glowing prefatory letter from Charles Morgan. The book then received a Second Impression that same month, it being followed by a Third and Fourth in August and a Fifth in September of that same year. Eiluned's mother, Eveline, whose own family home had been at St. David's in Pembrokeshire, was a friend of the author J.M. Barrie, who often came to stay at Glan Hafren during Eiluned's childhood.

Her later novel, *The Captain's Wife*, published in 1944, is primarily based within and around a thinly disguised St. David's. Its story possesses vividly descriptive powers concerning places and their, perhaps partly fictional(?), characters inhabiting that remote and picturesque peninsula of farthest West Wales. It includes a penultimate and heart-rending tragedy that overtakes a small boy, which unexpectedly assails the reader and remains unforgettable.

The Captain's Wife was followed, in 1951, by *In Country Places*, it being a charming collection of short essays upon widely diverse subject matter, and each respectively relevant to the Twelve Months of the Year. Many pages are interspersed with delightful pen-and-ink drawings by Gilbert Spencer, R.A., brother of Stanley Spencer, R.A., the latter perhaps better known, generally speaking, than his artistic relative.

In 1937, the London publishers B.T. Batsford added *The Land of Wales* to their already impressive and extensive series of books descriptive and illustrative of Britain's vast inheritance of rural and architectural riches. Eiluned and her brother Peter together collaborated on writing *The Land of Wales*, thereby sensitively extolling the delights of their Native Land.

During an uninterrupted period of thirty-five years, Eiluned Lewis became the longest contributor to the magazine *Country Life*, there founder of her regular and inimitably styled '*Countrywoman's Notes*'.

In 1996, her daughter Katrina, together with editor Glen Cavaliero, assembled a representative collection of her mother's exquisitely crafted writings, privately publishing them through the Finchcocks Press of Godhurst, Kent with the title *A Companionable Talent*. Their book, as does my *Boyhood's Recall, Maesmawr Hall*, includes, as it so happens, a respectively different set of wood-engravings by the eminent artist Agnes Miller Parker. During the 1930s, she created, in company of engraver colleagues Blair Hughes-Stanton and Gertrude Hermes, incomparable illustrations for the magnificent Limited Edition books printed by my aunts' private Gregynog Press at Tregynon, Montgomeryshire.

It remains my treasured privilege to have received permission, from a close relative of the late Agnes Miller Parker, to include twenty-two of her wood-engravings in this book. As native to beloved Montgomeryshire, as they were, I feel it valid to happily associate myself with my late aunts of Gregynog and with the late Eiluned Lewis, a close family friend, insofar as they had their creativity enhanced by inclusion of Agnes Miller Parker's consummate artistry. I am most fortunate to be likewise favoured.

Eiluned Lewis wrote two books of verse. They are *December Apples*, first published in 1935, and *Morning Songs* of 1944. Whilst living in a Kentish cottage in later years, she wrote *The Leaves of the Trees*, being her third novel.

In February 1937, Eiluned married the Scotsman Graeme Hendrey, an electrical engineer by profession but also a prolific amateur writer, with whom she enthusiastically travelled worldwide during his business commitments.

IN THE RIVER SEVERN,
AT BERTH-DDU,
THE GANGERS' TROLLEY

Courtesy:

The Countryman magazine

The silver Severn water
It winds its way at ease
Across the amber pebbles,
Beneath the alder trees,
And all day long its quiet voice
Is sweet to me as my heart's choice.

Then when the orchard grasses
Were flecked with shade and sun,
Bare-footed to the water
We boys and girls would run,
And leaping there would plunge and swim
Through broken lights and shadows dim.

First two verses of 'THE RIVER', From the Book of Verse of 1935, *DECEMBER APPLES*,
by Eiluned Lewis.

167

These delightful verses and the woodcut together remind me of similar innocent pleasures. Why 'innocent'? I ask myself. What else but the ecstasy of a summer's breeze and water's caress upon my nakedness? Why, then, a first and only quiver of vulnerability whilst acting Nature's Child – perhaps of fleeting guilt as on the river's grassy bank I played. Did some long-forgotten reproach in infancy cause momentary disquiet? – perhaps Old Adam? – who's in us all!

On one such occasion, I remember being on a high bank of the Severn, almost directly opposite Maesmawr, when my companion Derek, Evan's second youngest son, gave a cry of sudden disbelief, which was followed almost immediately by an ominous splash eight or ten feet below. The river is notorious here for its undercut banks, especially on the outside of bends where flood currents erode their soft faces of sand or clay. The thick pasture turf on top often remains undisturbed, giving whoever steps casually to the edge an utterly false sense of security. Derek had been thus deceived, and instantly fell into a pool of deep water. Fortunately he had, at the least, already learned the basic dog-paddle swimming stroke, and saved himself by thus paddling some yards downstream, where it was possible to wade ashore.

In that same year, 1943, aged eleven and with Maesmawr having become my home since my mother's death the previous December, I joined Gordonstoun School at Llandinam. Although I was then really too young for it, my nain asked a local boy, whose family she knew – he was five years older, and already a Gordonstoun pupil – to 'keep-an-eye' on me. He must have done so in an exemplary manner – 'exemplary' being a word I feel sure Kurt Hahn (the headmaster of Gordonstoun) used; indeed, I can vividly recall his heavily Germanic tongue slowly pronouncing it! My then appointed mentor continues to live in the Upper Severn valley; we see each other every so often, and our friendship has continued to flourish over the past sixty-two years.

I have never regretted my brief sojourn at Gordonstoun. Earlier, I briefly alluded in passing to Dr. Kurt Hahn. This book is no place for a detailed biography of him, and I am not qualified to write one, nor to embark upon a history of the School. Nevertheless, Hahn was such a towering figure, educationally, culturally, spiritually and – not least – physically, that I feel privileged to devote a few paragraphs to his memory, thus giving myself the opportunity, long after his death, and even longer since I was a very nervous eleven-year-old in his presence, to admit that the infrequent occasions on which I met him were DAUNTING! Meanwhile, my mentor, who was well into adolescence by that time, was adept at managing his own personal relationship with the 'Great Man', even if it did not reach a one-to-one basis!

Kurt Hahn was born in 1886 and studied in several of Germany's Academies before going on to Christ Church, Oxford. Returning to Germany, he became Under-secretary to Prince Max of Baden Baden, the Prince himself having been Principal secretary to Kaiser Wilhelm. In 1920, Hahn, then aged 34, was appointed headmaster of Salem School by Prince Max. The school took its name from Salem Castle on the Bodensee (Lake Constance), home of the Baden Baden family, who founded the school. Kurt Hahn remained Salem's headmaster until 1930. In 1921, he escaped assassination for his liberal and humanitarian opinions in a Germany heading towards the rise of Hitler. In 1933, Hitler imprisoned Hahn, but he managed to escape shortly afterwards to Britain, bringing with him most, if not all, of his predominantly German Jewish staff, as well as others. One of those was my housemaster at Llandinam, an Englishman who had driven Hahn out of Germany in his car, with the SS in hot pursuit – or so the story went. My biology and natural history teacher at Gordonstoun, who, with his German colleagues, had also managed to escape from Hitler, was the nephew of the great orchestral conductor Hans Richter, who at one time was conductor of the Hallé Orchestra in Manchester.

I do not know the circumstances which made it possible for Kurt Hahn to settle his former school in the north of Scotland; but this was what happened. The school was based at Gordonstoun Castle near Elgin in Morayshire, the former ancestral home of the Gordon-Cumming family. Hahn remained headmaster of the school (renamed Gordonstoun) from 1934 to 1953, including the period of its evacuation to Llandinam from 1940 to 1945.

As headmaster of Gordonstoun, and of Salem beforehand, Kurt Hahn possessed a very personal moral and spiritually educational vision, which he believed would permanently enhance the life of each pupil in the ever-changing world that they were destined to experience. Moreover, in that world of their adulthood, a world in which change would probably be predominantly for the worse, he wished to 'arm each for the battle of Life' and desired, furthermore, that each, through self-conduct, brotherly love and positive action for the good of their fellow men and women, would seek to make the world a better and happier place.

There were those cynics who, even in the midst of daily life sixty years ago, let alone today, saw Kurt Hahn's vision as a self-deluding crusade against the worship of materialism and increasing spiritual nihilism. But in Hahn's view, many of the world's ills were the direct result of insincerity and self-interest engendered by a lack of respect for, and unawareness of, the practical needs which many – the poor and the aged especially – had, and could not meet on their own.

Hahn's watchword for his school was thus 'service to the community'. During the War years of 1939 to 1945, the vast range of social services that are used by thousands of citizens today did not exist. Whilst many need the expertise of professionally experienced staff, others, like 'meals-on-wheels', are devotedly maintained by non-professionals who love their needy neighbours. Social help of that and a similar nature – such as shopping for the housebound – was an intrinsic part of the Gordonstoun ethos. While the school was at Llandinam, a wider application of the same principle was the fully trained and active affiliation of a number of senior boys to the National Fire Service at Newtown. The school's fully equipped and motorised brigade maintained a standby readiness for duty 'around-the-clock'. On one occasion, when my uncle Emrys discovered the old Hall's chimney well alight, the Gordonstoun brigade, being closer to Maesmawr than were the Newtown firemen, arrived on the scene first, and quite probably saved the old house from destruction by skilfully extinguishing the blaze. Moreover, both before and after the school's four year sojourn at Llandinam, a unit of senior pupils was kept fully trained and equipped to assist the Coastguard Service on the Moray Firth, Gordonstoun Castle being a mere half-mile from its southern shore.

Dr. Kurt Hahn, Headmaster, Gordonstoun School, Elgin, Morayshire, 1934–1953, and formerly of Salem School, Germany.

Courtesy: Jeremy Pryce and Scottish Provincial Press Ltd

Kurt Hahn's first and abiding axiom was to seek to instil in his pupils an all-embracing desire to uphold, through example, the great principle of Truth – to be true to one's own best aspirations. Hahn maintained his belief that this engendered neither personal selfishness and self-interest nor a self-conscious 'selflessness', the latter being frequently imbued with a mistaken sense of 'saintliness'. He passionately taught us to know that to be true to oneself enables one to be true to others.

Upon my joining the school at Llandinam, I boarded at the junior house, called Berth-ddu – the 'ddu' pronounced 'thee'. It is a small late Georgian mansion, c. 1820, two miles west of Llandinam. Built of silver-grey ashlar limestone, it perches prettily on a slight plateau at the foot of Allt-y-Moch, otherwise known as the 'Sugar Loaf', whose sharply defined crest, when viewed up the valley from Llandinam, looms eight hundred feet above Berth-ddu. The steep north-facing slope starts to rise, initially gently, a mere couple of hundred metres beyond the house's walled kitchen garden. The usual punishment for minor misdemeanours was for the miscreant to clamber up to the top of Allt-y-Moch and then slide down it before breakfast, dark winter mornings not excepted!

I thoroughly enjoyed the physical rigours of the School's regime, from my first day there. Each morning at about 7am, the entire 'house', apart from those with genuine heavy colds or other advantageous but temporary maladies, assembled on the entrance forecourt for the 'morning-run'. Clad only in shorts and gym shoes, a senior boy led off the shivering, teeth-chattering contingent, clad likewise, for a fast run to-and-from the Lodge at the main road. The shivering and chattering very soon became a pleasurable warming glow despite one's virtual nakedness. The run lasted about ten minutes, and was followed by a hot shower and then an icy-cold one before breakfast, which predominantly comprised plenteous bowlfuls of Swiss muesli made of porridge oats and chopped raw apple, soaked overnight in milk. That delicious form of gruel was prepared by the local jolly cook, Janet. It being Wartime, such luxuries as oranges and bananas for adding to the muesli were absent. Marmalade and jam were also very scarce at that time of National austerity and Wartime rationing. Hahn managed, somehow, to find and substitute for these a very concentrated orange jelly, almost reduced to a fruit 'cheese'. It was packed in large shiny tin cans, about twelve inches high, and was liberally and relentlessly spooned out at breakfast and afternoon tea.

The mornings were devoted to lessons and study. After lunch, it was mandatory that each boy lay flat and quiet upon his bed, either reading or napping, for thirty minutes. Outside activity then followed for the remainder of the afternoon, before evening lessons. In summer, activities included cricket, athletics and swimming, while in winter athletics were continued, together with rugby and hockey, this last being especially popular. Dr. Hahn was a fine and fast hockey player, despite his heavy build. Work in the walled garden was also needed, and so was the sawing and chopping of firewood. Another outdoor activity which was eagerly anticipated and usually occurred at weekends, when there was more time, was simple expeditioning into the oak woods behind the

house. These extended up into a deep, wooded, valley on the right of Allt-y-Moch, through which tumbled a rocky mountain stream with miniature waterfalls and little pools along its stony course. The smart little Dipper bird, black with white breast, was frequently seen perched on large stones in mid-stream, as was the Grey wagtail, the latter having

Grey Wagtail   Agnes Miller Parker, 1936

a bright yellow breast, and thus being easily mistaken for the Yellow one. On other exploratory daytime expeditions, further afield, we went up onto the bleak moorland behind Allt-y-Moch, which is now the location for the very extensive Llandinam wind farm. In my Gordonstoun days, only herds of wild mountain ponies roamed up there, because only an experienced and watchful human eye could spot the hazardous bogs, which the ponies instinctively avoided.

We were in the knowledgeable and capable hands of the late Captain Richard Annand, V.C., who was the first British officer to be awarded the Victoria Cross in the Second World War. He was serving as a Second Lieutenant of the Durham Light Infantry fighting in Belgium in 1940 when his batman received severe injuries in a ferocious engagement with the enemy, and lay helpless somewhere out in 'No-Man's-Land', between the opposing forces. Annand learned of this just as his Company commander had ordered a withdrawal. Despite his own severe wounds from previous fighting, seeing a wheelbarrow conveniently to hand, he pushed it back towards the enemy line, under machine-gun fire, in search of his colleague. Annand eventually found him, unable to walk because of his severe leg and head wounds. Lifting him into the wheelbarrow, Annand sought to push it back to the comparative safety of their own line. However, on the way a fallen tree barred the pair's progress. Annand then had no alternative but to place his batman in an empty trench and stagger on alone in search of his company H.Q. There he intended to get help for the rescue of the wounded man. Alas, Annand found the H.Q. abandoned, and collapsed from exhaustion and blood loss, to be found and rescued later by his colleagues. His batman, Private Joseph Hunter, was later found by the Germans, taken prisoner and sent to a Dutch hospital,

2nd LIEUT. R. W. ANNAND, V.C., Durham Light Infantry

Photo : BIPPA

When the Germans over-ran Belgium, 2ND LIEUT. ANNAND commanded a Platoon on the River Dyle beside a blown-up bridge. The Germans sent forward a bridging party. Annand and his men attacked, but when ammunition ran out completely, he himself advanced over open ground, with total disregard for enemy mortar and machine-gun fire. He drove out the whole party of Germans with hand-grenades. Wounded, he carried on. During the evening, he went forward once more with grenades and repeated his attack. Then, ordered to withdraw his men, he found that his batman was wounded and had been left behind. He returned at once and brought him back in a wheelbarrow, before losing consciousness as the result of wounds.

W555F

Postcard in 'Heroic Deeds of the War – V.C. Series'.

Courtesy: County Records Office of Durham County Council

The late Captain Richard W. Annand, V.C., the Durham Light Infantry. A delightful portrait of a great hero.

Courtesy: photographer John Attle

where he died a month later.

Promoted to the rank of Captain, Richard Annand was Gazetted on 23 August 1940. Prior to his heroic attempt to rescue Private Hunter, and despite intense mortar and machine-gun fire, which badly wounded him, he had made two lone and devastating grenade attacks on enemy bridge-repair parties. Although he recovered from his wounds at La Tombe, Annand was severely deafened. He was invalided out of the army in 1948, and devoted his life to the disabled, especially the deaf. (Courtesy: *The Times*, London, for extracts from its Obituary, dated 29th December 2004, of Captain Richard Annand, V.C.)

During the early years of his convalescence, Richard Annand spent some time at Gordonstoun, especially with us youngsters at Berth-ddu. We had a lot of fun with this jovial man, and he with us. He showed us how to light campfires with damp sticks, and how to bake potatoes in their skins in the fire's hot embers. From him we also learned the rudiments of map and compass reading. I can vividly recollect the claret-coloured strip of silk ribbon, about one and a half inches long, which was sewn onto the breast of his khaki battledress blouse, to represent the bronze Victoria Cross medal which, when not formally worn, was represented on the ribbon by a miniature Maltese Cross.

In 1979, when Captain Annand and his wife Shirley were the visiting guests of the officers of a Royal Navy frigate, she slipped off the gangplank adjoining the quayside and fell into the river. Richard, then aged sixty-five, without hesitation plunged in to save her from drowning, until both were rescued by the ship's crew. I feel that Kurt Hahn saw Richard Annand as both representing and fulfilling his Ideal of heroic young manhood, the archetype of John Bunyan's 'Valiant for Truth'. The Victoria Cross is 'For Valour'. Captain Richard Annand, V.C., died on 24th December 2004, aged ninety. Just before he died, he said to Shirley, "Darling, God has been so good to me. I have a wonderful wife and had a full life. I am ready to go." – **And all the trumpets sounded for him on the Other Side'.**

Courtesy: Imperial War Museum, London

After the afternoon's outdoor activities, and before tea, the morning's hot, then icy, ablutions again took place, in a steam-enveloped outhouse filled with naked boys teetering along soap-slippery wooden duckboards into the showers, before the dismal cry went up: "Hot water's running out!" Our morning dress comprised, for all ages, an open-necked pale grey flannel shirt, dark blue flannel shorts, dark blue wool, long-sleeved pullover, blue knee-high woollen socks and black shoes. After the pre-tea shower, we donned our evening dress, which was also worn on Sundays. This comprised a very pale grey-blue open-necked flannel shirt with, again, matching shorts and long-sleeved woollen pullover of the same inimitable Gordonstoun tone. This was also the colour of our light woollen knee-socks.

The head boy was called the 'Guardian', and beneath his eighteen years, a set of seniors, each known as a 'Colour-bearer', enforced a degree of authority below the school staff. The 'Guardian' and the 'Colour-bearers' each had an inch-long narrow strip of pale lavender-blue cotton tape stitched onto the left breast of their morning and evening pullovers, to signify their status. While it never occurred to me at the time, I later realised what a singular connection there was between Richard Annand's V.C. stripe, awarded for having heroically proved Kurt Hahn's axiom of 'selflessness for Truth' by rescuing a colleague in battle, and the Gordonstoun 'Guardian' and 'Colour-bearers', wearing a stripe of not quite the same hue while being instilled with that same axiom as pupils.

Gordonstoun had no day school, and its boarders had no opportunity of visiting their homes in term-time. However, I was an exception, the School giving me compassionate leave to enjoy alternate Sunday afternoons at Maesmawr, between 2pm and 6pm, in view of my mother having died the year before I joined Gordonstoun. My precious Sunday visits to Maesmawr were eagerly anticipated, but although Nain and my uncle would have welcomed my bringing a school friend to tea, perhaps the reason I never did was that the school only allowed me to enjoy that special leave for a few hours.

I had no bicycle of my own at that time, but was always able to borrow one from one or other kind and understanding boy who did. In hindsight, I should have asked Lord Davies if he would buy one for me, but I was rather in awe of him. I feel sure he would have bought me a bicycle had I felt the courage to ask. At that time, he was widowed and, unknowingly, was only to live for another two years. He occasionally invited me to lunch in the little house, Deildre, near his Plas Dinam home, then occupied by the school. I recall that our lunchtime conversation was rather limited. I was too young to know anything about fox-hunting, which was so dear to his heart, or his other great enthusiasm, the League of Nations, whose aspirations he would surely have explained to me, had I been some years older. Instead, I sat on the floor after lunch and enjoyed browsing quantities of *Country Life* magazines. Alas, it was not until years after his death that I learned that "Uncle David", as I knew him, had held my mother in such great affection. Had I known that when I visited him, I know that our brief relationship would have been altogether and happily different. He presumably, and I suppose understandably, felt shy of mentioning her to me so soon after I had lost her.

During the War, Berth-ddu still belonged to my uncle, Lord Davies. The house has a magnificent panoramic view across the narrowing Upper Severn valley. The river itself, from directly opposite Berth-ddu downstream to Llandinam's bridge, runs very close to the route of the former single-track railway, which was demolished in 1962. It ran from Moat Lane Junction to Llandinam, whose station was opened in 1859, up to Llanidloes, thence over the mountain to Rhayader and beyond. Berth-ddu boys swam in a deep river pool several pastures beyond, but roughly opposite to, the house. This beautiful spot was bounded, on its far bank, by a thick rocky stratum supporting the portion of the railway that ran past our pool.

Often whilst we swam there, the Great Western Railway's maintenance gangers happened to come 'pumping' up from Llandinam on a self-propelled four-wheeled trolley. I especially choose this term to describe the manner of their motion along the track. They rode aboard a heavy wooden chassis mounted upon two pairs of steel flanged wheels, similar to those of a truck or carriage but smaller. Each pair of wheels was mounted on a swivelling bogie at either end of the chassis. This enabled one or other of them to be turned at right-angles to the line of the rails, upon the chassis being raised by its occupants the few inches required to lift the flanges over them. That initial action allowed the chassis to swivel its second bogie, and thus the entire contraption was cleared from the track at the anticipated approach of a train. The wooden chassis accommodated four men, sitting one pair opposite the other on rudimentary benches. Between them, and centrally located on the chassis, extended a hinged wooden beam with a pair of handles at each end, capable of being worked up-and-down 'see-saw' fashion. This beam was somehow hinged at its centre upon an upright which formed the pivotal point of the 'see-saw' motion. Down from there extended a drive-rod mechanism which, in turn, was connected to the bogie wheels. Thus, when the beam was worked up-and-down, the trolley was propelled along. Any reader who has seen the great American actor of the silent film era, Buster Keaton, in 'The General', will recall Keaton, as the engine driver of that locomotive, chasing it on a gangers' trolley of very similar design.

177

SEREN ESCAPES

Maesmawr did not harvest a crop of oats every summer, its own acreage, excluding the fields of the three tenant farms, Dôl-Hafren, Red House and Ty-Mawr, being insufficient for a full annual rotation. However, when this cereal was needed, the agricultural contractor from Caersws, Messrs Tanners, brought machinery to sow, cut and thresh it – the latter in November or December. Before a brief description of the harvest field and the binder machine that cut the crop, I will look back – with amusement now, 'though it wasn't funny at the time – to a crisis of my own making that occurred when the oats were ready to harvest. It was a summer of beautiful weather, and the crop stood undamaged by wind. The field today no longer has the gate which once opened immediately right at the start of the Drive, and the hedge has been extended to replace it.

A new and weather-boarded stock-shed, painted black, had recently been built onto the north end of the old Dutch hay-barn, neither of which remain nowadays. The shed's first occupant was a pretty little chestnut Shorthorn heifer named **Seren**, which is Welsh for 'star', because she had a white flash on her forehead. During the first few days after her arrival, she was kept enclosed and quiet in her new quarters. Therein she was provided with thick straw bedding as an additional comfort to assist her in settling down in unfamiliar surroundings.

However, to my cost, this luxury did not prevent the little animal from taking any opportunity to enjoy herself beyond its comfortable confines.

Her intent caught me unawares. Before visiting her for a chat and a stroke, which I thought she would enjoy, I had opened the top leaf of the shed's stable door, hooking it back securely before unbolting the bottom leaf just enough for me to squeeze through without giving **Seren** the chance to escape – or so I thought! Seeing her opportunity, she quickly pushed past my futile efforts to stop her and, pushing the door further open with her nose, was instantly free. She rushed off, her tail in the air, through the cobbled yard, out past the stable-block, down the little lane that led to the Drive, across it – AND into the precious Maesmawr oats! When I breathlessly caught up with **Seren**, I saw that she had pushed through a thin part of Evan's previous winter's 'laying' of the thorn hedge that bounded the Drive. Worse was to come, as the naughty little animal excitedly rushed about, trampling the upright stalks and creating potential havoc. The harvesting machines of those days were inefficient at cutting cereal stalks flattened by wind or any other cause, and **Seren** was doing just that.

This crisis happened to occur on a Sunday afternoon, just as had the excitement of THE 'LOST' AEROPLANE, albeit the latter posed no problem – except for anxiety lest the pilot should fail to be airborne before reaching the Maesmawr Drive's trees. My uncle enjoyed his afternoon nap after the morning's service at Llandinam's Presbyterian Church and lunch at home. However, I had no alternative, whilst apprehensive of his reaction, but to alert him urgently to the trouble I had unwittingly and foolishly caused. When I awoke him from his 'forty winks', he was naturally enough a little displeased upon hearing my anxious tale. Quickly realising that the situation would need more than the efforts of himself and his 'hopeless' young nephew to capture **Seren**, he told me to run immediately up to White Cottage and summon Evan to the scene of potential disaster. When I got there, he was then at the twentieth of HIS 'forty winks'! However, Evan being such a willing and understanding soul, realising what a 'pickle' I had got myself into, he straightway abandoned his remaining 'winks' and rushed to the scene. There we found that my uncle had cleverly corralled **Seren** into a corner. Evan's rope halter was quickly put over her ears, and she was led back to safe-custody, whilst I was lightly admonished for being deceived by a cunning little calf.

DANDY AND DAVIS

I have always thought that **Dandy** came to Maesmawr upon an impulsive whim of my uncle Emrys. Being no expert on horse breeds, I can best describe **Dandy** as a chestnut cob with an attractive white flash on his forehead. He possessed unbounded youthful energy that, ideally, needed regular and strenuous work to consume it, but I doubt if the mercurial young gelding was ever given the healthy labour he so needed. When free and grazing in the orchard rookery, seeing Evan approaching with a halter, **Dandy** would imperiously toss his head and canter off with equine defiance of impending work.

Although the old stables, adjacent to the garages, were in perfect repair to house a horse, **Dandy** was provided with a sturdy, timber-clad stable of his own in the middle of the orchard rookery. Here there was open space, close beside the Roman Road's raised agger, which ran to the river bank, and where the high old trees did not impinge on the ancient track and flourished in rich soil, away from the Road's stony foundations.

I recall Evan – with me as his enthusiastic helper – painting the weatherboard cladding of **Dandy's** stable with tar-creosote. Today's so-called creosote is a pale substitute for the old preservative, whose thick and blackish liquid kept decay at bay for decades. It had an astringently pleasant smell that was apt to linger in clothing for days. In my self-appointed role as Evan's mate, I did not feel the part unless I wore an old sack over my shoulders, as he did – particularly when it rained. Thus Evan fitted me up with one small enough for me, which was difficult to find, securing it upon the chest of my smart new gabardine coat with a long nail pushed in and out of the sack, not dissimilar to a typical Roman device for the same utilitarian purpose. This was in the summer of 1941, the year before my mother's death, and she had bought my new coat especially for my holiday visit to Maesmawr. It was far from being suitable for wear whilst creosoting, and the astringent vapours remained in it until it was dispatched for dry-cleaning by Davis & Co. of Westbourne Park in London. In those days, any article of clothing that was not washable at home was set aside to be 'sent to Davis'. The firm's premises were – perhaps are still? – situated alongside the railway lines at the approach to Paddington Station, where the smoke of express train engines entering and leaving the metropolis drifted and hung around. The dry-cleaner's works comprised a series of 'zig-zag' glass factory roofs, with brick gables to each 'zig' and 'zag', built end-on to the innumerable rail tracks. Across each gable was painted, in large white capital letters, DAVIS THE CLEANERS. There were six or more of these painted gables stretching westwards towards Old Oak Common railway sidings. In the days of steam trains, before welded track superseded the bolted 'fish-plates' that held the lengths of rail together, the bogie wheels of express passenger trains went *tickety-tick-tickety-tick* as they sped over the rail-joints. Thus, whilst passing the dry-cleaners, about a quarter-mile out of Paddington, I imagined the bogies saying, "DAVIS THE CLEANERS – DAVIS THE CLEANERS", which they repeated for several minutes as the coaches rolled past. I never understood how clothes were returned in pristine cleanliness from such a smoky and grimy location. However, the daily 11.10am 'Cambrian Coast Express' from platform 1, which on many happy occasions took me and members of my family back to Wales, reminded us to send, when back home, our muddy trousers to "DAVIS THE CLEANERS – DAVIS THE CLEANERS" – *tickety-tick-tickety-tick-tickety-tick*.

Dandy would have been in his element as one of a prancing pair harnessed to Queen Boadicea's chariot, with whirling scimitar blades on its wheel-caps, challenging the cockaded cohorts of Sextus Julius Frontinus at their Roman fort at Caersws. Frontinus was the Governor of Roman Britain at the time of the subjugation of Wales in A.D. 74–78. But the nearest ***Dandy*** got to that Ideal was being harnessed between the shafts of a smart new wooden wagon, painted dark blue, with its pair of wheels fitted with pneumatic balloon-type tyres that might have been suitable for a Wartime fighter aircraft.

One morning, Evan and I clambered aboard ***Dandy's*** 'chariot', loaded with logs destined for the Georgian residence of Bron-felen, on the opposite side of the valley. We trotted up the Maesmawr Drive and down deserted Long Length, then turned right before the Dôl-Hafren bend, up the narrow lane over the railway bridge, a mile from Moat Lane Junction, and beyond to Bron-felen itself, where our load was tipped out.

We had not gone far on our return trip when it became increasingly obvious, both to us and to ***Dandy***, that his early oat breakfast had not been sufficiently digested for his comfort. The outward journey's motion had set the oats fermenting, and by the time we started for home, the pressure on the equine stomach was potentially explosive; poor ***Dandy*** had acute flatus, as it is politely described. Pulling his now empty 'chariot', whose relative lightness upon the balloon tyres induced an uncomfortable up-and-down motion of the wagon shafts, ***Dandy's*** own safety-valve began to relieve his gastro-pressure. It did so in short, sharp retorts as we trotted and bounced our way homeward. Evan said that he thought methane gas was very explosive, and he lamented having forgotten his matches. Had he remembered them, he said, we could have been assured of returning to Maesmawr 'double-quick', due to the expelled force of ***Dandy's*** repetitive reports. At that time, the name of Sir Frank Whittle, the jet engine's inventor, was unknown to me, but presumably not to Evan, who must have read some Wartime newspaper article on the intended development of jet propulsion after hostilities were over – and if the Allies eventually won the War, which was then far from certain.

But ***Dandy*** was spared a match-scorched posterior on the journey back to Maesmawr. Before we got home, his thunder had rumbled away as quickly as it had come – just as in Beethoven's Sixth Symphony, the 'Pastoral'. Upon being unharnessed from the wagon shafts, he galloped away, as free as air, onto the Roman Road's raised agger, which – today as it did then – runs towards the river and old Caersws beyond it. I can still recall the young cob's whinnying for Boadicea, who never came for him! Nevertheless, despite his yearning for her campaigns' chariot-shafts, at Maesmawr he was as free as the thunderous bolts he had blown at us.

Otter.

Agnes Miller Parker, 1937

182

THE PAIRS OF PIGS

At Maesmawr, a pair of pigs was reared every year, to spend their brief, but happy, lives housed in semi-detached sties, built of pinkish brick with a blue slate roof, in the farmyard. The sties were demolished after my time, but stood north of the BLACKSTONE engine-shed, close to the boundary fence along the Severn's pasture. In later years, I often wondered why pigs were reared at Maesmawr. Whilst I acknowledge that they provided sides of undoubtedly flavoursome bacon for a year's consumption, my nain bought beef and lamb every week from Caersws' butcher, Bryan Lloyd. Long ago, I used to ask myself why she did not obtain bacon and hams from him also. It was certainly traditional for remote farmsteads and cottagers, especially those with very little money, annually to rear and kill a pig because it provided meat, albeit of necessity salted, for the entire year ahead. I recall once entering a mountain farm high up on the Brecon Beacons whose kitchen-parlour's old ceiling beam was hung with so many flitches that they almost touched one another.

Maesmawr was undoubtedly not wealthy, but neither was it impecunious and thus needful of home-produced bacon for that reason. I can only surmise that the need for flavour was paramount, and only obtained by a most beneficial diet for the pigs. This was certainly provided at Maesmawr, and the end result, as ham

Photograph: Ellis-Jones

and bacon, proved its worth. The pigs were fed 'BOCM' nuts to maintain vitamin intake, and they also assisted in the disposal of many gallons of skimmed milk which would have been difficult to get rid of in any other way – certainly not by pouring it into the river! Each morning and evening, after milk-separation, a large bucketful of skimmed milk was emptied into the great oak cask of vegetable peelings, bread crusts, over-ripe tomatoes, raw cabbage, cauliflower stalks and other uncooked produce which comprised the bulk of their diet.

The pigs' ultimate demise, by traditional and very primitive methods, was undertaken by an old pig-sticker from Llandinam. I was, rightly, forbidden to witness any part of those pitiful proceedings, and had no wish to do so. I preface these Recollections of Maesmawr with two lines by the writer and poet Mary Webb: '*Long, long ago I thought on all these things: Long, long ago I loved them.*' The only thought, long ago suppressed, that I did not wish to remember was the annual demise of the poor pairs of pigs.

My uncle liked to give each a name – *Salt* and *Pepper* one year, 1939 – although *Salt* did not need his so early in his brief life. During one of the subsequent years – that which witnessed the German Army's siege of Leningrad, now St. Petersburg – the Maesmawr pigs were given the names *Zhukov* and *Voroshilov*, after two Russian Red Army generals. In the year of the British Eighth Army's invasion of Italy, my uncle named that year's pigs *Mussolini*, after the Italian dictator, and *Hirohito*, after the Japanese Emperor. The latter's name was then premature as regards the War with Japan, but Mussolini's (Il Duce) happened to be very relevant, as both the poor Maesmawr pig and he came to much the same fate, the pig hanging upside-down in Maesmawr's garage and Mussolini likewise in central Milan.

Before bidding the porkers adieu, I must mention that the rafters of their comfortable straw-bedded sty were very popular with nesting swallows and martins, despite the roof apex being a mere six feet or so above the brick floor. At that time, swallows and house-martins were very plentiful – so much so, in the War years especially, that their nesting sites were at a premium and at Maesmawr's eaves, the birds' most favoured place, latecomers had to find other

House-martin wood-engraving.
Margaret Tournour

places to build their nests. The pigsty roofs were the best alternative. Nests built under the house eaves and bargeboards were taken for granted. However, even in those now faraway days, to see martins darting in and out of the sty's opening, not much higher than was necessary for the pig to walk through, was an amazing sight. Moreover, their nests, in the apex of the sty's roof, were potentially liable to human interference, – although that never happened. Nevertheless, their self-protective instincts did not seem threatened in any way, and they were perfectly content to nest only four feet or so above their hosts' ears.

THE VANISHED COWS

Early one autumn morning, when dew lay heavy on grass and leaf, and glistening gossamer cobwebs stretched from every twig, gleaming in the hedgerow, Evan came out of his little White Cottage. Opening its wicket gate, he crossed an empty Long Length, and lifted the latch of the iron gate into the first of the Maesmawr pastures, just as he did three hundred and sixty-five days each year. But on this occasion, the unexpected was about to occur. The three house-cows had apparently disappeared. The first pasture, in which Evan always found them on his way to work, was empty. Perhaps, he thought, they would be in the next pasture, where the lush grass was even more luxuriant than in the first. When Evan reached the open gate between the first and second pastures, his perplexity increased when he found the latter also devoid of cows.

Had the 'Little People', thought he, spirited them away? Faeries are reputed to be fond of cattle. Or had a rustler made a night raid and stolen them? "Oh well," he said to himself, "I will have to tell the 'Missus', or Mr Emrys, without delay, that their precious cows have vanished." Anxiously, he walked through the second pasture's gate at its farthest corner, where it adjoined the bottom of the Drive, and crossed over the Drive into the little lane which, in those days, ran behind the east garden's shrubbery approach into the stable-block forecourt. There he listened attentively for any sound from his beloved cows. He

185

went around the corner of Walter's carpentry workshop and into the narrow cobbled yard between the cow-byres and the old Dutch hay-barn. Upon reaching the yard, he noticed that the bottom leaf of the byres' stable-door was closed, whilst the top leaf was open and hooked back to the wall. Evan was certain that he had closed both leaves the previous evening on his way home. (He knew that an unwelcome old rat was apt to spend a night in a byre, in preference to the hay-barn.) Suddenly, Evan was amazed to hear the unmistakable metallic *clink-clink* of a bright steel chain within. Peering over the stable-door, there he discovered the three cows, **Ayrshire**, **Ty-Mawr** and little **Seren**, contentedly chewing their cud and patiently waiting to be milked.

A very young aspiring cowherd – myself, of course – had arisen, even before the Faeries, and brought the docile beasts to their byres.

When I reached the top pasture, where they grazed and where Evan had expected to find them, I knew that it was overlooked by an upper window of White Cottage. I imagined that Evan had perhaps already seen me through it, and that my ruse might be spoilt even before it had begun. The three cows had looked up at me with relaxed surprise, but upon my softly calling "cow-cow-cow," as Evan always did, they had begun to follow me home.

Together we had made a slow ambling progress across the first pasture, through the gate into the second, which I had optimistically left wide open in the hope of my ruse being successful. The second pasture was crossed by our bovine procession, with **Ayrshire**, as senior cow, taking the lead as she always did. As we slowly approached the gate onto the Maesmawr Drive, which I had intentionally also left wide open to facilitate our progress, my young heart began to quicken. As I was following the cows and not leading them, I suddenly feared that **Ayrshire** – it would have been her very first time – might decide to turn left onto the Drive instead of crossing it. Such an outcome, if it had occurred, would certainly have attracted **Ty-Mawr** and **Seren** to follow her. There, facing them, seductively would have lain my uncle's precious lawns, and Nain's and Noel's precious herbaceous flowerbeds! My enthusiasm for the early morning ruse had overlooked that potential disaster.

Dear docile cows: they had always gone to-and-fro, twice-daily, along their familiar route across the Drive, up the lane to the stable-block and around the corner to their byres. No small boy's plan, successful or otherwise, was to alter their familiar route, so potential trouble for him, had the trio decided to graze Maesmawr's lawns, was averted. One by one, as into the Ark, the obliging cows ambled into their respective stalls. Their proud but greatly relieved cowherd followed them. Whilst I gently placed the shining steel-linked chain over each deep neck, they gazed at me with large and very soft eyes, as though to say, "*Moo, we'd never ever make trouble for you.*"

186

VERY EARLY

Very early we will go into the fields to-morrow
And wait beneath the budding elm-tree arches,
Till Earth has comforted her night-long sorrow
And dawn comes golden in the larches.

There's a little hush that falls when the airs lie sleeping;
The sky is like an empty silver bowl,
Till eagerly the blackbird's song goes upward sweeping,
And fills the aery hollows, and the soul.

There's a scent that only comes in the faint, fresh gloaming,
Before the crocus opens for the bees;
So early we will go and meet the young day roaming,
And see the heavens caught among the trees.

Mary Webb, FIFTY-ONE POEMS

JUST GOING FOR A WALK

THE OLD BELL

There, still, on Black-and-White brick wall,
Oft did I heed its peals o'er distance call;
Then dropped my rod, or bow, the bat-and-ball,
My nain to please at Maesmawr Hall.

M. E-J

Maesmawr's old bell, still today high on the north gable; it often pealed Gretta's urgent call, "Master Michael! Nain wants you!" Now rope-less and disused.

Photograph: Ellis-Jones

Poor Evan. He had hoped to walk her up the Maesmawr drive and out of sight down Long Length without my noticing, but there was little chance of that good fortune. They had not gone far when a piping voice called out, "Evan, where are you going?" There was no reply. "Evan, where are you taking her?" "We're going for a walk," he replied. "Where to?" "Not far," he said. "Can I come too?" "No, not today," Evan responded. "Why not?" "Nain might want you to take a message." "No she won't," the small boy retorted.

At that moment, Gretta's distant call was heard. "Master Michael! Master Michael! Nain wants you" – as she pulled on the rope of the old bell, sending its clear peal across the fields. "There you are," said Evan with great relief. "Nain

188

does want you." Back to the house scampered the little enquirer, and on went Evan, leading **Seren** by her halter to Dôl-Hafren, Maesmawr's first-of-three tenant farms, at the eastern end of Long Length. Today's constant road traffic down Long Length makes unimaginable the fact that sixty years ago it was perfectly safe and easy for a cow, or heifer, to be led by a halter along its verge.

Why were Evan and **Seren** walking to Dôl-Hafren? Why, for her to visit the bull, of course. How could dear Evan explain this fact of life to a tender ten-year-old? Nowadays it could be done more easily, but not  over half-a-century ago. In those faraway days, there was 'Children's Hour' on the wireless, innocence reigned, and what bulls did never entered my young head!

Cow.

Agnes Miller Parker, 1937

189

HARVESTING THE OATS

The agricultural contractor, both before and in the era of my childhood of which I write, fulfilled an essential function in small-scale farming, and in places like the Upper Severn valley, virtually all farms relied upon him, to a lesser or greater extent, at every season of the year. Maesmawr itself, and its three tenant farms in the neighbourhood, often called upon the contractor's services for one purpose or another. Messrs Tanners, from beyond Caersws, thus had many customers patiently, and in some cases perhaps impatiently, waiting for his help according to the season. That was especially so at harvest time, when the conjunction of ideal weather and a perfectly ripened grain meant that he was needed everywhere at once. Somehow the good-natured proprietor managed to oblige all his customers, there being a strong local farming spirit between most; and the great majority accepted that the contractor always did his best to serve them. When Maesmawr's harvest day arrived, and the machinery hove in sight at the top of the drive, we were all overjoyed that it was our turn, especially Evan, who loved his role as the 'binder-man', so-called, which opportunity did not occur every year, as I explained earlier. In preparation for the tractor and binder's arrival, Evan had previously sharpened his trusty scythe and cut several wide swathes of the standing crop, immediately within the field gate, to allow the machinery to enter and be best positioned for starting to cut the first outer swathe around the field.

The tractor was the most common model of those days, a dark-blue painted 'FORDSON Major', with orange-painted wheel-centres fitted with, in all probability, cross-tread Firestone tyres. The FORDSON of those faraway days had neither an enclosed cabin for the driver, nor a hydraulic drive for rear implements. The driver sat upon a capacious metal seat which, although of an ergonomic design best suiting the average farmer's posterior, nevertheless was frequently 'upholstered' with sacks as further comfort. The seat was bolted to a curved length of tempered steel which provided the driver with a welcome amount of 'spring' over bumpy terrain. He sat thus in all weathers, fully exposed to the pleasures of summer and autumn and often the vile cold and wet in the depths of winter. Not for him the modern 'leviathan' with its enclosed plastic cabin, complete with heater and also, if desired, a continuous diet of Radio 1. Apart from the old FORDSON engine's characteristic throb, its driver of sixty years ago was not very far removed, in his awareness of Nature's sounds around him, from the previous generations who drove their horse-teams in earlier centuries – granted that the former sat at his task and had not to trudge in the clay-clogging furrow, following a straining and nodding pair of Shires – the latter a lovely sight in itself.

I include a photograph of a typical corn harvest binder. Years ago there were hundreds of examples of that invaluable, but often frustrating, invention working throughout the country. They had a multiplicity of temperamental moving parts, many made by MASSEY HARRIS, a name closely associated with the harvest field, even into the era of the combine harvester. That spelled the humble binder's death-knell, but saved countless hours gathering up hundreds of bound sheaves by hand and standing them into *stooks*. A field of the latter was nevertheless one of rural life's most attractive late summer sights, forever remembered with nostalgia both by those who made them – thistles often included! – and those whose delight in them was solely because they were a beautiful reminder of a loved and long-vanished era of the harvest field.

The typical binder consisted of a steel chassis supported by a single broad-rimmed and spoked wheel. This wheel was treaded with bars of steel diagonally welded onto its six-inch-wide rim. The wheel was positioned at the pivotal point of balance of the entire machine, being approximately central beneath it. The binder was thus in effect self-supporting on the wheel, a triangular-framed tow-bar onto the tractor being almost solely for that purpose. The single wheel, by means of internal gearing, activated all the moving parts. It was wound up and down by means of a cranked handle, the winding-up being done after a small pair of demountable rubber road wheels had been fixed either side. Upon arrival at the crop field, the single wheel was wound down to take the weight of the binder, and the road wheels removed, pending replacement for transit when the work was finished. On the left-hand side of the chassis projected a platform, about five feet square, clad with light metal sheeting and fitted with several wooden rollers. Stretched tightly over them, by means of buckled leather straps, was a robust canvas sheet. As the rollers rotated, the taut canvas performed as an 'endless-belt' moving into, and then out of, the complicated mechanism within the body of the binder. Its purpose will become evident as my description continues.

The front (leading) edge of the aforementioned platform was fitted with a to-and-fro cutting blade, similar in action to a modern-day hand-held hedge-cutter but much larger. It was activated as the binder was towed, as was also a multi-vaned 'sail' poised directly over the platform, comprising lightweight wooden bars on the ends of metal rods radiating from a central hub. As the binder's platform was towed into the standing corn at the outer edge of the field, the to-and-fro cutter blade severed the stalk at four to six inches above level ground, leaving what is called *stubble*. The stalk immediately fell onto the rotating canvas, assisted by the stroking effect of the rotating 'sail' directly overhead. The sail could be raised or lowered, as appropriate, to the height of the standing stalks.

The cut stalks, upon being taken into the central mechanism by the slowly

Not an original Maesmawr photograph, but this is as the harvest was there. In this instance the 'binder-man' is temporarily out of his elevated seat while the tractor driver continues unconcerned. Note the 'sail', whose slowly revolving blades stroked the cut stalks onto the inwardly moving canvas sheet.

Courtesy: *The Countryman* magazine

moving canvas belt, were automatically gathered into bunches of pre-determined girth by a clever claw device. This device then pushed the bunches into the tying machinery, which wound stout twine around them to form a waist. The twine was automatically knotted and cut off, and the sheaf, thus bound, was ejected by means of another rotating internal claw, and fell upon the *stubble*. A sheaf was expelled every ten seconds or so, depending on the towing tractor's speed, which was determined by the density and stalk length of the crop being harvested. A huge ball of binder-twine, almost the size of a small football, sat on an external spigot and unwound as it was automatically drawn into the sheaf-tying mechanism.

Above and 'amidships' of this mechanical wizardry sat the 'binder-man', Evan in Maesmawr's case. He was perched high up on a tractor-type iron seat, and in front of him were several palm-release levers for adjusting parts of the moving assemblage, including the 'sail'. Every so often, as was to be expected from such a complicated but primitive machine, something would suddenly go wrong, and there would be immediate shouts of "STOP!" loud enough to be heard by the tractor driver, who otherwise was apt to drive on unaware that something was amiss. The trouble was almost always first seen by the 'binder-man' from his advantageous viewpoint, or by a harvester walking along beside the machine, and the problem most frequently concerned the sheaf-ejection mechanism and the twine-cutting knife, so that sheaves would bunch up within, or be ejected in two's or three's connected together with uncut twine. The first problem was the most frustrating, causing stoppages when time was pressing. However, taken as a whole, the now old-fashioned binder was an ingenious invention and an inseparable feature of happy 'old-time' harvesting. Around the field it went, the 'sail' gently turning whilst the old tractor *chugged* on and – with any luck – summer clouds drifted in the azure sky. Eventually, the crop was reduced to a small square in the field's centre, and here all the poor rabbits, fearful of fleeing their hiding place, were trapped until they were finally forced to flee when the last few swathes were falling to the binder's knife. Some ran away from my uncle Emrys' gun whilst others, in panic, raced towards him. However, being a first-class shot, he ensured that no rabbits escaped wounded, and I was glad that their demise was instantaneous.

Not an original Maesmawr photograph, but this resembles the crop of oats there, though here it is wheat that is being gathered into *stooks*, each comprising eight corn sheaves. Oat *stooks* commonly comprised only four sheaves, its stalk being less rigid than that of wheat.

Courtesy: *The Countryman* magazine

Not an original Maesmawr photograph either, but a similar scene. There, Messrs Tanners of Caersws brought their steam traction engine and threshing box to the stable-yard. The corn stack was traditionally built upon a thick bed of dry bracken, collected from the hill above Bron-felen in **Dandy's** wagon.

Courtesy: Beaford Archive

When the crop lay as bound sheaves, Evan, Walter, Noel and I (in my small way) gathered them up to stand as serried rows of *stooks* to dry in sun and breeze. A few weeks later, they were carted to the stack-yard and skilfully laid, with their heads facing inwards, one upon the other, to form the stack. Months later, at a time dependent on circumstances, the sheaves were threshed. In the meantime, the *stubble* was not ploughed before the onset of winter, but intentionally left for the welfare and enjoyment of free-range hens, who were provided with a capacious mobile hen-house in which they roosted and were shut up each night. Whilst foxes must have been present in the neighbourhood, perhaps the prevalence of wildlife provided enough food for them. I cannot recall knowing of a fox attacking the contented little flock, who happily scratched and pecked in the 'Seventh Heaven' of the *stubble* field. In that era of long-ago, it was common practice to leave generously-wide 'headlands', so-called, around the perimeter of arable fields. These provided an undisturbed habitat for many species of wildlife. Although they were so abundant, it continued to be viewed as good husbandry to provide Nature's creatures with the space and security so essential for their welfare, which had been theirs for centuries past.

Fox.

Agnes Miller Parker, 1937

HARVEST SONG

The noise of bells has sunk to rest;
The low grey clouds move softly on.
The land is still as Avalon,
Deep-breathing in its sleep, and blest.

For us the holy corn is spread
Across the quiet, misty dales
Towards the hyacinth hills of Wales,
To give our souls their daily bread.

For us that starling flock took wing,
And, like a silken banner blown,
Across the rippling corn has flown,
To teach our spirits how to sing.

A tiny hedge-bird chirps to me,
And down among the heart's-ease pass
The lowly people of the grass;
They preach to me of charity.

Mary Webb, FIFTY-ONE POEMS

196

'HIDE-AND-SEEK' IN THE STOOKS

While the oat *stooks* slowly dried in summer's warmth, I was fond of playing 'hide-and-seek' with my uncle's Welsh Springer Spaniel, ***Nell***, who briefly features in THE 'LOST' AEROPLANE. Our game often began in the stable-yard, where she had her kennel. I let her sniff a dog biscuit, while my uncle held her

by the collar. After that, I ran to the oat field by a circuitous route and jumped about in its *stubble*, making the widest leaps I could so as to interrupt my scent and make it difficult for ***Nell*** to follow it. My uncle gave me five minutes to run and leap about towards the field's farthest corner. When that time had expired, he blew once on his whistle to announce that he had released ***Nell***, who ran off in search of the denied biscuit. By that time I had found a *stook* of widely spread sheaves in which to conceal myself, with knees under chin and crouching on very spiky *stubble* in thin summer shorts. After several minutes, I spied ***Nell*** eagerly casting

Agnes Miller Parker, 1937

about some distance away, having occasional difficulty in tracing my scent due to my leaps, which confusingly broke the trail for her. Despite my intention she nevertheless came closer and closer to my hiding-place, while I tried to remain motionless, despite my increasing discomfort from the spiky *stubble*.

Just when I was certain that she would discover me, ***Nell*** suddenly turned as if to seek elsewhere. At that precise moment, mistakenly thinking she had missed her quarry, I pressed a knee against one of the sheaves concealing me.

197

Nell acutely heard the rustle of my movement and turned back to investigate. Suddenly the clever little dog was upon me, enthusiastically wagging her short tail at the thrill of finding me, and being given the biscuit that her search deserved.

Pheasant.

Agnes Miller Parker, 1937

My uncle's other sporting dogs, with whom he enjoyed local rough-shooting, were ***Jess***, also a Welsh Springer, and ***Wendy***, a very gentle auburn long-haired Red Setter. They each had a kennel on the dark-blue bricks that formed a pavement along the base of what were then the stables. Some of the diamond-pattern bricks, looking almost as new as when laid in 1910, remain, and stir little memories of happy times.

THE 'UP' NIGHT 'MAIL'

As the evening sun sank towards the sea's horizon, with Ireland beyond, and in the darkness of winter, Aberystwyth's station was the scene of the train's departure. You may ask, did the roof-boards of the brown-and-cream painted carriages each bear the romantic or mysterious destination of VENICE or TASHKENT, MOSCOW or BUDAPEST? Did Tiffany-style pink-shaded lamps stand central upon tables fronted by the windows and flanked by silk curtains in the opulent compartments' interiors? Alas, no! Neither did a smartly uniformed G.W.R. sleeping-car attendant stand on the platform beside the door of what would soon be his somnolent and rolling 'little world', a list of awaited occupants on a clipboard in his gloved hand. Instead, everything had the appearance of the mundane, moments before the departure of a regular and rather dull-looking train.

Nevertheless, the very mention of the 'Mail', as it was colloquially known, gripped a small boy's wild imaginings with a frisson of expectancy each time the name was mentioned. To others this may have seemed inexplicable, given that the train was merely going to Shrewsbury. Moreover, it was not scheduled to stop at stations (perhaps sensuously corrupting fleshpots?) such as Buttington, Breiddin, Plas-y-Court, Westbury, Yockleton and Hanwood Halts. What potential excitement or hazard could possibly present itself on such an utterly prosaic railway journey?

There stood the 'Mail', awaiting the guard's shrill whistle and the purposeful wave of his green flag, signalling that it was now permitted to depart. Attached to the set of 1st and 2nd class carriages was the ROYAL MAIL letter and parcel sorting van. At the head of the train, sturdily steaming quietly to herself, was coupled the 4-6-0 Manor Class locomotive. Her gleaming dark-green paintwork, polished brass-lettered nameplate and chimney ring exemplified her Aberystwyth 'shed's reputation for presenting immaculately prepared locomotives for service. The two who most frequently hauled the 'up' and 'down' 'Mail' train between Aberystwyth and Shrewsbury at this Wartime period were 'Hinton Manor', No. 7819 and 'Compton Manor', No. 7807.

This class of locomotive, being strong for its size and having a relatively short wheelbase for running through tight curves with ease, except for giving a slight 'kick' at the approach to Commins Coch Halt, hauled both passenger and freight trains. Moreover, the Manor engine was fully capable of hauling a heavy train up the 1:56 track gradient at the westerly approach to 'Top Sawyer' David Davies' stupendous rock-cutting at Talerddig. This is about midway between Machynlleth and the now empty site of Moat Lane Junction, the latter having been demolished years ago.

'Torquay Manor', No. 7800 (Swindon-built 1938) displays the elegance of her potential power.

Thus, promptly at 6pm at Aberystwyth's terminus, the guard's flag and whistle having been acknowledged by her driver, either 'Hinton' or 'Compton' Manor's speed regulator was opened for her to begin, with increasing speed, to haul the 'Mail' out into open country. Beyond lies the track beside the River Dovey's estuary, thence to Machynlleth, up the long Llanbrynmair Bank and the even steeper Talerddig one, after whose summit the line either runs level or else gradually falls the remaining miles to Shrewsbury, via Newtown and Welshpool.

Shortly after leaving Aberystwyth the 'Mail' ran the high and curving embankment before Bow Street, a magnificent daytime spectacle for steam train enthusiasts, a plume of white smoke streaming from the locomotive's chimney and the entirety presenting a classic example of 'God's Wonderful Railway' – the G.W.R., hastening into the glorious coastline and mountain scenery of western mid-Wales.

During the eighteenth-century's era of the horse-drawn long-distance Mail coach, that which ran between Aberystwyth and Shrewsbury traversed the rutted and deserted mountain track in the vicinity of Dinas Mawddwy. However, whilst the route might often have appeared deserted to the intrepid occupants of the jolting coach, it frequently concealed the much-feared band of robbers known as the *Gwylliaid Cochion Mawddwy*, the 'Red-haired Brigands of Dinas Mawddwy'. The purses and – if they met with brave but ineffectual resistance from the Mail coach guard's cumbersome blunderbuss – the lives of the occupants also were threatened by those often merciless highwaymen.

When the 'Mail' train halted at Machynlleth, its ROYAL MAIL sorting van was opened to receive the bagfuls of letters and parcels. In addition, and more frequently carried than one might expect, were wads of scruffy, wrapped banknotes destined for pulping. It was the latter commodity that quickened the small boy's vivid imagination, as he pictured it attracting the attention of the *Gwylliaid Cochion Mawddwys'* successors. It was his bizarre notion to imagine the 'Mail' train, halted at Machynlleth, being there especially equipped with a protective posse of armed and official vigilantes, travelling unseen within the ROYAL MAIL sorting van. Mindful of the true tales concerning the eighteenth-century *Gwylliaid Cochion Mawddwy*, the boy, in his fantasy, enjoyed bringing their violent ambushes forward by about a hundred years, so that the drama would now take place on the Aberystwyth to Shrewsbury 'Mail' train, thus:

'Merlin' and 'Earl of Powis', in charge of a heavy train, triumph up the penultimate 1:56 gradient leading into 'Top Sawyer' David Davies' deep Talerddig rock-cutting on 6th August 1938.

Photograph: the late Ifor Higgon
Courtesy: Gwyn Briwnant-Jones

Having left Machynlleth, and about nine miles up the line, the ever-slowing heavy train, as it runs up the long Llanbrynmair Bank after Commins Coch, is suddenly set upon! A horde of the *Gwylliaids'* descendants stream out of the trackside oak woods, brandishing pistols and shrieking to each other in Welsh as they ride bareback on the native, highly-strung breed of mountain stallion, in the style of the fearsome Russian Cossacks. The brigands' loosely aimed bullets ricochet, with a 'Western' film's inimitable whine, off the Manor locomotive's impenetrable boiler, as she 'barks' in valiant tractive effort up the relentless incline. Her regulator handle is fully open, her fireman furiously shovelling coal into the blazing firebox to provide the maximum steam pressure, hopefully to enable the train to outpace its assailants, who relentlessly pursue it – for the soiled banknotes! The doors of the ROYAL MAIL van are swung open for the defending posse within to return gunfire. The exchange lasts for a while, until the combination of superior force from the van and the horses' slowing pace enables the train to gain ground and leave its adversaries far behind.

In reality, of course, this fanciful scenario never occurred. There was no thrilling headline in the Montgomeryshire newspaper announcing 'ARMED ATTACK ON "MAIL" TRAIN BELOW TALERDDIG'. Instead, and as always, its passengers and precious contents were unmolested, the former somnolently lulled into safe travelling contentment by the slow, rhythmical *tick-tick-tick-tick* of the carriages' bogie wheels steadily passing across the rail joints secured by the old-style bolted 'fishplates'. Up and over Talerddig's demanding 1:56 final incline steadily rolled the 'up' 'Mail'. Immediately east lies the bog which nineteenth-century 'Jeremiahs' prophesied would prevent David Davies from traversing it with his Newtown to Machynlleth Railway. His innate engineering skills proved them wrong. 'Top Sawyer' merely diverted the stream that created the Talerddig bog and triumphantly laid his ballast and track across it!

It was at the Long Length rail-over-road Crossing, which interrupts the Newtown to Llanidloes main road, that I, aged upwards of ten, excitedly and often awaited a close, but momentary, acquaintance with the 'up' 'Mail'. That was my best vantage point, in daylight or dusky evening, after a short bicycle ride up Long Length from Maesmawr. There, upon dismounting, I waited with my left cheek pressed hard against the wire mesh of the huge timber-framed Crossing gate that now barred the road against the impending onslaught of iron and steam shortly to thunder over it. An ancient motor car or a wheezing and rattling lorry often drew up at the closed Crossing gates, the driver turned its idling engine off, and in the ensuing total silence, we waited for the locomotive's approaching whistle to Mrs Davies.

The G.W.R. Company's Statutory warning notice, an iron plate fixed to the top of a sturdy wooden post, stood imperiously beside the track, tersely stating that 'NO UNAUTHORISED PERSONS ARE PERMITTED ON THE RAILWAY, BY ORDER'. Although I was well known to Mrs Davies, this Notice forbade her to allow me to stand beside her within the confines of the gates, lest the slipstream suction of the passing train pull me off my feet to disaster. Thus I had to press my cheek against the mesh, in an attempt to get the best possible view of the curving track towards Caersws. The Ideal was frustrated, but it was instantly forgotten as the 'Mail' hove into sight.

'Compton' Manor or 'Hinton' Manor came thundering towards the Crossing, her bright red buffer-plate surmounted by a pair of white-painted paraffin lamps. The locomotive's surging power was accentuated by the thrusting horizontal to-and-fro motion of the piston-slides, which was transferred to the

'Cockington Manor', No. 7806 (Swindon-built 1938) is oiled by her driver, Montgomeryshire County Councillor H.R. Humphreys, J.P., at Aberystwyth 'shed'. Perhaps prior to hauling the 'up' 'Cambrian Coast Express'?

Photograph: Gwyn Briwnant-Jones

huge spoked driving wheels, three each side, by the shining steel connector-bars, as the dark-green polished 'iron-horse' galloped through the road Crossing. As she passed, hauling her obedient carriages, a sudden whiff of scalding steam and hot oil assailed my nostrils, while my ears were assaulted by a cacophony of heavy mechanical movement, metallic ringing and rattling that seemed to shake the ground beneath.

As 'Compton' or 'Hinton' passed in swirling white smoke and steam, I felt a wave of radiated heat from her boiler, as if she was demonstrating the tremendous effort of surmounting Talerddig. My excited wave to the driver and fireman, half-seen through the enveloping smoke, was always returned as the 'Mail' ran onwards to Moat Lane Junction, passing the 'Home' and 'Distant' signals which had earlier nodded consent for her progress.

After the cataclysmic thunder of the Manor, the rhythmical *tick-tick-tick-tick* of the carriage wheels was a leisurely sound, fading into silence as the dependable red tail-lamp on the guard's van was gradually lost to view. As it disappeared, I wondered whether the intrinsic metre of the *ticking* carriage bogies, varying in response to changes in speed, sometimes coincided with the deft posting of letters into the ROYAL MAIL van's 'pigeon-holes' – *tick-tick-tick-tick* to 'Llanfairpwll-this' and 'Llanfairpwll-that' – all destined for dawn delivery onto Wartime doormats, near and far.

I bicycled back to Maesmawr feeling fulfilled by my quest, at least until the next time. Close (but safe) proximity to 'Compton' Manor or 'Hinton' Manor – perhaps even 'Cockington', on occasion – imbued my clothes with a characteristic *scent*. I always tried to make sure that I wore the same the next morning when I was with Walter in the BLACKSTONE'S engine-shed. Then he would say, "Where have you been, Master Michael? Oh, I know – you went to watch the 'Mail' go by!"

Geese.

Agnes Miller Parker, 1937

THE 'LAST' TRAIN
from
MOAT LANE JUNCTION

Many years ago, a famous 'Western' film called 'The Last Train from Gun Hill' was made and released. Its principal character was the law-upholding sheriff, who personified 'Good', the co-principal being the lawless cattle thief who, with his accomplices, represented the 'Bad'. I cannot recall the gripping story's details, but Kirk Douglas was the sheriff and the villain was Anthony Quinn.

The plot of 'The Last Train' concerned the sheriff, who had ridden into town on an earlier train (to Gun Hill) to arrest the 'bad guy' and had only an hour or so to apprehend him before the last train of the day arrived. On the train, the sheriff would take the trouble-maker to face Justice at the County town's assizes, and in this intent, after great suspense for the film-goer, he was successful. The train's engine *whoo-whooed* away from Gun Hill as only 'Western' engines can, the 'bad' guy's chums dead on the platform, shot by the sheriff's accurate deployment of his *mother-of-pearl*-handled revolver.

My taid and my uncle Emrys were both High Sheriff of Montgomeryshire in their day, that being 1911 and 1939 respectively. Their ceremonial dress for that appointment was very splendid, but I do not know whether it included a silver star upon the breast, this being the older and – many would say – much superior equivalent of the 'Western' sheriff's *tin star*. However, of one thing I am certain: that neither my taid nor my uncle Emrys had to take his 12-bore shotgun and dress himself in silver-buttoned black coat, matching velvet knee-breeches, silk stockings and silver-buckled leather moccasins for a desperate encounter with villains at Moat Lane Junction, resulting in the capture of the ringleader to stand trial at Welshpool Assizes.

No: my 'last' train from old Moat Lane was not the last that ran from there to Llandinam, Llanidloes, and thence over the mountains to Rhayader and beyond. The final passenger train on that line ran in 1962, followed by the end of freight traffic in 1975, the latter having been required until then for transporting cement for the Clywedog reservoir dam, which was then being constructed above Llanidloes.

My 'last' train ran in a different direction, along the Shrewsbury to Aberystwyth railway whose stations and halts west of Moat Lane Junction (as was) are Caersws, Pontolgoch, Carno, Llanbrynmair, Commins Coch, Cemmaes Road, and Machynlleth. These comprised the Newtown and Machynlleth Railway, which was built by 'Top Sawyer' David Davies, as I mentioned earlier, and opened on 3rd January 1863. On that day, the first train to carry passenger traffic started from Machynlleth.

My uncle Emrys, High Sheriff of Montgomeryshire in 1939, in the Judge's Procession from Newtown Parish Church to the County Assizes, preceded by the Sheriff's chosen Chaplain, the Reverend Dr. Richard Jones, D.D., of Llandinam.

Courtesy: Ruth Lambert, David Owen Owen

AT THE COURT AT BUCKINGHAM PALACE,

The 9th day of March, 1939.

PRESENT,

THE KING'S MOST EXCELLENT MAJESTY IN COUNCIL.

Sheriffs appointed by His Majesty in Council for the year 1939 :—

WALES.

North and South.

Anglesey	Major Sir George Llewelyn Tapps-Gervis-Meyrick, of Bodorgan, Bt.
Breconshire ..	John Wilfred Rowlands, of 25, Cholmeley Park, Highgate, London, N.6, Esq.
Caernarvonshire ..	John Thomas, of Cefn, Llanengan, Abersoch, and 3, Mollington Road, Wallasey, Cheshire, Esq.
Cardiganshire ..	Col. Bertie Taylor Lloyd, of 20, Great Darkgate Street, Aberystwyth, M.C.
Carmarthenshire ..	David John Thomas, of " Brookhurst," New Road, Llanelly, Esq.
Denbighshire ..	John Lockett, of Maesmor Hall, Maerdy, Corwen, Merioneth, Esq.
Flintshire	Geoffrey Summers, of Cornist Hall, Flint, Esq.
Glamorgan ..	William John Treseder Treseder-Griffin, of Lisvane House, Lisvane, Cardiff, Esq.
Merionethshire ..	Arthur Edward Campbell Lloyd Jones-Lloyd, of Moelygarnedd, Bala, and Newton Cottage, Chester, Esq.
Montgomeryshire ..	Evan Emrys Jones, of Maesmawr, Caersws, Esq.
Pembrokeshire ..	Daniel Daniel, of Ffynone, Boncath, Esq.
Radnorshire ..	Loftus Otway Clarke, of Boultibrooke, Presteign, Esq., C.I.E.

Printed under the authority of HIS MAJESTY'S STATIONERY OFFICE
By HARRISON AND SONS, LTD., London.

(302/19201)T Wt. 8068 20/1 3/39 H & S Ltd. Gp. 392

207

New High Sheriff of Montgomeryshire

Mr. E. Emrys Jones, Maesmawr Hall

Mr. E. Emrys Jones, Maesmawr Hall, Caersws, was on Thursday pricked as the new High Sheriff of Montgomeryshire in succession to Mr. J. Howell Evans.

Mr. Emrys Jones is the son of Mrs. and the late Mr. Edward Jones, a former High Sheriff of the county. A Liberal, he has been mentioned as a possible Independent Liberal candidate for the county. He is keenly interested in agriculture, and is a popular sportsman, being an excellent angler.

An enthusiastic musician, he is a member of the Executive Committee of the County Music Festival, and is treasurer of the Llandinam and District Choral Society, of which he is also an active singing member.

Mr. Emrys Jones was born at Trewythen, Llandinam, in 1897, and received his early schooling at Caersws Council School, from whence he proceeded to the Leys School, Cambridge, for whose rugby XV he played regularly. He was also a member of his school's shooting team for three years in succession. He proceeded to Caius College, Cambridge, from where he enlisted and served for four years in the Royal Army Service Corps in the mechanical transport attached to the London Defence.

He has taken an active part in local government affairs. From 1928 to 1931 he represented Llanwnog on the County Council, and from 1931 has represented Llandinam. He is a member of most of the County Council's committees, and the L.E.A., and is chairman of the Public Assistance Committee. He is also a member of the Newtown and Machynlleth Area Guardians Committee.

He has been a manager and correspondent of Llandinam Grouped School for some years, and also of Caersws Council School. He is an elder of Llandinam Presbyterian Church, a treasurer of the Forward Movement, and a trustee of Montgomery County Recreation Association.

Mr. Emrys Jones is also a vice-president of Caersws Recreation Association, and was chairman of the Boy Scouts Association and treasurer of the Caersws Branch of the L.N.U. He is a director of the Ocean Coal Co. Ltd., and also of Ocean and Wilson's Ltd., London and Cardiff. He is deputy chairman of the Dinam Estates Co.

In 1932 he was made a magistrate for the county, and sits regularly on Caersws Bench.

LLANDINAM

CHAPLAINCY – Mr. Edward Jones, Maesmawr Hall, High Sheriff of Montgomeryshire, has appointed as his chaplain the Reverend Richard Jones, Calvinistic Methodist minister, Llandinam, the chapel attended by Mr David Davies, M.P., and the Plasdinam family.

(1911)

Courtesy:
Powys County Times

AT THE COURT AT BUCKINGHAM PALACE,

The 4th day of March, 1911.

PRESENT,

THE KING'S MOST EXCELLENT MAJESTY
IN COUNCIL.

WALES.

NORTH AND SOUTH.

Anglesey,	Major William Augustus Lane Fox-Pitt, of Presaddfed, Bodedern Valley.
Breconshire,	Roger Jeffreys Powell, of Maespoth, Senny Bridge, Esq.
Cardiganshire,	George Fossett Roberts, of Laura Place, Aberystwyth, Esq.
Carmarthenshire,	Thomas Griffiths, of Glaumor, Burry Port, Esq.
Carnarvonshire,	Thomas Edward Roberts, of Plas-y-Bryn, near Carnarvon, Esq.
Denbighshire,	Alfred Hood, of Strathalyn, Rossett, Esq.
Flintshire,	Arthur Phillips Roberts, of Coed du Park, Mold, Esq.
Glamorganshire,	William James Tatem, of The Court, St. Fagans, Esq.
Merionethshire,	Colonel Lewis Owen Williams, of Borthwnog, Dolgelly.
Montgomeryshire,	Edward Jones, of Maesmawr, Caersws, Esq.
Pembrokeshire,	Evan Davies Jones, of Pentower, Fishguard, Esq.
Radnorshire,	James Lutter Greenway, of Greenway Manor, Nantmel, Esq.

Printed by EYRE and SPOTTISWOODE, Ltd.,
Printers to the King's most Excellent Majesty. 1911.
For His Majesty's Stationery Office.

Appointment as High Sheriff of Montgomeryshire;
Evan Emrys Jones in 1939, and his father Edward Jones in 1911.

Courtesy, respectively: Alex Galloway, Clerk of the Privy Council,
David Owen Owen, my cousin

Two engines drew it, especially for the long and steep ascent up to and through the rock cutting at Talerddig. The twenty-two carriage train was hauled by the locomotives 'Countess Vane' and 'Talerddig', with David Davies and the young Marquess of Blandford riding on the former. The Marquess played '*See the conquering hero comes*' on a cornet, and at Caersws station the train passed under an arch bearing the inscription 'MR DAVIES FOR EVER'. He was then aged forty-five.

Many years later, the train that I now recall from my boyhood left Moat Lane Junction at about 9 o'clock every Saturday night. I especially loved to hear it on dark windy nights, when I had already been tucked up in bed by Gretta, my prayers said, in the orchard bedroom. I heard the engine's long shrill whistle, seemingly twisted on the wind in the several seconds it took to float across the intervening fields. The initially slow and steady *chuff-chuff-chuff* gradually got faster as the train gathered speed and ran the long curve between Moat Lane and

My dearest Gretta from Trefeglwys, Maesmawr's senior housemaid and my nain's beloved personal maid. Photograph 1935. Gretta often pealed the old wall bell calling me to the house from play, and tucked me up in bed each night, her loved 'Master Michael', in the years that followed my mother's death.

Courtesy: Sharlene Jones

the Long Length Crossing. A second whistle warned Mrs Davies, the gatekeeper, of its imminent approach – too late if she, dear soul, had not left her cosy fireside, for the umpteenth time in her many years as custodian, to open and close the gates.

That mighty pair, whose perfect balance enabled their keeper merely to push them with a gentle hand, have long since been replaced by the present ones – functional, but not handsome as their predecessors were. The gate-span of the Long Length rail Crossing is the widest on the entirety of what used to be the Great Western Railway. The pair of gates I remember so well each comprised one huge tapered baulk of Baltic pine, supported by long diagonal bracing and a frame which was clad with metal mesh. At dusk, the large paraffin lamps which stood fixed upon the centre of each gate were lit, their red and green lenses shining forth until dawn was sufficiently advanced for them to be extinguished. All was painted white. The

Receiving the 'token' at Caersws station; a G.W.R. safety device, each being a signal key controlling its own section of single-track railway, preventing head-on collisions.

Courtesy: Gwyn Briwnant-Jones,
his photograph

gates were a magnificent sight.

As 'my' train's distant *chuff-chuff* of departure from Caersws became fainter and finally inaudible, I wonder if I thought about all those on board, that windy Wartime night? Almost certainly not; my boyhood mind was not troubled by Man's inhumanity to Man. If I had then been of mature mind to do so, I would surely have reflected that many of the passengers had husbands, brothers, sons and daughters somewhere far away, serving in the Forces and in potential or real peril. Moreover, many on that train were returning to their homes in lampless streets – the 'blackout', as it was called – some from tedious business meetings perhaps, and others from similarly tedious ration-book shopping in those drab days of austerity.

Thus they dozed or deeply slumbered westwards, on the Great Western's 3rd class cushioned comfort, in dimly lit but cosily warm compartments whose sepia photographs, framed above the upholstered seat-backs – 'The sands at Porthcawl', 'Low tide at Tenby', 'Caernarfon Castle' and other delightful views of Wales – reminded their occupants of happy pre-War days. Central between the photographs were, on one side of the compartment, a mirror, and on the other, a map of the entire Great Western Railway System, an original copy of which I possess. All the routes are shown in scarlet lines of three widths, thick, medium and thin, indicating principal, secondary and minor lines respectively. Every station and halt, including those on freight branches, is marked and named; the Welsh coastline is outlined by a thin blue line, and St. George's Channel (the Irish Sea), and the English and Bristol Channels are in pale blue.

At the rear of 'my' train, in his van, gently swayed the guard, his red and green hand-flags furled for the night beneath the flap of a capacious leather

Gleaming dark green and polished brass 'Bradley Manor', No. 7802 (Swindon-built 1938) has just descended the long Llanbrynmair Bank, and runs her afternoon 'Cambrian Coast Express' towards Commins Coch Halt, bound for the Aberystwyth terminus. Note track gangers' sturdy shelter, with chimney for winter-warming fire and essential tea kettle!

Photograph: the late D.S. Fish
Executors are sought

shoulder-bag of the kind that railway guards of that era never seemed to be without. Weary, but still keenly alert, as was required of him whilst on duty, he sat, a long day to-and-from Shrewsbury nearing its welcomed end, the newspaper's crossword studied yet again. When his train – for it was HIS, officially – halted at each station, he alighted onto the dark platform. No glimmer of lamp or light – the 'blackout' regulations were all-inclusive – showed along its length. When all was clear and the doors were closed, excepting that of the guard's van, he shone the green lens of his paraffin hand-lamp towards the driver awaiting the signal. The driver acknowledged it with a short *toot*, and then could be heard the sound of the engine's straining power – *CHUFF-chuff-CHUFF-chuff* – as the train drew away into the enveloping darkness. Those few passengers who had alighted were by then also gone into the night; none therefore saw their train's tail lamp glow brightly red by its unfailing paraffin flame, none heard the characteristic and clear *ting-ting* ring from the signal-box, nor saw its sole occupant, in the yellow lamp-glow, grasp a signal-lever handle with a cloth, lest moist hands rust any amongst their gleaming row.

Long after 'my' train had left Caersws, Mrs Davies-the-Crossing had brewed herself some strong tea to dispel sleep for many hours to come, for on some nights she had to stay awake until after midnight, when she opened the gates for an occasional 'Saltney Goods' train to rumble past. These freight trains were shrouded in Official secrecy, but were believed to carry munitions from the marshalling yards at Llandeilo to Saltney, on the outskirts of Chester. Their long procession of creaking and squeaking trucks never disturbed my slumber. Lying warmly awake, and by kind fortune safe in that Wartime night, I was lulled by Maesmawr's hooting owls and the sighing of a lessening wind, and – whispering *'chuff-chuff'* in soft reply – I fell contentedly to sleep.

THE MOUNTAIN TREE

Montgomery's hills are deeply brown,
In Merioneth the sun goes down,
And all along the Land of Lleyn
The spate of night flows darkly in.

Come away to the mountain tree!
Cinnabar-red with fruit is she.
We'll watch the stars, like silver bees,
Fly to their hive beyond the seas.

Mary Webb, FIFTY-ONE POEMS

THE STEAM LORRY

One day each week, this mechanical 'Leviathan' *chugged* past the top of Maesmawr's Drive. I never knew where it had come from, nor where it was going, but it was always heading in the direction of Newtown – and perhaps far beyond? They were built at Shrewsbury in great numbers and before that at Glasgow, as the following, 'A Short History of SENTINEL Waggons', explains. (SENTINEL always used two g's in Waggon.)

Seven thousand, one hundred and forty of these 'giants of the road' were built and registered between 1906 and 1930. They were ordered from, and exported to, all parts of the world, in addition to the many that 'stayed at home', contentedly trundling around the British Isles.

The original 'Standard SENTINEL' engine design, and the 'Super SENTINEL' engine which followed in later years, were incorporated into a wide range of alternative bodies. These were:

Typical example of the weekly SENTINEL STD steam lorry. Note chimney through the cab's roof, chain-drive to one pair of wheels, solid rubber tyres, no side glass or windscreen (!), but prominent pair of acetylene gas lamps.

Courtesy: Anthony R. Thomas

Model:

STD. . . . *Standard Waggon*
SUP. . . . *Super-Sentinel Waggon*
T. . . . *Super-Sentinel Single-Geared Tractor*
TDG. . . . *Super-Sentinel Double-Geared Tractor*
PORT. . . . *Portable Engine and Boiler*
Type:
6T. . . . *6 Ton Flat or Sided Waggon*
5T/3WT. . . . *5 Ton Three-Way Tipping Waggon*
6W. . . . *6 Wheeled Super-Sentinel*
/T. . . . *Tipping Waggon*
/ET. . . . *End Tipping Waggon*
/P. . . . *Fitted with Pneumatic Tyres*

I have especially chosen to illustrate the Standard SENTINEL 6T because it is the model that most closely resembles the lorry that I remember made its weekly journey past Maesmawr. The fact that the illustrated one was based in Liverpool is irrelevant to my recall of over sixty years ago, but the photograph's clarity shows the marque's salient features, which I glimpsed as they rushed past me and disappeared. These include the windowless cabin with the central chimney within it which passes up through the roof, the underneath portion of the steam-boiler, the chain-drive to one rear wheel, the solid rubber tyres, and the large pair of acetylene gas front lamps. All these, and other features too, were compounded as the SENTINEL trundled past the waving small boy excitedly waiting for it by the Lodge gates. I can still clearly picture the sooty faces of the driver and his mate, the whites of their eyes peering down at me from the high cab, the oily whirr of the chain-drive, the black smoke drifting from the chimney, the rumble and rattle that accompanied the machine as it sped on around the Dôl-Hafren bend, the mighty clamour dying to silence as it disappeared from sight.

A Short History of Sentinel Waggons

The first Sentinel steam waggon was built by Alley & McLellan Ltd of Glasgow in 1905. They had made ships engines, hoists and steering gear for 30 years but wanted to expand their range and get into a new market. Up to 1901 heavy loads had been carried by traction engines towing trailers and lighter loads by horse and dray. The new legislation allowed light steam waggons which would carry their load on their own chassis. Many new manufacturers emerged but Sentinel was to prove the most successful.

The success was mainly due to the unique boiler design and the robust construction, patented by Stephen Alley the son of the company's founder. In 1915 war work caused the Glasgow works to be desperately short of space and a new steam waggon factory was built in

215

Shrewsbury in only 9 months. In 1918 Stephen Alley sold all his shares in Alley & McLellan Ltd and bought the whole Shrewsbury concern setting it up as a new company.

These early waggons were later to be known as Standard Sentinels. The boiler was mounted vertically at the front and consisted of an inner and outer shell forming a water jacket. Criss-crossed within the inner shell were 48 tubes, so the flames went round the tubes which carried the water. This made a very lightweight but highly efficient steam producer. It was totally opposite to conventional horizontal boilers used on traction engines and locomotives, where the fire goes through the tubes surrounded by the water, which design was used by competitors such as Foden. On the Sentinel, the fire grate was at the bottom and the chimney at the top which carried away the hot gases. The coal was kept in bunkers behind the driver and mate, who were seated either side of the boiler. There was a lid in the top of the boiler which enabled the mate to stoke the fire through an open area down the centre, so that coal could drop

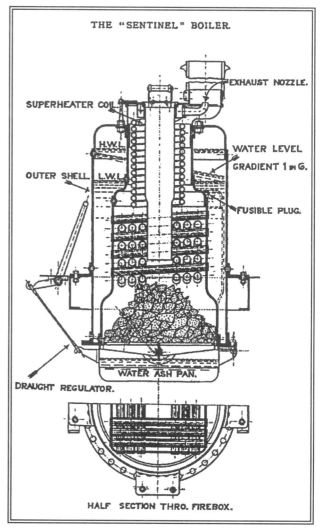

THE "SENTINEL" BOILER.

EXHAUST NOZZLE.

SUPERHEATER COIL

H.W.L.

WATER LEVEL
GRADIENT 1 in 6.

OUTER SHELL L.W.L

FUSIBLE PLUG.

WATER ASH PAN.

DRAUGHT REGULATOR.

HALF SECTION THRO. FIREBOX.

Half-section through the SENTINEL STD boiler. Coal was kept behind the driver's 'mate', who dropped pieces of it down the central tube in front of him, after removal of the 'lift-off' lid! Note water-filled pan cooling spent ash. On all operational routes it was essential to know where top-up water was readily available –last resorts being horses' drinking troughs and even roadside ditches.

Courtesy: Anthony R. Thomas

into the fire. Below the fire was an ash pan filled with water to keep it cool. Water was kept in a large tank under the chassis at the back of the waggon and pumped into the boiler by an engine-mounted pump.

Unlike all traction engines, and the Foden engine, where the cylinders and cranks were mounted on top of the boiler, the Sentinel had a self-contained two-cylinder double-acting engine mounted under the chassis behind the driver's cab. This could be assembled on a bench and fitted later to the waggon. The back axle had a differential gear with a chain drive from one end of the crankshaft.

All these features made a light vehicle with maximum load-carrying capacity on the flat platform at the rear. Several manufacturers later tried to copy these ideas, including Foden, but with much less success.

By 1923 many steam waggon builders had ceased production, leaving a handful of makers of which Sentinel and Foden were the main contenders. Stephen Alley expanded production by reorganising the factory into flow line methods to produce the new 'Super-Sentinel' waggon which had a unique differential built into the engine crankshaft, again a Stephen Alley patent. Weight was saved wherever possible to increase the legal load capacity from 6 tons to 7 tons.

This enabled Sentinel at least to 'buck the trend' away from steam to the new petrol lorries. Sentinel produced over 600 Super-Sentinels at their peak in 1924. However, by 1927, the year they produced their new DG, double-geared, Super-Sentinel model, production was down to 400. They had made tipping waggons from the early days and also 28 other body styles, but they made their first rigid six-wheeled waggon with the DG6 and later a world first DG8 eight-wheeler with four wheel steering.

The Road Traffic Act of 1930 limited the axle weight which penalised steam vehicles due to the extra weight of the boiler, coal and water. It also limited top speed to 12 mph on solid tyres but allowed 16 mph on pneumatics. In 1931 Sentinels came out with a new lightweight DG on pneumatic tyres. Many owners of earlier Supers also had them converted to pneumatics to take advantage of the higher speed. Some owners however did not and a few were still around in the years just before the War.

Sentinel's last effort was a very light-weight waggon introduced in 1933 called the 'S' type which stood for shaft-drive. This had a completely new engine which had four-cylinders and single-acting, with a two speed gearbox and shaft drive to the rear axle, very similar to the modern petrol engined lorries of the day, and still considered the most advanced steam waggon ever built. Again, four, six and eight-wheeled versions were made in flat, sided and tipper bodies or tankers and tar sprayers.

Foden made their last steam waggon in 1935, after which they went over to petrol or diesel, but the S type Sentinel was built up to 1938 when War work took over, having produced only 400 in the five years of production.

In 1951 they produced a batch of 100 S6 tipper steam waggons for the Argentine Coal Board and one to try and interest the British Coal Board. These were the last commercially-built steam waggons anywhere in the world. The boiler in these waggons was to the same basic design as the first waggon built 45 years earlier.

A RIDE ON THE DEAN 'GOODS' FOOTPLATE

Evan had a good friend, a Mr Corfield, who lived in a cottage just across the river bridge from Caersws, and was a train guard on the Great Western Railway at Moat Lane Junction, the familiar old station from which, at Maesmawr, were pleasantly heard the brief shrill whistles of shunting engines, or the longer purposeful ones of express trains departing to Aberystwyth or Shrewsbury. It was, even then, strictly forbidden for any unauthorised person to ride an engine's footplate. Nevertheless, kindly Mr Corfield intended to give Evan's young friend the treat of a lifetime. The guard must have persuaded or – more likely in the circumstances – had the willing co-operation of the engine driver to facilitate the unofficial venture.

I must have walked roughly a mile from Maesmawr, up Long Length – empty of cars and lorries, as usual – to the railway Crossing and thence down the lane to the Junction. On my way, I passed the Llandinam and Caersws Home Guards' headquarters, a black corrugated iron *Nissen* hut squeezed into the narrow apex of a field immediately adjacent to one of the mighty rail-Crossing gates. Only the brick base of the old hut remains today. Within its summer-stifling heat and icy winter cold – perhaps in the latter a coke-fuelled stove was lit? – my uncle Emrys, as the Contingent's Commanding Officer, planned the locality's defence strategy in the event of a German invasion. I include a photograph of the Llandinam and

The Llandinam & Caersws 'Home Guard' platoon in 1942. Its Commanding Officer was my uncle Emrys, seated centre.

Courtesy: Jeremy Pryce

Caersws 'Dad's Army' of Yesteryear in which fifty-two men and two women are present. The latters' role in such a potential crisis is worthy of speculation – even now, after an interim of sixty-three years. The *Nissen* headquarters could not possibly have contained fifty-four people, even if, like wrens in extreme cold, they all crammed into the *Nissen* 'nest' for my uncle's orders prior to frosty night exercises in the surrounding fields. There must have been a descending chain of command commencing with my uncle, as C.O., down to sergeants and corporals who ordered the plentiful privates to do 'this-and-that'.

At Moat Lane Junction, I was met by Mr Corfield, who introduced me to the jovial engine-driver and his similarly cheery fireman. They told me that there were some coal-trucks in the Newtown goods railway sidings, full of OCEAN coal that had to be brought back to the local coal-merchant's yard – that was why their DEAN engine was going down, alone, to pull them back. I must, as a matter of interest, mention that OCEAN coal, which was subsequently renamed OCEAN & WILSON'S, was one of the vast coal-mining projects founded by 'Top Sawyer' David Davies. My uncle Emrys was a director of OCEAN & WILSON'S.

DEAN 'Goods' engine shunting at Moat Lane Junction in both their heydays; almost certainly the one that took me down to Newtown.

Photographer: the late Stanhope Baker
Courtesy: Gwyn Briwnant-Jones

One *toot-toot* and we were off, quickly gathering speed down the curving single track and beneath the little lane bridge leading up to Bron-felin, which **Dandy**, Evan and I had crossed with our load of logs. On we sped towards old Penstrowed and under the bridge that carried the main road from Newtown where, on the Caersws side of the bridge, I had met aunt Bess in her chauffeured Rolls-Royce.

As the engine only had herself and a coal-tender to propel, she swung about down the track, without the restraint of any burdensome trucks. The return journey with the loaded OCEAN coal-trucks would have been more stable. In an attempt to hang on – although I was in any case prevented from falling down by being partly protected between the burly engine-driver and his strong-shouldered, coal-shovelling fireman – I grasped the iron safety-bar lowered across the steps which gave access to the footplate from the platform and trackside. With this to hang on to, and helped by the sandwiching support of the two-man crew, I felt less likely suddenly to disappear through the narrow gap between engine cab and coal-tender into the blurred haze of trackside vegetation, wooden fence-posts and the occasional white-painted gradient indicator that rushed past.

After some while, the driver settled his well-endowed posterior, clad in dark blue oil-bespattered dungarees, on a tiny (for him) wooden seat hinged to the cab, which, when needed, folded down for use in similar fashion to a church misericord. Thus seated, and in a position to peer through one of a pair of little round glass portholes either side of the engine's tubby and grimy boiler, he relaxed, safely grasping the regulator's handle to control our speed towards Newtown. The diagonally disposed regulator handle was surrounded, on the cab's front panel and between the porthole windows, by a seemingly haphazard array of copper pipes of several sizes, some of which were connected to circular, glass-fronted dials with needle pointers to black numerals, not dissimilar to those in the BLACKSTONE'S battery-room at Maesmawr. One small copper pipe led to a bracket-mounted square jar of toughened glass in which the water level was measured against a set of calibrations for some purpose or other.

The fireman, meanwhile, suddenly operated a lever that opened a hefty pair of iron fire-box doors which slid apart from each other in grooves, top and bottom, about nine inches above the footplate. The ferocious glow of the flaming coals within was akin to the mouth of Hell, as typically depicted in mediaeval 'Doom' paintings.

Satisfied that his 'Hades' did not need immediate replenishment from the huge stack of coal in the tender behind him, the fireman levered the doors closed again. This induced the instant return of the chilly draught which rushed around within the cab and also around a pair of young knees, rather unsuitably clad in short trousers for such an exhilarating ride.

In due course, the red and white painted bar of Newtown's 'Home' signal hove into view with an affirming nod, whilst the 'Distant' signal, with its 'bird's-mouthed' bar of black and yellow, remained horizontal on their shared and lofty trackside gantry. My thrilling but tantalisingly short trip neared its end. In some anxiety lest G.W.R. authority should chance to see a bare-kneed boy on the footplate, the driver began to close the DEAN'S regulator a mile before Newtown station, and we came to an intentional halt at an unattended and minor crossing, enclosed by a pair of field gates. From there, a little lane ran towards and met the main road into Newtown. Today, a housing estate engulfs it, a few hundred yards west of the fire-station. At the crossing, the engine-driver and his mate bade me "Goodbye" as they helped me down the steep iron steps from the foot-plate to *terra firma*. I never saw them again, but I have never forgotten the treat of a lifetime they gave me.

I cannot remember how I got back to Maesmawr, but surely not by walking the four miles on the main road? I believe that my uncle Emrys must have met me in the old Vauxhall car, having previously ascertained from Mr Corfield how long the engine ride from Moat Lane would take. It is equally likely that he had secretly contrived with Evan and guard Corfield to obtain the ride for me. It was just the sort of school-holiday surprise they would arrange. Moreover, Mr Corfield was a member of the Llandinam and Caersws Home Guard and, as I have already mentioned, my uncle was its Commanding Officer. A case of 'wheels-within-wheels'!

Weasel.

Agnes Miller Parker, 1937

221

ST. JOHN, CHAPTER XIV, VERSES 1-18

I never enquired of my beloved nain why she chose these verses for me to learn by heart, but she remained gently persistent in her frequent and quiet requests that I recite them to her, at least as far as I had committed them to memory. A favourite moment of hers for asking to hear my little task was when we drove by motor car to attend Sunday morning service at Llandinam's Presbyterian Church, or as she and I strolled beside the tall hazel hedge that ran closely parallel to the raised agger of the old Roman Road in the pasture immediately east of Maesmawr's stable block, as it was then. Nuts grew plentifully in the hedge, and seemingly there were no squirrels, not even the delightful Red ones, to steal them. The fun was to find 'sixers' – a cluster of six ripening nuts on one stalk. As my nain strolled on, wearing – if it was wet underfoot – rubber overshoes called *galoshes* to protect her Edwardian indoor shoes, her little and rather stout pet Camarthenshire corgi, **Peggy**, waddled in front and showed the way. I lagged some yards behind, hoping to delay or postpone Nain's asking to "hear John Fourteen". A prosaic indoor place to render my recitation was the dairy, when turning the handle of

Red Squirrels.   Agnes Miller Parker, 1946

222

the milk-separator. Nain would occasionally enter to inspect the cream or fetch some eggs, and she would once again say in that lovely voice of hers: "Dearest, I'd like to hear St. John."

Looking back now, across the intervening sixty-two years, I know that she desired to instil in my young mind these words of New Testament comfort and reassurance following the recent death of my mother, her adored eldest daughter. St. John's writing in this chapter is of great solace, commencing with verse 1: '*Let not your heart be troubled, nor let it be afraid* …' and continuing to verse 18: '*I will not leave you desolate; I will come unto you.*' I progressed well with memorising it until I reached verse 8, where I always tripped up at this 'tongue-twister': '*Philip saith unto Him, Lord, show us the Father and it sufficeth us.*' After that verbal hurdle, I could never recover my composure to recite further verses without apprehension, and the nearer I got to the dreaded *sufficeth us*, the more certain I became that it lay in wait – which of course it always did.

I know to this day that my nain wished me to learn up to and including '*I will not leave you desolate; I will come unto you.*' Even if I never reached that verse confident of its recitation – and I don't think I ever did – nevertheless I knew in my innermost heart the certainty of never feeling desolate for as long as I remained with her at our beloved Maesmawr.

HAZEL BUDS

Now breaks the sheath and spreads the leaf!
The banks beneath, the branch above,
Are set with nests, are homes of love.
So good-bye, grief!

With restful haste and gentle strife
Pink hazel stipules are unfurled,
Pink dawns are flung across the world.
So welcome, life!

Mary Webb, FIFTY-ONE POEMS

LLANDINAM PRESBYTERIAN CHURCH

A kindly stonemason, whom I recently found repairing the Church's roadside wall after a passing lorry had careered through the pavement railings, offered me the vestry key. Outwardly the Church could, with some justification, be described as a little – or perhaps very – intimidating, depending on aesthetic taste. The editor of the book *Powys*, from the series *The Buildings of Wales*, says of its exterior: 'Ornate in an idiosyncratic 14th century style by Szlumper and Aldwinkle'. Mr Szlumper, or his architect partner – perhaps both – designed an inspired interior, even if the exterior did not meet the same standard. Such is the former's quality that *Powys* calls it 'fine', a commendation that I heartily endorse.

Llandinam's Presbyterian Church today; scene of many Sundays' hymn singing, and my family's joys and sorrows across the years.

Photograph: Ellis-Jones

In my frequent visits there during my boyhood, the minister Dr. Richard Jones' scholarly sermons ensured that no inattentive worshipper lay 'szlumped' asleep in a pew's furthest corner! During the entirety of Dr. Jones' Llandinam ministry, from 1907 to 1947, he, his wife Violet and their family lived at Penybryn, at the end of a steep driveway behind the church, and screened from it by mature trees. During my recent visit, I glimpsed some modern residential development beyond the trees, suggesting perhaps that Penybryn's former large garden had been encroached upon? When I was a pupil at Gordonstoun, a number of boys, myself amongst them, were billeted upon the Doctor and Violet for several terms. As one of the terms was in deepest wintertime, we were kindly met after our nightly walk from Plas Dinam to Penybryn, which was just over a mile, with steaming mugs of *Ovaltine*.

Provided with the vestry key, I entered a vast and reverberant room. During the Victorian and Edwardian eras, this had primarily served as the venue for Sunday School; large numbers of children from the surrounding countryside attended this mandatory gathering every week, almost without exception. The Maesmawr family's attendance at the Sunday morning service was also mandatory, and the party included whoever was staying, be they family or friends. My nain imposed this rule with gentle benignity upon both the young and the not-so-young. As I loved singing hymns, I didn't mind too much being deprived of the enjoyable pottering about amongst the farm buildings and on the river bank which I would otherwise be doing. Where better than amongst a Welsh congregation to sing the great Welsh hymn melodies: *Gwalia, Hyfrydol, Aberystwyth, Ebenezer* and *Talyllyn*? Their instinctive gift for harmony and adorning the melody enabled many there to sing without stave music.

The Maesmawr party always arrived in good time for the Sunday morning service, my uncle Emrys driving the elderly black Vauxhall motor car, and those staying at Maesmawr following in their own cars for the short journey of about ten minutes. My nain sat in the Vauxhall's front passenger seat and her companion Gwen and I sat in the back seat. Unknown to Nain, but watched with amusement by Gwen, I often spent the journey examining and counting the several varieties of 'fruit' which generously filled the dished crown of her Sunday-best hat in front of me. The 'fruit' was protected from the potential assaults of imaginary blackbirds by a circular piece of finely meshed millinery net extending to the rim of the hat. Nain possessed a wide variety of Sunday hats, almost as wide as the variety of imitation cherries, elderberries, blackberries and strawberries which clustered on those deemed appropriate for summer and autumn Sunday wear. During the brief car journey its interior quickly became imbued with the astringent scent of camphor-oil, which wafted from both Nain's and Gwen's long coats, the residue of the crystalline mothballs which were kept in clothes cupboards to keep destructive moths away. The sugar-cube sized deterrent had a second unintended but effective use: to clear the heads of singers, in much the same way as did a nasal inhaler called *Benzadrine*, which was then available from any chemist's shop. By the time we arrived at the Church, our clear noses and vocal chords were in fine fettle for W. Williams' mighty hymn: '***Guide me, O Thou great Redeemer, Pilgrim through this barren land***', sung to the melody *Cwm Rhondda*.

The old Vauxhall was parked beside the church, in the narrow lane that leads to Penybryn, and my uncle scurried to the vestry, there to attend to whatever matter of church business had arisen during the previous week. The service began promptly at 10 o'clock. In the ten minutes before it started, Nain, Gwen and I walked around to the Gothic-style arched doorway that led into the Church. There we greeted members of the family, friends and acquaintances, with a perfunctory kiss on the cheek or a brief handshake. Seldom absent were my aunts Gwendoline and Margaret Davies. They came the five or so miles from

225

Gregynog, cruising through the narrow lanes in their black Daimler, driven by their chauffeur Walters, who awaited the service's conclusion and then drove them home again.

The Maesmawr pew was in the Church's west transept wing, directly opposite the fine pipe organ built by Connacher of Huddersfield in 1908, which was a gift from Gwendoline and Margaret's father, Edward Davies, the son of 'Top Sawyer'. (I mentioned all of them at the outset of these Recollections.) Prior to purchasing Gregynog from their brother David (later 1st Baron Davies) in 1924, the sisters lived with him at Plas Dinam, the family home on the east flank of Llandinam. Whilst there, Gwendoline regularly played the Connacher organ for services; and at home she played her violin, which was a Stradivarius named the 'Parke'. The Gregynog pew was in the east transept, which – perish the thought! – was within a small boy's easy call or waving distance from ours, if one had dared! The organ console was entirely hidden from the majority of the congregation by a crimson curtain, hung with brass rings from a brass rail. Nevertheless, the organist had a clear view of the minister, perched aloft in the cushioned comfort of his pulpit.

In my boyhood the organist was Mrs Benbow, whose playing was much admired. She slowly rode to the Church upon a high and old-fashioned lady's bicycle whose rear-wheel spokes were effectively prevented from ensnaring her long skirt and coat by means of a series of taut cords stretched fanwise from the central hub to fixings along the curved edge of the mudguard. Incidentally, someone told me long ago that the Connacher organ's wind-chest was water-powered. If that was true, Mrs Benbow's playing of Johann Sebastian Bach's great Chorale-Prelude *Wasserflüssen Babylon* would have had great poignancy!

Dr. Richard Jones was blessed with a fresh rose-pink-cheeked complexion, even at the age of seventy-two. He had snow-white hair and wore the blackest of black clerical attire, with a matching waistcoat whose lower pocket snugly held a gold watch, its chain hanging from the top buttonhole. When he was about to listen to, or to expound on, some serious or deep matter, Dr. Jones had the quaint habit of pursing his lips into a little 'rosebud', which he then pressed gently with the tip of his index finger.

His scholarly Sunday sermons and formal addresses made to Montgomeryshire assemblies and groups were eagerly heard, especially when the gathering was of his religious *Persuasion*. Capacity congregations and audiences were delighted by his erudite wisdom, to which he frequently added more than a modicum of theatrical *gravitas*, which enabled him to enrich his theme in the great Tradition of Welsh preachers. Every so often, Dr. Jones would give a special short address of gentler hue for "the young amongst us" – the young, of course, including myself, dressed in my Sunday-best of creaseless cream cotton shirt and tie, grey flannel short trousers, white ankle-socks, well-polished shoes and neatly brushed hair.

The preacher, be it Dr. Jones or a visiting minister, addressed his congregation from the elevated pulpit that stands centrally against the Church's far wall. The pulpit is ornately made of polished mahogany, and fitted with a little door in its waist-high side reached by a short flight of wooden and carpeted steps. These rise from within a raised platform one step above floor-level, which is enclosed by a balustered handrail. The area within it is called, in Welsh, the *set fawr*, the 'Big Seat'. Nowadays the *set fawr* is an historically surviving feature from before the 1689 Act of Toleration, which freed Nonconformists from the previous State-supported repression and persecution of their chosen form of worship. During that period of frequent harassment, Nonconformists often held their worship clandestinely in remote farmsteads and barns. Nevertheless, even there the preacher – often an itinerant 'field-preacher' – was potentially exposed to threats or much worse from local mobs. Protection from abuse, threats or attack was provided by a group of the strongest available men-folk, whose physique matched their faith, or more so! These stalwarts sat in a protective semi-circle, the *set fawr*, around the preacher's central rostrum, which was perhaps no more than a mound of trodden hay or straw.

When the congregation had settled themselves and an expectant silence had fallen, the vestry door quickly opened to reveal Dr. Jones, or his visitor, who ascended the pulpit steps in stately fashion. After silently closing its little door, he settled himself upon the ample cushions, surveying all from his 'eyrie', whilst the soft strains of the introductory organ voluntary were concluded and gently died away. During its final bars, my uncle Emrys silently emerged through the vestry door and crept to his accustomed seat close by the organ console's crimson curtain. He sang beautifully and preferred doing so there, with several tenor and bass colleagues, rather than with us in the Maesmawr pew directly opposite. His reason was probably to distance himself from Gwen's rather overt vibrato upon the alto clef, to which she was apt to give voice when singing the most soulful or emotionally-infused hymns.

One of my favourite hymns was Bishop Heber's '***Holy, Holy, Holy, Lord God Almighty! Early in the morning our song shall rise to Thee*** …' As the ten o'clock service often opened with it, its timing was, by accident or design, most suitable. The second verse similarly begins: '***Holy, Holy, Holy***', and continues with: '***All the Saints adore Thee, Casting down their golden crowns around the glassy sea.***' That phrase, '***Casting down their golden crowns***', imbued my boyhood mind with some deep, yet at the time wholly intangible, imaginings of aesthetic beauty.

In later years I happened upon William Blake's ethereal paintings of '*The Sons of the Morning*' from '***Job***', which the composer Ralph Vaughan Williams magnificently set to music between 1927 and 1930. Both in those and in other depictions by Blake of winged, diaphanously-robed angelic figures praising God in a star-spangled Firmament, my boyhood's intangible imaginings were made manifest.

227

Those paintings gave pictorial substance to Bishop Heber's Saints '***Casting down their golden crowns upon the glassy sea***', that most beautifully, yet spiritually, enigmatic vision which had touched my boy's heart at a time of personal grief.

So, having been let in by the stonemason, for the first time in sixty years I sat alone in Llandinam's Presbyterian Church, immersed in its elegant spaciousness whilst a flood of autumn sunlight illumined its walls and handsome pews, unchanged by Time. Much water has passed under my 'Bridge of Time' during those years – an often 'turbulent river' too, in many ways. Musing there in my own inner silence, whilst sitting in the old Maesmawr pew, the outer silence often broken by the passing roar of road traffic, I emotionally saw everything as it had been long ago. There was, still, the now empty little brass card-frame at our pew's entrance. Its white insert had said MAESMAWR HALL. There I had sat, tucked close to my beloved nain, on the long pew cushion which still remained. There I had sung, with piping treble, beside Gwen with her soulful vibrato, about Saints with golden crowns and a glassy sea. There, behind that very crimson curtain, had pedalled Mrs Benbow, finger-substituting a perfect legato upon the three manuals' ivory keys.

For a while I stood at the spot in front of the high pulpit where once had come so many members of my family; those with joy in their hearts upon marriage, and those with sorrow and Hope around a departed one who, for a last hour, was still amongst them. There had taken place my mother and father's wedding in 1927, and those of her younger sisters Megan and Mari in 1928 and 1937 respectively, and my taid's funeral in 1937. My mother Beryl and her sisters were all married from Maesmawr, their home from childhood. My mother's funeral service in 1942 and her mother's, my nain's, in 1947, were both held privately in the old Hall at Maesmawr.

Dr. Richard Jones, M.A., D.D., had officiated at them all, except, sadly, at Emrys' funeral in the Presbyterian Church, for he died five months before Emrys, in July 1947. Thus both sad ceremonies were held where they had so devotedly served and worshipped for many years. The epitaph on Richard and Violet Jones' grave in St. Llonio's Parish Churchyard at Llandinam, where many of my family are buried, reads: '***A man shall be as an hiding place from the wind – as the shadow of a great rock in a weary land***'. [Isaiah Ch.32, v.2] He was surely that man to many at Llandinam, including my Maesmawr family and myself when I was a little boy. We were all blessed to shelter in his great kindness and his warm humanity.

I thanked God for my maternal family's love of me and for my love of them, in which I include all those dear friends at Maesmawr remembered in these Recollections. Returning the vestry key to the helpful stonemason, I bade him a grateful goodbye and drove contentedly away.

FAMILY EPITAPHS, ST. LLONIO'S CHURCH, LLANDINAM

M. E-J

In Abiding Memory of
ELIZABETH BERYL

my Mother
on the

Centenary of her Birth
30ᵗʰ April 1898–1998

Rev. **EVAN JONES**
Brynhafren
Born February 2ⁿᵈ 1808
Died February 14ᵗʰ 1897
'The memory of the
just is blessed'

EDWARD JONES OF MAESMAWR HALL
November 12ᵗʰ 1854 – June 19ᵗʰ 1937
'Dyrchafaf fy llygaid i'r mynyddoedd,
o'r lle y daw fynghymhorth'
('I will lift up mine eyes unto the hills,
from whence cometh my help')

ELIZABETH BERYL *(my Mother)*
April 30ᵗʰ 1898 – December 1ˢᵗ 1942
'Life is Eternal and Love is Immortal'

MARY ELLEN JONES OF MAESMAWR HALL
February 26ᵗʰ 1863 – April 10ᵗʰ 1947
'Great in her heart and lovely in her ways,
and in her mind replete with beauteous things'

EVAN EMRYS JONES OF MAESMAWR HALL
March 10ᵗʰ 1897 – December 4ᵗʰ 1947
'Full in the face of heaven upon these hills
He died; nature's true lover, of His kind
Beloved as loving,
And by the sighing of the mountain wind
He soundly sleeps'

They are all gone into the world of light!
And I alone sit ling'ring here;
Their very memory is fair and bright,
And my sad thoughts doth clear.
Henry Vaughan (1621–1695)

'WHITHER MUST I WANDER?'

Home no more home to me, whither must I wander?
Hunger my driver, I go where I must.
Cold blows the winter wind over hill and heather;
Thick drives the rain, and my roof is in the dust.
Loved of wise men was the shade of my roof-tree,
The true word of welcome was spoken in the door –
Dear days of old, with the faces in the firelight,
Kind folks of old, you come again no more.

Home was home then, my dear, full of kindly faces,
Home was home then, my dear, happy for the child.
Fire and the windows bright glittered on the moorland;
Song, tuneful song, built a palace in the wild.
Now, when day dawns on the brow of the moorland,
Lone stands the house, and the chimney stone is cold.
Lone let it stand, now the friends are all departed,
The kind hearts, the true hearts, that loved the place of old.

Spring shall come, come again, calling up the moorfowl,
Spring shall bring the sun and rain, bring the bees and flowers;
Red shall the heather bloom over hill and valley,
Soft flow the stream through the even-flowing hours;
Fair the day shine as it shone on my childhood –
Fair shine the day on the house with open door;
Birds come and cry there and twitter in the chimney –
But I go for ever and come again no more.

from: SONGS OF TRAVEL,
Robert Louis Stevenson (1850–1894)

Yet shall I come again;
And ever stay.
M. E-J

231

JOY

'The spring of joy! The spring of joy! I have not found it.'
So my soul questioned and complained each day.
I asked the singing thrushes where it lay;
They cried — 'We never built or sang around it.'
I questioned of a harper, passing by
To a festival;
He said — 'I know of no such spring at all.'
This my soul heard, and wept most bitterly.
We wandered hand in hand
By many towns and hamlets, weary-hearted:
For those we questioned could not understand,
Or else they smiled in silence, and departed.
But, when the sun
Had left us in the dusk, mysteriously
Came One,
Who stood and called my weeping soul, and she
Unclasped her hand from mine and ran from me
Like a blown leaf to shelter. Kneeling low —
'The spring of joy!' I heard her say;
'Oh, great Wayfarer of the world, you know —
Let me know too — the way.'
I did not hear their colloquy, for they
Were both withdrawn from me;
But when she came again, as one who brings
A treasure, she was carrying tenderly
Some little rosy things
Like seeds. 'We go to plant sweet love,' she said,
'In pain's deep forest.' Then she pointed where
The dark trees loomed. I cried — 'Oh, soul — not so!
No spring of joy is there.'

She answered — 'None the less, at dawn we go.'
Like wraiths among the heavy shadows speeding,
Through trees as dark as night, as dumb as death,
We travelled, my soul leading.
Afraid at every breath,
When she stooped oftentimes to plant a seed,
I whispered — 'Speed, oh speed!
This place is wild and evil, full of harm.'
And yet she trembled not, but, gravely calm,
She said — 'There will be so much less to fear
For others, since the way that was so drear
Will be afire with flowers where we have been.'
But still she wept, and murmured wistfully —
'I thought to-day that we should both have seen
The lovely spring of joy!' Then carefully
She planted love's last seed, and we passed on.
And there, at the edge of the forest, gleamed and shone
A little rocky, rose-encircled spring,
So fair, so fresh, its music made us sing.
And One
(Oh, marvel!) held a cup for us, and said —
'I knew that dark way led
Straight here. Come, stand in the sun
And share with me.'
Then my soul knelt, and I,
Among the white and glistening flowers around it,
And drank the vital water with ecstasy —
So glad because through grief and love we found it,
The spring of joy!

Mary Webb, FIFTY-ONE POEMS

THE

𝔐ontgomeryshire Express
and Radnor Times,

TUESDAY, MARCH 7TH, 1911.

ST. DAVID'S DAY
CELEBRATIONS
IN
MONTGOMERYSHIRE.

**UNIVERSAL CELEBRATION
BY SCHOOL CHILDREN.**

CAERSWS

In common with other elementary schools in the county, Caersws children joined in the general celebrations by performing a specially prepared programme (**approved by the Board of Education**) in the morning, and having a half-holiday in the afternoon.

The child attending the Caersws school has every incentive to be a Welsh patriot. In this respect the school is blessed in a patriotic Welsh schoolmaster in Mr Rees, whilst **Mr Edward Jones, Maesmawr Hall**, the chairman of the managers, and Mr Richard Jones, Pendinas, the correspondent, are Nationalists of the most pronounced type. Added to this the child has constantly before its eyes the names of such eminent Welsh men and women as Robert Owen, Socialist; Richard Wilson, landscape painter; Ann Griffiths, hymnologist; Richard Roberts, inventor; and last, but not least, Ceiriog, whose names are painted on the walls of the main building, and all of whom have a strong link with the county and some with the immediate locality.

The chair at Wednesday's proceedings was occupied by **Mr Edward Jones, Maesmawr Hall**, and he was supported by Mr Richard Jones (chairman of the County Education Committee), **Mrs Edward Jones, Misses Megan, Beryl, and Mari Jones, and Miss Stratton, of Maesmawr Hall, Mr Carey Morris, Llandeilo**, Mr J.E. Mills, Mr J. Evans, Mr E. Jones (managers), and Dr Davies Rees.

The Red Dragon was prominently displayed in the school, and the children wore a daffodil or a leek on their breast. The next item was penillion singing by **Miss Megan Jones, Maesmawr Hall**, who for one so young made a very commendable effort to accomplish the very difficult task of singing **penillion to harp accompaniment**. Miss Nancy Richards (**Telynores Maldwyn**) and Miss Beryl Jones (in Welsh costume) played the accompaniments.

The Welsh air, "Harlech," was followed by a **duet on the harp by the two young ladies already mentioned**, and **this item was very excellently given and well received.** "Cuckoo dear" was next rendered by the children, in English, after which **Mrs Edward Jones gave an address on "Love of country."**

THE ADVICE OF A LADY

Mrs Jones said that it was to love of country that they in Wales owed their very existence as a nation, for if their ancestors had not had an intense love of their country, the Welsh nation would have been entirely merged with that of the English. Although their land was conquered, the spirit of the people remained free and unsubdued. Above all, they kept to their grand language, which was to-day as rich and expressive as ever. **Mrs Jones** said that the boys and girls of to-day ought to learn Welsh as a duty to their free and independent forefathers, who kept alive the language and spirit of their gallant little nation.

The children should also cultivate a real love for Welsh scenery, for its beautiful hills and valleys, its rivers and grand mountains. They should love the music of Wales, as its melodies were amongst the most beautiful in the world, whilst the harp was one of its sweetest instruments. They should also feel themselves ready to perform some sacrifice for those they loved most dearly. In what way were they going to carry on the traditions which had been handed down to them? Wherever they went when they grew up, they should carry with them strong impressions of their native land and a warm affection for its people, and at all times keep up the honour of Hen Walia Anwyl, Gwlad y Gan (applause).

The hymn tune, "Aberystwyth," to the words "Jesu, lover of my soul," was next sung by the children.

LLANDINAM

On the afternoon of St. David's Day there was quite a distinguished and representative gathering in the Council School, **when due honour and respect were paid the departed Saint. Mr Edward Jones, Maesmawr Hall** (chairman of the Managers) presided, and was supported by **Mrs Jones, Misses Beryl, Megan, and Mari Jones, Mrs Edward Davies (Plas Dinam)**, Mr T. Morgan Owen, Mrs and Miss Morgan Owen, and Miss Hughes (Llwynderw), Mrs James Jones (St. Llonio's Vicarage), Dr Rees (Caersws), **Rev and Mrs R. Jones (Penybryn)**, Mr Meddins (Cwmlwydin), Mr Evans (Gellidywyll),

Mr Evans (Penrhyddlan), Mr J.R. Hones (headmaster) and Mrs Jones, Miss Manuel, and Miss O.M. Rees. **The leek or daffodil was conspicuously worn by the majority of the children, teachers, and visitors**. The singing of the good old Welsh tune, "Crugybar," to the words "From Heavenly Jerusalem's towers," by all present opened the proceedings. An excellent musical programme was well sustained throughout. Addresses were given by Dr Rees on "St. David," which was most instructive and concise, just what might be expected from such a keen archaeologist and antiquarian. Mrs James Jones most earnestly and eloquently set forth the claims of our Patron Saint to be worthy of emulation, and **implored the children to strive after perfection, to be truthful, honest, straightforward, and persevering as children, in order to become good men and women, to endeavour to equip themselves for the battle of life and the glorious hereafter**. Mr Morgan Owen very wittily spoke of the origin of the Patron Saints of the British Isles. He also exhorted the children to try and follow in the footsteps of St. David. His was quite a scholarly address. Then followed the **Reverend R. Jones with his usual well chosen remarks. The Chairman was also quite up to his usual standard.** *Selections on the harp of Welsh airs, including a duet, were given by Miss Nancy Richards (Telynores Maldwyn) and Miss Beryl Jones,* Maesmawr Hall. **We are indebted to Mr and Mrs Jones for this musical treat**, which not only the children, but all present thoroughly enjoyed. **Both young ladies wore Welsh costumes**, which added a more decidedly characteristic nature to the proceedings. "My native land" was nicely recited by Miss Evelyn Bennett. At the special request of the master, **Mrs Edward Davies** – who is ever mindful of the welfare of the children – gave a short and inspiring address.

It is to be hoped that the good seed sown on the celebration may blossom and bear fruit. The usual votes of thanks to the Chairman, speakers, harpists, and master were given with ringing cheers.

Mrs J.R. Jones played the accompaniments on the organ and Miss M. Savage and Miss Jessie Savage on the piano. The singing of "God save the King" closed the interesting gathering.

It is safe to say that March 1ˢᵗ, 1911, will be fixed in the memory of those present as long as life lasts, and let us hope it will be the means of fostering amongst the rising generation a greater love for, and pride in, one's own country.

GATHERING OF NEWTOWN WELSHMEN

Quite 250 Welshmen and Welshwomen assembled at the Crescent Schoolroom on Wednesday night, when a banquet and public meeting was held in celebration of Dydd Gwyl Dewi Sant. A committee had been formed some weeks ago to make preparations for the event on an extensive scale, and this was undoubtedly accomplished. The secretarial duties were carried out by Mr Ivor Jones, M.A., and Mr P. Wilson-Jones. The luncheon was provided by Mr Evan Benn and Mr D. Bunford, and this was of quite a substantial character, and was much enjoyed.

At the subsequent proceedings,

MR EDWARD JONES, MAESMAWR HALL, Presided, and in referring to the celebrations which had taken place at the schools during that day, said that he hoped they would result in making a lasting impression on the minds of the children. **It was something extraordinary to find the Board of Education countenancing the movement to celebrate St. David's Day in Wales. He hoped that attitude would grow and continue during the years to come**. Welshmen had reached high positions in society and in the State, and they hoped that the spirit of St. David would be felt by the Welshmen of the present day (applause).

CHURCHSTOKE

There is so little Welsh, either of feeling or language, on this side of Offa's Dyke, that no attempt was made to celebrate St. David's Day here.

Courtesy: *Powys County Times*

Author's note.

In the aforesaid 3ʳᵈ paragraph, which reports the CAERSWS celebrations, Mr. Carey Morris of Llandeilo is included amongst the Maesmawr Hall party. He was the portrait painter who, at that time, was engaged upon the standing portrait of my mother, included herein and signed and dated, 'Carey Morris 1911'. He returned to Maesmawr the following year, to paint my uncle Emrys' seated portrait, seen in the dining room. Miss Stratton, also included in the Maesmawr party was, most probably, the family's governess before my mother and her sisters went to Wycombe Abbey School, and my uncle to the Leys School at Cambridge.

M. E-J

MAPS

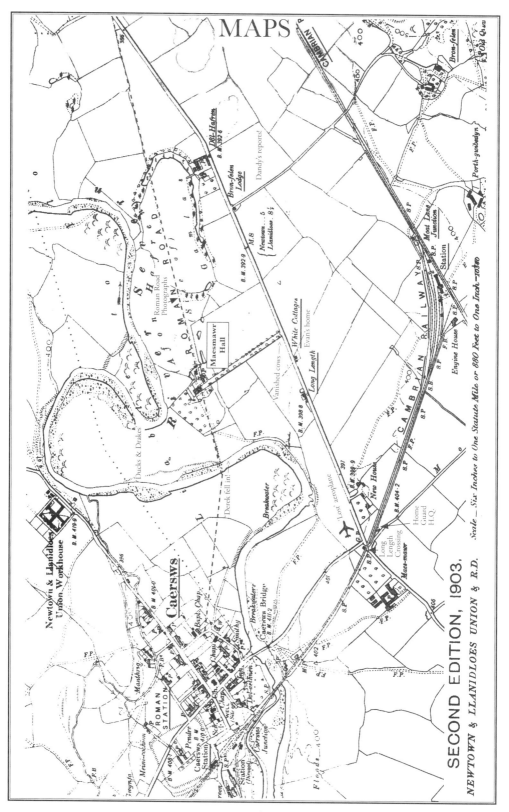

SECOND EDITION, 1903.

NEWTOWN & LLANIDLOES UNION & R.D.

Scale — Six Inches to One Statute Mile or 880 Feet to One Inch — $\frac{1}{10560}$

236

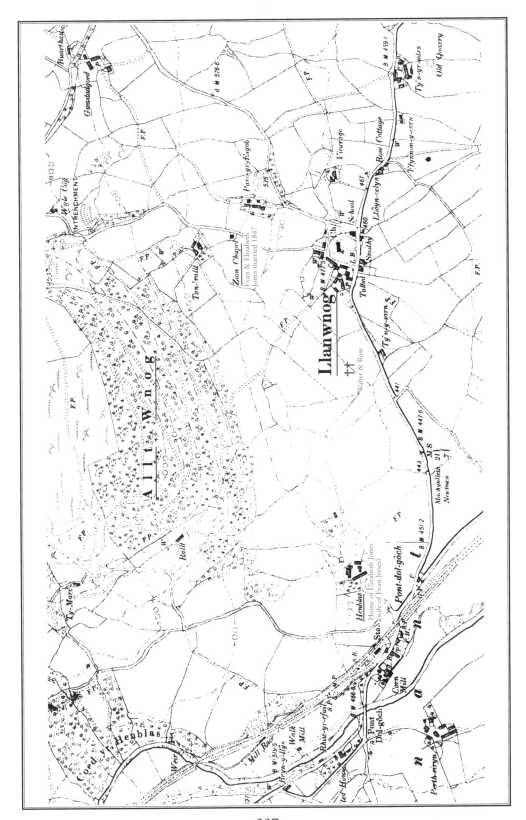

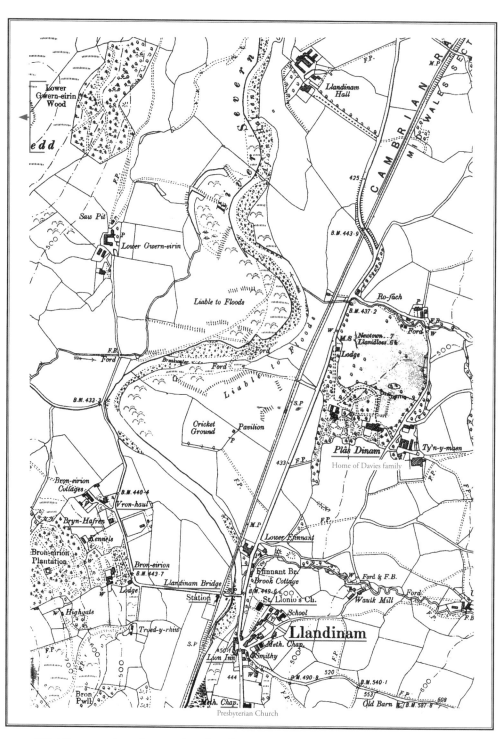

NB: The maps have been reduced to fit on the page, and therefore are not to scale.

238

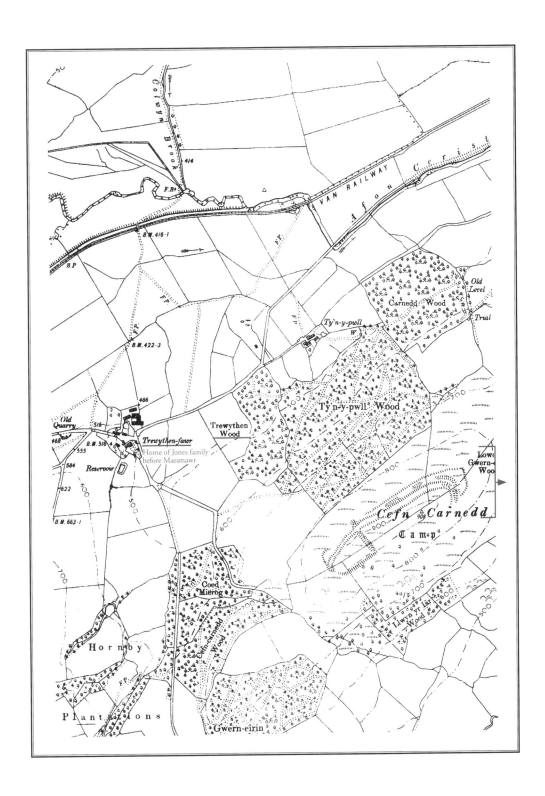

My tales are told;
As I grow old
Friends' mem'ries hold
As treasured gold
Until – Beyond,
Again behold!

M. E-J

Endpapers:

Front: Harp Engraving
Courtesy: Amgueddfa Cymru and Sain Ffagan Amgueddfa Werin Cymru.

Back: A photograph of 'THE MOTHER AND HER SON'. Bronze of 1907. Sculptor:
Wilhelm Lehmbruck, 1881–1919. Now in the Folkwang Museum, Essen, Germany.
(©1961 Rembrandt Verlag, Berlin; permission sought)
Dust jacket :
Photographer: the late Hugh Creighton

Swans.

Agnes Miller Parker, 1937